MANITOBA MILESTONES

Bridgen's of Winnipeg.

LOWER FORT GARRY
FROM THE AIR
IN 1927.

MANITOBA
MILESTONES

BY

MARGARET McWILLIAMS

WITH MANY
ILLUSTRATIONS AND MAPS

TORONTO & LONDON
J. M. DENT & SONS LTD.

First Published in 1928

Printed in Great Britain by
Hazell, Watson & Viney, Ld., London and Aylesbury.

TO

MY HUSBAND

354.

PREFACE

No one can write the story of the growth of any country, no matter how small, without being debtor to many men for the knowledge which informs and the spirit which interprets. So it is with me. Right gladly do I own myself debtor to Ross, and Gunn, and Hargrave, and Begg, and Bryce among those who no longer write ; and, as well, to J. W. Dafoe, Esq., and to Dr. C. N. Bell, and to Professor Chester Martin among those who still discuss the problems of our province.

So generous and kindly has been the help given to me that to name all to whom I am under obligation is impossible. Gratefully, however, I acknowledge special indebtedness to His Grace the Archbishop of Ruperts Land, to Hon. T. A. Crerar, to Hon. A. B. Hudson, and to H. S. Seaman, Esq., for valuable papers and books lent me, or for careful discussion of difficult points. The aid which I have received from Dr. Daniel McIntyre is among those services of friendship for which there are no adequate thanks.

Acknowledgement is hereby made and thanks offered to those publishing firms which have kindly given me permission to reproduce pictures or to make quotations from books published by them : The Ryerson Press, The Oxford Press, Glasgow, Brooks and Company, The Hudson's Bay Company, and Simpkin and Company.

Acknowledgments for the pictures are made under their reproductions.

CONTENTS

LIST OF ILLUSTRATIONS

IN COLOUR

IN HALF-TONE

LIST OF ILLUSTRATIONS

IN LINE

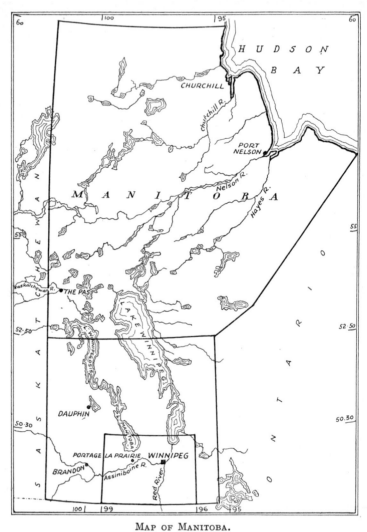

MAP OF MANITOBA.
Showing successive enlargements of the Province.

MANITOBA MILESTONES

CHAPTER I

EXPLORERS

ONE sunny morning, in the spring of 1652, three boys slipped past the sentry of the stockaded fort of Three Rivers, on the south side of the great St. Lawrence, to go hunting in the woods beyond. That they should not be going off thus they very well knew, for the Iroquois, enemies of the French, were on the warpath and were known to be close at hand. But the sun was shining, the spring breezes blowing gently, the birds calling them to adventure. So off they went—three of them—led by the brave and gay young Pierre Radisson, who was now about seventeen and had lately come from old France to New France, as Canada then was.

Even that spring air must have been full of warning, for it was not long before the two friends of Pierre became frightened and decided to turn back. Laughing at their fears Pierre went on alone until, at a distance of perhaps nine miles, he found he had shot all the birds he could carry and he, too, turned his steps homeward. Whistling as he went, he all but fell over the bodies of the other two —tomahawked and scalped. Then Pierre felt fear and started to run for the gate. From the grass all around Indian heads rose, watching him then as they had watched him early in the morning laughing at his timid friends and going bravely on by himself. There was not the slightest chance of escape, but, because he had been brave and because the Indians admired bravery above all things, he did not meet the usual fate of captives but was adopted into a family of Mohawks, who had recently lost a son. His French name, Pierre, was changed into the Indian " Orimha," also meaning a stone, and for two years he lived the life of a young Mohawk brave.

Once, indeed, in that time he tried to escape, but the torture and threatened death by burning which followed taught him the heavy penalties that would attend another unsuccessful attempt. But, though happy in his life, the call of his race was strong, and he accepted the offered aid of the Governor of one of the English forts in what is now the state of New York. In that fort he lay hidden for days while his Mohawk brothers and sisters wandered outside calling plaintively for Orimha. He returned to Quebec by the long way around of Amsterdam in Holland, rejoining his family after an absence of two years, having gained in that time a knowledge of the ways and the tongues of the Indians which was to be of the greatest help to him in days to come.

The great business of Frenchmen in Canada 300 years ago was to send wealth back to France in the form of furs, and into that business Pierre threw himself with all his heart. Expedition after expedition he made, not, as an entry in the famous *Jesuit Relations of* 1655 says, " in great galleons, or long-oared barges, but in little gondolas of bark." So the Indian canoes seemed to the French priests. In all of these he had the company of his brother-in-law, Medart de Chouart, afterwards Sieur de Groseilliers, whose first wife was a daughter of that Abraham Martin after whom the Plains of Abraham were named, and whose second was young Pierre's sister. Never did these two undertake an expedition but they met and conquered dangers, which seem now so great and terrifying as to be almost unbelievable ; never did they come back empty handed, bringing always great cargoes of furs, which went to enrich others than themselves— governors of New France and nobles and king's favourites in old France.

By the winter of 1658–59 Radisson and Groseilliers, pushing ever westward, had found their way to Lake

Michigan, to the farthest point west the white man had yet reached, as far as authentic history can now tell us. Unexpectedly, they found the Iroquois on the war path. Without hesitation Radisson led the Algonquin Indians, always the friends of the French, who were accompanying him, against the Iroquois with such success that not one escaped. Nor, this task over, did he hesitate about pushing farther into the unknown land. " Our mind was not to stay here but to know the remotest people," he wrote in his journal, " and because we had been willing to die in their defence these Indians consented to conduct us."

With such eagerness did they push on that the coming of spring found them on the waters of the upper Mississippi, the first white men to see that mighty river. Farther to the west they travelled and back to Lake Superior. Then came a year of exploration in which they heard many tales of the great water which lay to the north where the best beaver land would be found, before Radisson and Groseilliers returned to Quebec. Arriving at Quebec with sixty canoes ladened with 200,000 francs' worth of furs they received public honours, such as were seldom given, for they had come just in time to prevent the three ships in the harbour sailing empty for France. They had saved the season's trade. Unknown to those who did them honour, they had accomplished much greater things ; for they had discovered the great North-west of this continent, and had opened the canoe route by the Ottawa and Nipissing rivers along which trade between the East and the West was to pass for the next century and a half. Thus, full of praise and honour, they returned to their homes in Three Rivers.

But the glory and the financial safety which Radisson and Groseilliers had brought to New France soon passed from men's minds. Soon, too, it failed to satisfy them. Fired by what they had heard from the Indians of the western lands and of the great sea to the north, these two adventurers now determined to find that overland route to the great water of which word had been coming to

Quebec and Three Rivers for almost a generation. So, in the spring of 1661, they applied to the Governor for permission to make this journey, for without that permission no man was allowed to go to the interior. But the Governor, Baron D'Avaugour, would only consent if they in turn would promise to give him half of the profits of the expedition. Radisson indignantly rejected these terms, but determined not to give up because of the Governor's refusal. A little later he and Groseilliers, who was now captain of the soldiers at Three Rivers, stole away from the settlement and started out upon their great adventure. That winter they spent somewhere in the present state of Minnesota, near Lake Superior, threatened all the time by starvation and by hostile Indians, but making many explorations. Spring found them again at Lake Superior whence, accompanied by the friendly Crees, they set out to find the way to Hudson Bay. It was on this journey, somewhere west of what is now Duluth, that, fearing Indian attacks, they built in two days the first fort placed by white men in the north-western part of this continent.

Of this fort built by two lone men in the wilderness of the North-west, 2,000 miles from any help, we have a description. It was built in the shape of a triangle with its base on the water side. Unbarked logs were used for the walls and the roof was of branches interlaced. The door was on the water side and in the centre of the earthen floor, so that the smoke might go out through an opening in the branches, was the fire. A hewn log served for a table ; two more with pine boughs spread on them for a bed. But, if they were to rest, there must be sentries. Radisson provided these by stringing cords, carefully concealed, through the grass and branches of trees around the tiny fort. To these cords he fastened bells. More than once during that long winter, they were roused from sleep to stand on guard by the ringing of those bells. Then Radisson, knowing the eagerness for fire-arms of the Indians, among whom the news of two white men living alone spread rapidly, invented another protection.

Rolling twisted tubes of birch-bark he filled them with gunpowder and ran them in a circle around the fort. By putting a torch to the bark he showed the astonished Indians a circle of fire spluttering and leaping from point to point. That to the Indians meant magic. With magic they would not interfere, and the white men were, therefore, safe.

That Radisson and his companion came presently to the shore of a great sea, there seems to be little doubt ; but whether the great sea was James Bay, or Lake Winnipeg, or even the waters of Hudson Bay itself, is still a matter of dispute. There is at least a possibility that they gazed on Lake Winnipeg. What is certain is that they found the waters that flowed to the north, and thus learned that the overland route to Hudson Bay was possible, and that there was a vast expanse of land, where, in numbers that no man could count, lived the fur-bearing animals.

Almost exactly fifty years before Radisson and Groseilliers saw these waters flowing into the north, Henry Hudson had discovered the bay into which the rivers emptied, using for his voyage charts prepared by George Weymouth who preceded him to the straits. He did not, however, come into the territory which is now Manitoba, but spent the dreary winter of 1610–11 on the shores of James Bay. When spring once more brought open water, Hudson sailed to the north, but the mutiny which had long threatened, now broke out into open struggle. There were not enough provisions to take them all to England and the mutineers determined to set Hudson, his young son and seven sick men adrift in one of the ship's boats. One hero among them all, the ship's carpenter, volunteered to share Hudson's fate and with his carpenter's chest was also placed in the open boat. The mutineers then sailed away leaving the little company to meet death in the waters of the bay or on one of its islands. The manner of that death, the place of it, is one of those mysteries which there is now little hope that we shall ever solve.

The news of Hudson's death was carried home by the treacherous members of his crew, who, for some unknown reason, were never punished. It stirred other men, first, to search for him, and then to carry on the work which he had undertaken—that search for the western sea, a passage to which, it was then thought, would be found by rivers

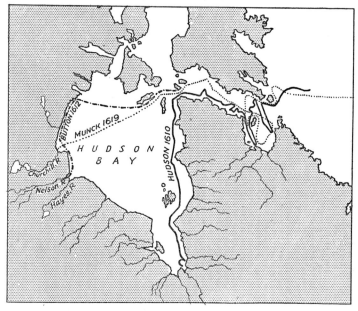

Fig. 1.—Map showing the routes taken by Hudson, Button and Munck.

flowing through this new land. For it was this, and no thought of a rich fur trade, which brought the British seamen to the new world.

Something more than six months after the crew of Hudson's ship, the *Discovery*, reached England, Thomas Button was off on his way to search for the lost explorer. His voyage was backed by a great company of adventurers and merchants, who were organized as " The Company of Merchants of London, Discoverers of the North-West Passage." They confidently hoped that Button and his two ships, the *Discovery*—in which both Weymouth and Hudson had sailed—and the *Resolution*, would come sailing home from India or China. So confident were they that King James I actually gave Button letters of credence which he was to present to the rulers of such far eastern countries as he might reach.

Button did succeed in reaching the western shore of Hudson Bay far to the north. Sailing down the coast, he apparently missed the Churchill River and came to rest in the mouth of the Nelson River, which he named Fort Nelson after his sailing master, and there he wintered. So, in 1612, came to Manitoba the first white men of whom we have certain knowledge.

Though he searched again the following summer, Button had to return without having found either Hudson or the passage which he had been sent to seek. He had, however, charted for all who followed him the entire western shore of the bay. Almost every year, thereafter, found some adventurer setting out on the quest, but it was not until 1619 that any of these searchers came to that part of the bay which is now Manitoba. The first of these was a company of Danes, captained by Jens Munck. Their ship fought its way through the ice and across the bay, coming to harbour in what is now the Churchill River.

" There," says Jéremie, a French chronicler, writing nearly a hundred years later, " they put their ships in to winter quarters and housed themselves as best they could, much as would be done by people who knew nothing about the country, and who had no forethought in providing against the intense cold. In the end they suffered so much misery that when sickness broke out among them, they all died during the winter without a single native being aware of what had happened. When spring came the ice went out with its usual impetuosity and carried away their ship and everything in it except an eight-pounder brass cannon, which was left behind, and which is still there."

Danish records, however, show that the ice had left them the smaller of their two ships, and that in it Munck, with two other survivors out of the sixty-five persons who had gone to Churchill, reached Europe the following September.

Eleven years later, there came two other expeditions, both British, one led by Captain Luke Fox of Hull, and the other by Captain Thomas James of Bristol. Both these men came to what is now Manitoba and both returned saying the passage was not to be found through Hudson Bay. Thus this hope died, and for more than a quarter of a century there were no more voyages.

It is one of the interesting things in a story crammed with interest at every turn, that when adventurers came once more to the bay, it was under the leadership of the Frenchmen, Radisson and Groseilliers. Stranger still that these two who had discovered the tributary waters to the south as French subjects, came now to the bay as agents for the British between whom and the French there was little love.

Furs, rather than the western passage, were now the objects of men's search. From the moment when Radisson and Groseilliers had seen the waters flowing to the north and had realized that there was great wealth in furs to be reached by the sea, in the land through which these rivers flowed, they had determined to share in it. Their first step was to hasten back to Three Rivers with a cargo of furs valued in present-day money at $300,000. But their great tidings and the fortune in furs brought no forgiveness for leaving without permission from the avaricious Governor, and when he got through with the business of fines, and taxes, and what, in these days, would be called graft, Radisson and Groseilliers had just about $20,000 left.

They returned to France seeking vainly redress and support for their new venture. They made two attempts themselves, disastrously, and had reached the end of their resources, when they were persuaded by Sir George

Carteret, a special British Commissioner in New England, to accompany him to England.

It was the time of the Black Death, when grass grew in the streets of London. The Court was at Windsor and thither went the two Frenchmen. Radisson seems to have caught the fancy of Charles II, for the King made the two a living allowance, kept them near the Court, where they met Prince Rupert, and finally wrote a letter to the Duke of York directing him as head of the navy to lend the Frenchmen a ship in which to make an expedition on behalf of England. In 1668 they set out in two ships, Radisson in the *Eaglet*, Groseilliers in the *Nonsuch*. But disappointment again came to Radisson. The *Eaglet* was injured and had to turn back. He was forced to leave to his partner the work of making this first voyage. Groseilliers wintered at James Bay and brought back so rich a cargo of furs that the nobles and merchants organized that " Company of Merchant Adventurers Trading into Hudson's Bay " which made the western prairies British, while Eastern Canada was still French. The first expedition sent out by this Company, as well as later ones, was led by the gallant Frenchmen. Under their direction too, were built trading centres— or forts, as they were called, at different points in the Hudson Bay and to these forts the Indians came to trade.

Though they brought home enormous wealth, Radisson and Groseilliers remained merely the men of the Company, receiving not too generous treatment. The French, claiming the territory around the bay, sent emissaries to win Pierre back to his French allegiance, and finally, both he and his brother-in-law, all their faults forgiven, and much honoured, returned to France. Just ten years after his first voyage into the bay Radisson was back, but in a ship carrying the French flag. This time he decided to explore inland and, leaving his brother-in-law to build a fort south of Fort Nelson, Radisson came up the Hayes River exploring the route to the interior. Thus he charted the course which hunters, and traders, and settlers followed for 200 years and more (*Fig.* 6).

In the struggle which France was making to retain her hold on the new world, and in particular the possession of the fabulous wealth of the land around the bay, Radisson played a great part. But the French, especially after the death of Colbert, France's great finance minister, seem not to have trusted him. They confiscated his furs and sought to force him to bring his English wife and children to France. By a ruse he escaped to England where the Hudson's Bay Company welcomed him gladly, and took him back into their employ. In 1684 he sailed once more in an English ship into the bay and brought back so rich a cargo, that the Company paid a dividend of 50 per cent.

No more honours came to Radisson, though he remained many years in the service of the Company. His salary, large, perhaps, in the beginning, appears, for most of his period of service, to have been only about $250 a year, and, though occasionally augmented by special grants and by dividends on a small share of stock, was not sufficient for his family of wife and four children. Records of this part of his life are few, but minutes of the Company show that in 1700, being then a man of sixty-five or six, he petitioned for the post of warehousekeeper and was refused. Ten years later, on July 12th, there is this record : " the secretary is ordered to pay to Mr. Radisson's widow, as a charity, the sum of six pounds." Nineteen years elapse and then there is this entry, found by Agnes Laut in the records of the Company under date of 1729 : " the secretary is ordered to pay Mrs. Radisson, widow of Mr. Pierre Esprit Radisson, who was formerly employed in the company's service, the sum of £10 as a charity she being very ill and in great want." Radisson had shown the way to the Western States and to Western Canada ; he had shown the men of France and England how to gain enormous wealth ; of his death and burial there is nothing known and his children ate the bread of charity.

Whoever may have been the first white man to step on the soil of Manitoba there is no doubt, since the discovery of his journal two years ago in Carrickfergus, Ireland, that Henry Kelsey was the first to cross her prairies and to see the buffalo grazing upon them. Kelsey has always been a fascinating figure in the story of the exploration of the North-west, but the truth as told simply in his journal is much more stirring than the tales which tradition has built around him. Perhaps after a silence of nearly 250 years he should be allowed to speak for himself in the unpunctuated English, with its odd abbreviations, which he wrote. "In 1683 I went out in ye ship lucy Jno outlaw commandr. In '88 after 3 indians being employ for great reward to carry letters from hays river to new severn they returned without performing the business altho paid then I was sent with an indian boy and in a month returned with answers." His success in this his first trip in Manitoba brought him a more stirring adventure. "In '89 Cap James Young put me & ye same Indian boy a shore to ye north-ward of Churchill river in order to bring to a commerce ye Northern Indians but we saw none although we travelled above 200 miles in search of them."

It was not of his own will that Kelsey turned back even at the end of that 200 miles. Tom Savage, as he called the Indian boy, would go no farther, and "called me a fool because I was not conscious of the danger," says Kelsey. It was on this trip that Kelsey saw the musk-ox, a detailed description of which is found in the journal. He was the first white man to see these curious animals and called them "buffillo."

Kelsey's skill in travelling the unknown country brought him to the attention of the officers of the Company in London eager "to bring to a commerce" the Indians of the interior. Already, as Kelsey himself relates, they had been seeking this trade vainly through the help of Groseilliers whom the British always called Gooseberry.

"In '90 ye Company employed," writes Kelsey, "2 frenchmen viz. Gooseberry and Grammair ye former at £80 annm ye latter at 40 to go amongst ye natives to

draw ym to a trade but they did not go 200 miles from ye
factory." When Groseilliers failed the Governor of
York Factory received instructions to send this lad,
probably about twenty years of age, back with the
Indians who had come to trade at the factory. On the
12th of June 1690 he set out with the Stone or Assiniboine
Indians.

> " Then up the River I with heavy heart
>   Did take my way and from all English part
>   To live among the natives of this place
>   If God permits me for one, two years space.
>   The inland country of good report hath been
>   By Indians, but by English yet not seen
>   Therefore I on my journey did not stay
>   But making all the haste I could upon our way
>   Gott on the border of ye Stone Indians country
>   I took possession on ye tenth Instant July
>   And for my Masters I speaking for ym all
>   This neck of land I Deering's Point did call.
>   Distant from hence by Judgment at ye best
>   From ye house (York Factory) six hundred miles southwest
>   Through rivers which run strong with falls
>   Thirty-Three ' Carriages ' (portages) five lakes in all."

In the spring, Kelsey sent back for more supplies. He
spent the next summer going further into the country
of the Assiniboines, there to make a peace between
warring tribes. In the remarkable rimed intro-
duction to his journal he goes on to describe the
country.

> " The Ground begins for to be dry, with wood
>   Poplo and Burch with Ash thats very good
>   For the natives of that place wch knows
>   No use of better than their wooden bows
>
>   .   .   .   .   .
>
>   And now will give account of that same countrys soil
>   Which hither part is very thick of wood
>   Affords small nuts with cherryes very good
>   Thus it continues til you leave the woods behind."

It was just at this point, as he tells in the journal proper, that he saw the buffalo.

"August 19th (1691).—Now we sett forward again the ground being more barren than it used to be ye Indians having seen great store of Buffalo but killed none.

"August Ye 20th.—Today we pitched to ye outermost edge of ye woods this plain affords nothing but short round sticky grass and Buffillo and a great sort of bear wch is bigger than any white bear and is neither black or white but silver haird like our English rabbit ye Buffillo like wise is not like those to ye Northward their horns growing like an English ox but black and short."

The next entry in the journal is of the first buffalo hunt seen by the white man.

"August Ye 23rd.—This instant ye Indians going a hunting killed great store of Buffillo Now ye manner of their hunting these Beast on ye barren ground is when they see a great parcel of them together they surround them with men wch done they gather themselves into a smaller Compass keeping ye Beast still in ye middle and so shooting ym until they break out at some place or other and so get away from you."

Five hundred and eighty-nine miles south-west from Deering's Point, Kelsey travelled before he turned back, making in all a journey of 1,189 miles in a south-easterly direction from York Factory. Where his route passed exactly, what precisely are the points of which he speaks are still to be discovered. Men who know the country well hazard the guess that Deering's Point was close to the Pas and that the end of his journey was probably in the Swan River country.

For another thirty years or more Kelsey served the Company in the country around Hudson Bay, even making trips to the Eskimo country "to gather ye trade," and to "look for ye Copper." His journal ends in 1822, when he was recalled by the Company. It is interesting to speculate as to whether the two intrepid explorers Radisson and Kelsey ever met. Certainly

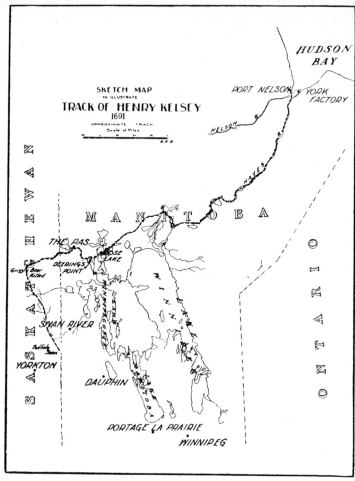

Fig. 2.—No precise information of the exact route taken by Henry Kelsey in his explorations inland has yet been found. This map shows the route which men, now in the service of the Hudson's Bay Company, and familiar with the territory, think he took on his journey of 1,189 miles south-east from York Factory to Deering's Point and thence to the prairie, where Kelsey watched the first buffalo hunt ever seen by a white man. The map, with the extracts from the journal, are published through the courtesy of the Company.

Radisson was at York Factory after Kelsey came out as a boy.

Explorations were continued from Hudson Bay, partly still in search for the western sea, but more in the interests of the fur trade. Though most of these travellers passed through what is now Manitoba they were chiefly interested in the country to the west and to the north. Some of their names are great ones in the history of the North-west. Samuel Hearne, who explored chiefly in the north country, discovered the Coppermine River, the fame of whose copper deposits had spread among the Indian tribes for hundreds of miles. Philip Turner was the first surveyor sent out by the Imperial Government. Peter Fidler, his successor, travelled for thirty years through Manitoba and the North-west and is known to have kept journals which would be invaluable if the mystery of their whereabouts could be solved. David Thompson, the first man to descend the Columbia River from its source to the Pacific Ocean, did much of his exploring in Manitoba in that network of waterways which lies between the Nelson and Churchill rivers. He also came south into the valley of the Assiniboine as far east as the Souris River.

In the meantime another great explorer, the first of Canadian birth, was coming westward from New France.

" The cause of North American exploration owes much to the man of New France," writes Lawrence J. Burpee, " and to none does it owe more than to Pierre Gaultier de la Vérendrye. No explorer ever accomplished so much under such extraordinary difficulties. His story is the story of a man who, having set himself a gigantic task, not for his own profit but for the glory of his native land, followed it unflinchingly in spite of obstacles of every kind, in spite of wearing discouragement, in spite of misrepresentation and calumny, until at last death intervened, the task incomplete but notable in its incompleteness."

La Vérendrye was born at Three Rivers in 1683 and, being the son of the Governor, passed naturally into the army. He saw service in America, and Newfoundland, and fought at the battle of Malplaquet in Flanders, where, with nine wounds, he was left for dead upon the field. In the time of peace which followed Marlborough's victories, there was little of adventure to be found in the army, either in the old world or the new, and adventure was what La Vérendrye craved. He returned to Canada and was sent to the far post of Nipigon, to the north of Lake Superior. Some time after he arrived there came to him an Indian, named Ochagach, with stories of the great lake beyond Superior from which there flowed to the north a great river. Paddling down it Ochagach had come to water which ebbed and flowed, and heard of salt water beyond. These stories revived in La Vérendrye the dream of his boyhood that he would be the discoverer of the western passage of which all men were then talking, and he determined to follow this search. Returning to Quebec, he laid his plan before Beauharnois, the Governor. If the King of France would but give him one hundred men, equipped and their wages guaranteed, he would undertake to lead them to that western sea. But Louis XV had no interest in new world exploration and the fur monopoly of the country he was about to explore was the most the friendly Governor could secure for him.

With this monopoly La Vérendrye was able to enlist the aid of the merchants in Montreal and in the summer of 1731, accompanied by three sons, Jean-Baptiste, Pierre and François, by his nephew, Christopher du Frost, Sieur de la Jémeraye, who had recently been in charge of a post on the Mississippi, and by soldiers and voyageurs, he set out upon his quest. There were about fifty men in all in the party, which included Father Messager and Ochagach as guide.

Seventy-eight days after they left Montreal, they reached Kaministiquia at the west end of Lake Superior. Wearied with their journey, envious at the sight of other canoes setting out to return to the villages on the St. Lawrence, alarmed by the approach of winter, La Vérendrye's men refused to follow him farther. The best his persuasion could bring about was that half the crew would go forward with Jémeraye, if La Vérendrye and the other half would remain at Kaministiquia with the supplies. Forward then went Jémeraye and Jean-Baptiste and, reaching the Rainy River, built Fort St. Pierre on the Minnesota bank. Trade with the Cree Indians was fruitful, and many valuable furs went back to Lake Superior in the spring in charge of Jean-Baptiste.

In June of the next year, exactly a year from the time he had left Montreal, La Vérendrye started for St. Pierre. Astonished Indians responded to the gifts he distributed on arrival by collecting fifty canoes and offering to conduct him to the Lake of the Woods. Tired as he and his men were, they set out at once and in August were in the " great lake " of which Ochagach had spoken. Again winter threatened and Jean-Baptiste had not arrived from the post at Michilimackinac, whither he had gone to trade his furs for supplies. So, on a peninsula running out into the lake, La Vérendrye built the second fort, naming it St. Charles in honour of the friendly Governor, Beauharnois. According to the record of Father Aulneau, who joined them the following year, this fort had four rows of posts or palisades twelve to fifteen feet high and had several rough cabins inside.

Here La Vérendrye spent the winter, and in the spring sent Jémeraye to Montreal to reason with his merchant partners, who, not realizing their wild dreams of profits, were not giving him adequate support. Meantime his sons, Jean-Baptiste and Pierre, pushed on to the shores of Lake Winnipeg and there built Fort Maurepas close to the site of the present Fort Alexander. Jémeraye brought back bad news. The merchant partners would not yield to his persuasions. La Vérendrye himself returned to Montreal and Quebec and succeeded in convincing his associates that they would reap large profits if they would but continue their support, but for that support he was forced to pay a heavy price. " I had before leaving," he wrote, " ceded to my tradesmen the privilege of trading and the business of the posts I had established." He returned to Fort St. Charles in the autumn, the supplies coming by slower travel behind him.

Fearing starvation La Vérendrye sent Jémeraye and part of the force to winter at Fort Maurepas, where they could fish and hunt, and, for the first time, the white man lived on the shores of this inland sea.

The worst fears were realized. Ice blocked the rivers before the supplies could be brought up. The fishing and the hunting failed. Spring found La Vérendrye and his men keeping themselves alive by eating parchment,

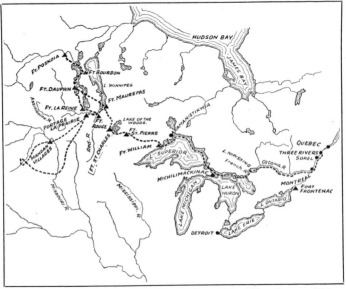

Fig. 3.—Map showing the explorations of La Vérendrye and his sons and the posts they established.

moccasin leather, roots and their hunting dogs. In the first days of that spring, while still waiting anxiously for the delayed supplies, his sons came from Fort Maurepas with word that Jémeraye had died three weeks before on his way to help La Vérendrye. With supplies exhausted, ammunition running out and his trusted lieutenant dead, La Vérendrye might well have given up. Instead he determined to rush three canoes with twenty voyageurs

to Michilimackinac for supplies and powder. Father
Aulneau decided to accompany them. Led by Jean-
Baptiste they set out on the afternoon of June 5th landing
at the island known as Massacre Island to pass the night.
Now while La Vérendrye had been away, a few Crees
playing with their new toys, guns, had fired without reason
on some wandering Sioux. When the angry Sioux asked
who had fired upon them, the Crees replied with a laugh,
" the French," and the Sioux, rejoining their band,
determined to kill the first white men they should find.
Fires lit by Jean and his voyageurs attracted their
attention. Judge Prudhomme, through whose researches
the actual scene of the slaughter was discovered, suggests
that the Sioux landed on the island by making overtures
of peace. At a given signal these Indians, following their
crafty custom, fell upon the Frenchmen and killed them
all, though how they managed to surprise them so completely is another of the unanswered questions. It only
serves to intensify the tragedy that two or three days later
came the supplies for which La Vérendrye had been
waiting so long and so anxiously. With them came
Louis, the fourth and youngest son, whom his father had
left behind to learn map making.

While at Fort Maurepas La Vérendrye's sons had
crossed Traverse Bay and had gone beyond Elk Island,
and so had seen the vast expanse of Lake Winnipeg.
They had also heard of a river which flowed in from the
south. When refusing to yield to the all but overpowering
discouragement, La Vérendrye decided to take all his
forces to Fort Maurepas, he and his sons, or it may be the
sons alone, while the father made another trip to reassure
his merchant partners, followed around the shore and
found the mouth of the Red River. Probably in the
summer of 1738 the whole party came up that river as far
as the mouth of the Assiniboine—the first white men of
whom we have certain knowledge to reach the site of
Winnipeg. It is likely that they also went on farther
south since one of La Vérendrye's early maps shows a
Fort de Bois on the Red River about the present inter-

3

national boundary.   At the same time de la Marque, who
had come up to reinforce La Vérendrye, built the first
of the forts at the forks of the Red and Assiniboine
rivers, calling it Fort Rouge.   La Vérendrye and his
party had already gone farther west along the Assiniboine
and were building Fort de la Reine somewhere near the
present town of Portage la Prairie.

But what seems from the point of view of to-day a most
important result of their exploration, was to La Vérendrye
and his son only a step in the realization of their dream
that they might be the discoverers of the way to the
western sea.   Fort Rouge at the forks, soon abandoned,
and their main fort, de la Reine, near Portage la Prairie,
were but bases from which to set out on further search.
From the Indians who came to trade, they had heard of the
Mandans, a people living to the south-west, who, in their
turn, knew a people who knew of the western sea.   To
the Mandans La Vérendrye determined to go (see Fig. 3).

Undaunted by the approaching winter and waiting only
long enough to finish building Fort de la Reine, he suddenly,
on the morning of October 16th, 1738, had all his men
mustered in the fort.   From the fifty-two soldiers and
voyageurs, he picked out the twenty most fit to stand
the hard journey overland which he was about to undertake.   To these twenty was given the necessary equip-
ment of powder, balls, axe and kettle.   Two days later
Pierre and François hoisted the French flag, the bugle
sounded the march and away went the little band.   Three
or four days after they started, they were joined by a band
of 200 Assiniboines which soon increased to 600.   The
presence of so many Indians much delayed the march
since it was necessary to stop to hunt the buffalo and to
make pemmican to support them on the way.   It was
the end of November before they came in touch with the
Mandans but, on December 3rd, at the head of his small
band of white men and 600 savages, La Vérendrye, the
French flag flying before him, marched into the presence
of their great chief.

Bitter disappointment awaited him.   The Mandans

were not white as he had been told. They did not know about the western sea. All that he could learn from them was that somewhere to the south-west there was salt water. He could not expect them to support his party for the winter and so, in intense cold on December 8th, he set out on the return march. It was late in the year ; they must march to the north-east in the face of the biting northern wind of winter ; they would cross treeless country and there would be no fuel for fire. What wonder if his men now feared to set out upon that threatening journey. A day or two after starting La Vérendrye fell ill—but, cold and hungry and racked with pain as he was, he led his men steadily forward. Not until February 10th, more than two months after leaving the Mandans, were they safe under the rude shelter of Fort de la Reine. " Never in my life," he wrote in his diary, " did I endure so much misery, pain and fatigue as on that journey."

Some time not long after his return, La Vérendrye, ill and harassed by trouble with the partners in Montreal, sent his sons northward. They discovered Lake Manitoba and on the west side of it built a fort which they called Fort Dauphin. Either from Lake Manitoba or from Lake Winnipeg they discovered the Saskatchewan River which they called the Poskoiac, and built Fort Poskoia (see Fig. 3) where now is the town of The Pas. In the spring of 1742, accompanied this time by his youngest brother Louis, Pierre de la Vérendrye set out for the country of the Mandans. From that country they travelled to the most easterly spur of the main range of the Rocky Mountains, reaching the Bighorn Mountains shortly after the New Year. Now surely, their dream would come true ; from the top of the mountains they would gaze on the western sea. But again disappointment was in store for them. The Bow Indians, who had led them to the mountains, fearful of the onset of the Snake Indians on their defenceless women and children left in camp, refused to wait for the Vérendryes to make the climb, which, as we now know, would not have revealed the Pacific Ocean, and forced them to retreat in the teeth of a terrible blizzard. On their way back they buried on the line of march a leaden plate bearing the arms of France and an inscription on one side—on the other, roughly cut, their names and the date. That was in the summer of 1743. In the spring of 1913 a little girl found that tablet across the river from the city of Pierre in North Dakota. " For thirteen years," as Agnes Laut sums it up, " they had followed a hopeless quest. Instead of a western sea, they had found a sea of prairie, a sea of mountains and two great rivers, the Saskatchewan and the Missouri."

The tale of the La Vérendryes ends in sadness. They were involved with their creditors. An ungrateful government, professing to believe that they were making themselves rich rather than searching for the fabled sea, took from them their monopoly and gave it to a court favourite, de Noyelles. They were not even allowed to salvage their own property in the forts they had built. In six months de Noyelles had shown he could not manage the Indians ; and La Vérendrye, restored once more to favour, was decorated with the Order of the Cross of St. Louis and given a commission to go west again. Sending his son ahead, La Vérendrye eagerly began his preparations to follow in the spring, but in the midst of them, on December 6th, he died in Three Rivers.

His sons hoped to have permission to continue the work. But their claims were ignored ; even the provisions their father had sent forward were confiscated, and their monopoly rights were given to another Court favourite, St. Pierre. But he, too, failed, the end of his expedition being spectacular. Like La Vérendrye, he made Fort de la Reine his base. Unlike him he could not control the Indians. One day, when he was in the fort with only five Frenchmen, 200 Assiniboines, apparently in hostile mood, entered and took possession. St. Pierre first ordered them to leave, and then, with his own hand, put four of the leaders outside. Still they would not go and St. Pierre took desperate measures. He writes in his journal,

" I seized hold of a blazing brand, broke in the door of the powder magazine, knocked down a barrel of powder over which I passed the brand telling the Indians in an assured tone that I expected nothing at their hands and that in dying I would have the glory of subjecting them to the same fate. No sooner had they seen my lighted brand and my barrel of powder with its head staved in, than they fled."

So, shortly after, did the French, and the Indians burned the fort behind them. With them ended the search of the French for the western sea. Already the fur traders were following quickly on the trails blazed by the explorers.

CHAPTER II

FUR TRADERS

No record has come to light of the value of that first cargo of furs carried to England from Hudson Bay by Groseilliers. But it must have been great for, in haste and with as much secrecy as might be, the men who had backed the first venture organized the Hudson's Bay Company. King Charles II, by royal charter given to his cousin Prince Rupert and a few of his friends, brought into being " The Governor and Company of Adventurers of England Trading into Hudson's Bay," as its formal title was and is. Though they did not know it at the time, it was a great kingdom which the company was receiving. " All the land, countries, and territories upon the coasts and confines of the seas, streights, bays, lakes, rivers, creeks and sounds," as well as the whole trade and commerce of all those " seas, streights, bays, rivers, lakes, creeks, and sounds, in whatsoever latitude they shall be, that lie within the entrance of the streights commonly called Hudson's Streights " became the property of the Company. The territory was to be called Rupert's Land after the Prince, who became the first Governor. This Company was not only to control all the land, which, when extended at a later time to include British Columbia, was 2,800,000 square miles in extent, but they had greater powers than had the King of England, even then, over his own realm. Prince Rupert and his seven associates had, as well as their absolute monopoly of trade, the power to make laws, to plant colonies, to build towns and forts, and to maintain armies. No British subject might so much as set foot upon the territory without their consent, and for all this wide extent of land and all these rights the Company was to pay to the King two elks and two black beavers "whensoever, and as often as, we our heirs and successors shall happen to enter the said countries, territories and regions." As a reason for all this bounty on the part of the King, the charter declared that the Adventurers had "at their own great cost and charge undertaken an Expedition for the Discovery of a new Passage into the South Sea and for the finding some Trade for Furs, mineralls and other considerable Commodities." By these, the King said, he hoped to gain for himself and for his kingdom "very great advantage."

But it was not of the size of their territory, nor of the complete power over it, which their charter gave them, that the founders of the Hudson's Bay Company were thinking, but rather of the riches to be derived from the new world. Groseilliers had built Fort Charles, the first post in James Bay, and a second post at Moose River was established the year after the Company was organized. In the time when Radisson was back with the French he built the post on the Hayes River which became the headquarters of all trade for years, and as York Factory is still the headquarters of trade upon the bay. At the mouth of the Churchill River the Company built Fort Prince of Wales. Ruins of this fort, which afterwards was made one of the strongest fortifications on the continent, may still be seen. It was over 100 yards long on the north and south sides, and its walls were from 37 to 42 feet in thickness. On the walls were mounted forty guns. Eighteen years after the building of their earliest fort, Fort Charles, the Company had forts at five other places, Hayes River, Moose River, Port Nelson, New Severn, and Churchill River. Having established these posts it was a long time before further efforts in this line were made. In 1749, when a vain attempt was made in the British Parliament to upset the charter, the Company could show only six forts, as testimony to what it was doing to explore the passage to the western sea, and it had in its employ only about

120 men. A fragment of the Kelsey journal was submitted at this enquiry, but had the officers of the Company had that full journal its story of exploration would have been much more effective.

During all this time the Indians had been bringing their furs down to the bay. Arrived at a fort, they camped outside the stockade, and began the business of selling their furs by drinking as much liquor as the

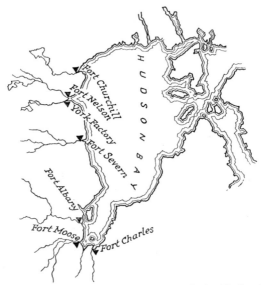

Fig. 4.—Map showing the early posts of the Hudson's Bay Company around Hudson Bay.

traders would supply. Though it had been watered before being given to them, its effects were serious and it was usually two or three days before they were ready for business. When that time came, the Indians were admitted to the fort with their furs, the skins were inspected and the price to be paid for each one was indicated by little notched sticks or quills. Taking his little sticks the Indian passed on to the store where, displayed for his benefit, were the things he longed to possess—axes, guns, blankets, mirrors, beads, and so on.

All prices were reckoned by the Hudson's Bay Company in beaver skins, not in money, and tokens were later made to represent these values. A list made out for the trading of 1783 gives an idea of the prices charged the Indian for the goods traded for his fur. For a blanket six beaver must be paid, ten or twelve for a gun, three for a pair of breeches or two handkerchiefs. But, if he wanted a brass kettle, one skin would do for it, as it would for three-quarters of a pound of beads, or two pounds of sugar, or a pair of shoes, or two of the much-desired looking-glasses. For a gallon of brandy he paid four beaver. This price list is one which was used for the southern district, that is for James Bay. At York and Churchill prices were higher, for, as the Company records show, " the French being not so near these places, cannot interfere with the company's trade so much as they do at Albany and Moose River where they undersell the company and by that means carry off the most valuable furs."

Once the trading was over the Indians quickly dispersed into the wilds whence they had come and the business of sorting and packing the furs for shipment kept all employed. Once a year two ships sailed into the bay, one for York and one for James Bay, carrying the supplies for the Company's men and the goods with which they were to trade. Discharging these they reloaded with the skins and sailed away as soon as might be in order to get through the straits before the ice formed again.

Though Radisson had brought home cargoes of such great value, that in 1690 the Company had trebled its stock without calling for any cash payment, and in addition had paid a dividend of 25 per cent., the trade was not always successful. Before the end of the century the Company had suffered losses to the amount of £1,000,000 or more. Most of the losses were the result of the struggle with the French for the mastery of Hudson Bay, for the French King was not willing to

acknowledge the right of his brother of England to grant
away this land and the monopoly of its furs. By 1697
the Hudson's Bay Company had been able to keep only
a small foothold at Fort Albany and for the next sixteen
years the French controlled the territory around the
shore of Hudson Bay. Then the Treaty of Utrecht in
1713 restored the whole of the North-west to England and
so to the Company. Recovery was rapid, for by 1720
the Company was able to treble its stock again, selling
the new stock to the shareholders for a cash payment
of only 10 per cent.

But no treaty made in the old world could settle the
fur war in the new. Even more serious than the open
warfare of the French Government, and much more
continuous, was the fight of the French traders. This
was true whether these traders held licences from the
Government of New France or were of the free-trader
class who harassed English and French alike. While
the British custom was to wait at Hudson Bay for the
Indians to come to their posts to trade, the French had
from the beginning adopted the method of going into
the interior to seek the Indians and buy their furs.
Thus when the French penetrated into the country
tributary to Hudson Bay they were able to intercept
the trade to the British posts and thus draw into French
channels the furs coming from the country beyond
Hudson Bay. Threatened thus with the loss of their
trade, the Hudson's Bay Company decided to follow
the policy which Henry Kelsey had initiated fifty years
before. They sent Anthony Hendry with a flotilla of
canoes and 400 paddlers up the Hayes River to visit the
Indians and buy their furs. Nine hundred miles to the
west, across what is now the province of Saskatchewan,
Hendry led his men, discovering the Saskatchewan River
and wintering somewhere between the present cities
of Edmonton and Calgary. It was on the return journey,
when his boats were ladened with furs, that there took
place the only meeting of which history tells us between
men of the British and French nations in the interior of

From an old H.B.C. print.   John Ross Robertson Collection, Toronto Public Library.

INDIANS VISITING THE GOVERNOR.

this country, while eastern Canada was still New France. On the Saskatchewan River, about 150 miles above that Fort Poskoia which the La Vérendryes had built about ten years before, Hendry found a French post, Fort de la Corne. There he was entertained by La Corne, the officer in charge.

It did not take Hendry long to realize some of the ways in which the French were able to take the trade from the English. " The French," he says, " speak several Indian languages to perfection ; they have the advantage of us in every shape and, if they had Brazile tobacco, which they have not, would entirely cut off our trade." When Hendry came in touch with the Blackfeet Indians he tried to induce the great chief to come to Hudson Bay to trade with the British. Then he learned another advantage of the French.

" White man, I have heard thy message," replied the Chief, " but the fort is far off. Our young men ride the plains like the wind but they know not the skill of the paddles. They live not on fish but on the flesh of the buffalo. They are the lords of the plentiful plains, while we hear that those who go down to the fort, ofttimes starve on the way. Therefore we cannot go to the fort though we thank thee for coming this long way to invite us." " His remarks I thought exceedingly true," adds Hendry.

With the conquest of Canada in 1763, the French traders disappeared from the west, but their places were taken by others who carried on a more skilful and much more relentless war against the Hudson's Bay Company. Attracted by the wealth to be won, English and Scottish merchants came to Montreal and, joining with Canadians there, employed the coureurs de bois and the voyageurs who had been trading under the French régime. Thus to the greater skill of the French in intercourse with the Indians was now added the keener mercantile sense of the British. This trade from Montreal was carried on partly by companies and partly by private traders. Four years after the conquest the " pedlars," as the

Hudson's Bay Company people, all men from Great Britain, contemptuously called the Montreal traders, were as far west as Fort de la Reine and that same year James Finley penetrated to the Saskatchewan. Another three or four years and forts had been established on the Saskatchewan and Churchill rivers, thus effectively intercepting the Indians on the way to Hudson Bay.

Now the Hudson's Bay Company, realizing at last that it must meet this competition point by point or give up the struggle, began to send men into the interior and to establish post for post. One of the first to go was Samuel Hearne, who built on the lower Saskatchewan a fort which he called Cumberland House. Its very name enraged the Montreal traders, many of whom were Jacobites, for it was, obviously as an insult to them, named for that Duke of Cumberland whom they termed " the Butcher of Cullodon." It was also at an exact point to spoil the plans which they had been making to outwit the Hudson's Bay Company, and its construction marks a turning point in the history of that organization.

The presence of so many traders in the field was bad both for the traders and for the Indians. All manner of practices were employed to induce the Indians to sell the furs to the first man on the spot, or to rob the successful trader of his booty. Alexander Henry has left in his journal a description of things as they were at the Grande Portage, at the west end of Lake Superior, where the men bringing up supplies from the east met those who had been trading in the interior. He " found the traders in a state of extreme reciprocal hostility each pursuing his own interest in such a manner as might most injure his neighbour. The consequences were very hurtful to the morals of the Indians."

Such competition was no better for trade then than it is now and there was, moreover, danger of an Indian war. An outbreak of smallpox checked both the danger and the trade. When the plague had passed and trade began to revive, the great merchants at Montreal saw that more organization was necessary and in 1784, led by the two Frobishers, Benjamin and Joseph, and Simon McTavish, organized the North-West Company. The advantages of the new Company were great. To begin with their head offices were in Canada, and they were thus more closely in touch with the actual trading operations. Then they had at their command most of the men skilled in the trade in the years of the French régime, the coureurs de bois, French, or half French half Indian, all of them sympathetic with the Indian and skilled in his ways. Moreover this Company adopted a new method of dealing with the men who directed the work in the field. It made them real partners in the business, calling them " the wintering partners." Some of them had one share, some two, and all joined in the direction of the Company, meeting for consultation once a year at the Grande Portage, the point of crossing from Lake Superior into the Lake of the Woods and Winnipeg River route which these British traders used instead of the Nipigon or Kaministiquia routes used by the French. Thus the men engaged in trade for the new Company were working for themselves, sharing in the gains they made, whereas the men of the Hudson's Bay Company were still working on salaries, and meagre ones at that. The fact that the governing committee of the Hudson's Bay Company lived in London and knew very little about actual conditions in the North-west was also a serious handicap. On the other hand, the Hudson's Bay Company had the great advantage of being nearer their field of operations. Their supplies were brought to Hudson Bay by vessels from the old country, and had only to be transported from that point by canoes; whereas the North-West Company had to put its canoes in the water at Montreal. It followed that the Hudson's Bay Company was able to get its traders into the field almost a month earlier than the " pedlars " from Montreal.

At the time of the organization of the North-West Company there were about 500 canoe men in its employ. Half of these travelled over the route from Montreal to the Grande Portage in canoes which could carry 4 tons weight of supplies and were operated by eight to ten men. The other 250 men were employed in taking the goods into the interior and they travelled in smaller canoes which would carry a ton and a half, and which required four to five men each.

These boats left Montreal in the spring as early in May as possible, came by Michilimackinac, where they

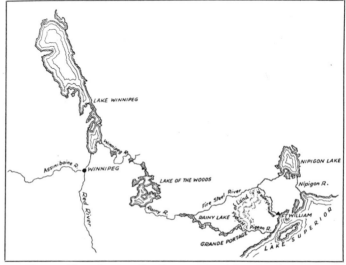

Fig. 5.—Map showing the three routes taken by fur traders from Lake Superior into the Lake of the Woods :

1. Via Nipigon Lake and Fire Steel River.
2. Via Kaministiquia River and Fire Steel River.
3. Via Pigeon River and the Grande Portage.

got fresh supplies, and reached the west end of Lake Superior early in July. About fifteen days were required to transfer the goods across the nine-mile portage and pack them into the canoes for the inland journey. Two-thirds goods and one-third provisions were carried, thus obliging the men engaged in the inland trade to depend upon the natives for the additional food required. In the *Voyages of Sir Alexander Mackenzie* is to be found a graphic account of this annual meeting by a man who often saw it.

" It is, indeed, very creditable to them as servants that, though they are sometimes assembled to the number of 1,200 men, indulging themselves in the free use of liquor, and quarrelling with each other, they always show the greatest respect to their employers, who are comparatively but few in number, and beyond the aid of any legal power to enforce due obedience. In short a degree of subordination can only be maintained by the good opinion these men entertain of their employers, which has been uniformly the case, since the trade has been formed and conducted on a regular system."

The annual business meeting, which soon came to be held at Fort William instead of at Grande Portage, was the great event in the life of the North-West Company. Here the Montreal directors, arriving in gaily decorated canoes with cooks and butlers and servants and a plentiful supply of wines and liquors, met the men who had been the winter before enduring the rigours of the west. By day they conducted their work on an absolutely business basis. Accounts were made, profits distributed, new " wintering partners " elected, if there were vacancies. By night great banquets, which seem almost impossible so far in the wilds, were held at which the drinking of the liquor brought up from Montreal was the great feature. The business ended, the Montreal men returned to luxury, the " wintering partners " to the hard life of the fur trader.

The Nor'-Westers did not have everything their own way. They had always to fight the Hudson's Bay Company once that organization came into the interior to meet them. But in the beginning their efforts were directed more against other companies, particularly that organized at the same time as the North-West by Peter Pond and Peter Pangman, and three years later absorbed into it, and the X.Y. Company organized by Alexander Mackenzie, who was dissatisfied with his treatment by the North-West Company after his wonderful voyage of discovery to the Pacific Coast. Mackenzie's company had a longer life, from 1798 to 1805, but in the end was absorbed into the North-West. There were also free or independent traders to be fought, the last of these coming to the west in 1805. Against all these the Nor'-Westers carried on a fierce warfare which had no rules. The comment of Alexander Ross, who worked for both the North-West and the Hudson's Bay Company, sums up the matter.

" The North-Westers, high in their own estimation, professed to despise all others and threatened with lawless violence all persons, who presumed in the ordinary course of trade to come within their line—a line without limits, which fancy or caprice induced them to draw between themselves and all others. Many needy adventurers from time to time sought their way into the Indian countries from Canada ; but few, very few indeed, ever had the courage or the good fortune, if good fortune we might call it, to pass Fort William. And if, in a dark night or misty morning, they had passed the forbidden barrier, vengeance soon overtook them. Their canoes were destroyed, themselves threatened, and their progress impeded in every way, so that they had to return ruined men."

The Red River country had early become a stronghold of the North-West Company. From its plains the Indians went out to hunt the buffalo and to make pemmican, the food upon which all fur traders relied. This was made from buffalo meat, cut into strips and dried, then pounded fine, put into sacks of the buffalo hide and mixed with the hot fat of the buffalo in the proportion of four to five. Packed thus it would keep for months and would sustain life even though no other food was available. In its new policy of following the Montreal traders to their outposts, the Hudson's Bay Company came south into the Red River territory in 1793 and the following year built Brandon House on the Assiniboine River about seventeen miles below the present Brandon. Two years afterwards they established a post near Fort de la Reine. Such was the competition around this point that at one period there were no fewer than five separate

By permission of the Governor and Committee of the Hudson's Bay Company.

YORK FACTORY ABOUT THE MIDDLE OF LAST CENTURY.

posts or forts there. Just when the Hudson's Bay Company came to the place where Winnipeg now stands is not so certain. British independent traders, perhaps, built a fort here—a fort was any stockaded post—as early as 1780 or 1781. The forks of the two rivers was always a marked spot and served as a rendezvous for the traders coming from James Bay and from Lake Superior. Here cargoes were resorted and repacked for the various routes to the north and west. But we do not seem to be on any certain ground as to the actual existence of a post here until 1803, when Alexander Henry established on September 27th, at the Forks, an outpost of his regular station up the Red at Pembina. This fort was not a success and was abandoned after one winter, but three years later John McDonald of the North-West Company built here Fort Gibraltar on the north bank of the Assiniboine right at its entrance into the Red. This fort became the headquarters of that Company's fur trade and of its operations against the Selkirk Settlement.

The Hudson's Bay Company was now in a better position to carry on the fight. It had its posts throughout the country. It had taken into its service many of the Métis, or men of mixed European and Indian blood, and through them it was better able to deal with the Indians than when its trade was done by its Scottish clerks only. Most of all it had a good reputation with the Indians. Edward Umfraville, who left the Hudson's Bay Company to enter the service of the North-West, put it on record that the English traders, as the Hudson's Bay Company men were called, had the advantage of a better reputation in character and trade among the Indians. In one way particularly the reputation of the Hudson's Bay Company stands high. Its officers had always been reluctant to sell the Indians liquor, understanding well, as all white men who came in contact with them understood, the peculiar susceptibility of the Indians to what they called " firewater," and the extremely dangerous effects it had upon them. When in the pressure of competition the Hudson's Bay Company

4

was forced to use liquor freely, it nevertheless stood ready to give it up, as appeared in an effort which was made to get the British Parliament to forbid altogether the sale of liquor to the Indians. This Company put itself on record as ready to agree to the legislation, since its men judged it would not be harmful to the fur trade. The North-West Company men looked at it differently, however, and used all their influence successfully to have the matter dropped.

But the North-West Company, by acquiring complete control of the trade from Montreal, was also in a stronger position to carry on the fight, which it did with a whole-hearted adoption of the policy that might made right. On neither side did the men who carried on the actual struggle hesitate to use all methods to win.

Of this struggle many thrilling stories survive. One or two will serve to illustrate the way of this war, for such it became. Once the Hudson's Bay Company men, hearing that a party of Indians with their furs had made its camp forty miles away, invited the Nor'-Westers, whose post was near their own, to a dance, secretly sending four sledges to get the Indians' furs. Furious when they discovered that they had been tricked, the Nor'-Westers waited their turn. Meeting a Hudson's Bay Company party on the way to another Indian camp to which they also were bound, they started a camp fire and passed around the liquor. The Hudson's Bay Company men drank freely, but the more wily Nor'-Westers poured most of theirs on the snow. When at last the Hudson's Bay men fell asleep, the Nor'-Westers tied them to their sledges and started their dogs on the return to the fort, while they themselves went forward and got the furs. Sometimes violence, rather than trickery, was used. In May 1806 one of the Hudson's Bay Company traders stationed near Fort Albany had his house broken into by the North-West men, who seized and held him and his men, while others seized the furs. Another Hudson's Bay Company factor and all his men at a post on Lake Winnipeg were not only assaulted but dangerously wounded by a party of Nor'-Westers who came to seize their furs. Alexander Ross describes the situation thus : " their (the North-West Company) servants pillaged their opponents, destroyed their forts and trading establishments, as suited their views, and not infrequently kept armed parties marauding from post to post, menacing with destruction and death everyone that presumed to check their career till at last party spirit and rivalry in trade had changed the whole social order of things and brought about a state of open hostility."

Already in 1803 the Parliament of Canada, alarmed at the violence of the struggle, had passed an act which allowed the Government to take cognizance of crimes committed in what were known as the Indian Territories. Little came of it, however, partly for the reason that the North-West Company directors had ways of their own of influencing the courts so near at hand, so remote from the Hudson's Bay Company offices in London. How the struggle would have ended is still a matter of argument, though the odds seem to have been with the Nor'-Westers. But an unlooked-for event changed entirely the course of development. This was the coming of the settlers, an event of even greater interest than the fur trade, with all its tales of romance and daring. It was these settlers who, caught in the midst of it with disastrous effects upon themselves, were yet the means of bringing to an end the fierce warfare of the fur traders.

CHAPTER III

To the dream of a passage to the western sea, to the dream of great wealth to be won from the fur trade, there was added another dream as a driving force in the development of the great North-west, of which Manitoba was the beginning. This time the dream was of a great free British colony in this unknown land, and the seer of that vision was Thomas Douglas, Earl of Selkirk. It is one of the ironies of which history is full, that he should have been drawn to that dream by reading the *Voyages from Montreal on the River St. Lawrence through the Continent of North America to the Frozen and Pacific Ocean in the Years* 1789 *and* 1793," by Alexander Mackenzie. For the author of that book, which, it is said, attracted the interest of Napoleon, was to be one of the bitterest enemies of the plan by which Lord Selkirk sought the realization of his dream.

Lord Selkirk was a pioneer in thinking of emigration as a remedy for economic distress in the old land. For the people of Ireland, harassed with the disorders following the rebellion of 1798, for the simple agricultural people and fisher folk of the Scottish Highlands, presently to be evicted from their homes that the owners of the estates might raise sheep, Lord Selkirk dreamed of free, happy, prosperous homes in the new world. In his enthusiasm for his plans he formally offered to the Secretary of State " to devote his personal exertions and the best years of his life to the service of his country in carrying them into execution."

But this idea, though generally accepted now, was new then, and Lord Selkirk could get no co-operation from the

British Government. Two settlement projects were attempted before he came to the great effort of his life. The first was made in Prince Edward Island, to which eight hundred Scottish settlers were taken in 1803. Success marked the early years of this colony. The second experiment was tried in Upper Canada, in Baldoon, a tract of land between Lakes Huron and Erie. Here, owing to opposition from the " Family Compact," much discouragement was met, and, though the settlement continued until the American invasion in the war of 1812, it did not take root in the country.

It was about the time of his marriage into one of the leading Hudson's Bay Company families in 1807 that the interest of Lord Selkirk in Rupert's Land revived. He was still unable to interest either the Government or the Company in his plans for settlement. But he had a remarkable faith in the possibilities of this western country.

" In so vast an extent of country," he wrote in his *Sketch of the Fur Trade*, " there must, of course, be great varieties of climate; but there is a breadth of at least twelve or fifteen degrees of latitude as fit to be inhabited as many of the well cultivated countries of the North of Europe ; and within this range extensive districts may be found that are preferable both in soil and climate to any of the remaining British colonies on the Continent of North America. It is a very moderate calculation to say that if these regions were occupied by an industrious population, they might afford ample means of subsistence to more than thirty million of British subjects ; and these immense resources of national wealth are to be lost sight of forever for the sake of a trade to the gross amount of £200,000 or £300,000 per annum."

Lord Selkirk determined that those resources should not be lost, and proceeded to buy up the stock of the Hudson's Bay Company, which was then having one of its times of low value. He induced his family to do the same, with the result that in May 1811, the directors granted to him a tract of land 116,000 square miles in extent, taking in parts of the present province of Manitoba

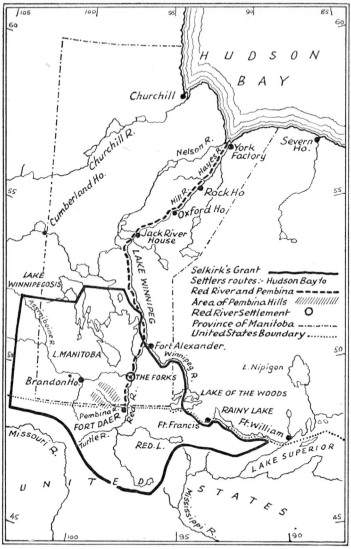

Fig. 6.—Map showing the grant to Lord Selkirk and the route travelled by the early settlers from Hudson Bay to Red River and Fort Daer.

and of the states of Minnesota and North Dakota. It was to be known as Assiniboia, and in return for this grant Lord Selkirk pledged himself to establish there at his own expense a settlement.

There was no delay in setting about the business of planting this settlement in the heart of the North American continent. The fulfilment of Lord Selkirk's plans was made possible by the fact that just now began in Scotland the cruel evictions of the crofters. On July 26th, 1811, the first party sailed from Stromness, not without being harassed considerably by agents and friends of the North-West Company. Too late, the North-West Company realized the destructive effect on its trade of Lord Selkirk's plans and bent every effort to foil him.

Traders and indentured servants to the number of 106 made up the first party, the plan being that the servants should go at once to Red River to build shelters for the real colonists who would follow the next year. The bad fortune which was to pursue this colony throughout its early days was soon in evidence. This particular voyage was the latest and longest known up to that time, and the party did not reach York Factory until September 24th. Boats for river travel had been sent out on the vessel, but, through the quarrels of petty officers, these were, unbelievable as it seems, carried back to Scotland. It was not possible to go to Red River that year ; there was no accommodation for so many at York Factory ; so Miles McDonnell, sent out as first Governor of Assiniboia, led his men to a spot twenty-three miles away on the north bank of the Nelson River ; there they built an encampment and spent the winter amid hardships almost unbearable and rendered worse by bitter disagreement among themselves.

During the winter boats were built at York Factory, and on July 6th, 1812, Miles McDonnell and twenty-two men, all he thought well to take with him, started up the Hayes River towards the " Land of Promise," as he wrote to Lord Selkirk. On August 30th they arrived at Red River and landed at the spot where the Hudson's Bay

Company had a trading post on the east bank opposite the mouth of the Assiniboine. Here, five days later, Miles McDonnell took possession of Assiniboia by formal proclamation, there being present, besides his own party, three men of the North-West Company, one of whom was his own brother-in-law, and a few Canadian "freemen" and Indians. McDonnell chose a spot a little down the river from the Forks—it was later known as Point Douglas— and set his men to work building a fort and breaking land. He was astonished to find that the Hudson's Bay Company men had made no preparations at all for their coming. They had, he wrote, " not one bag of pemmican or any other article of provisions reserved for us." No crops were possible that year, and food must be had, so McDonnell went off up the river to the Pembina Hills. Here the buffalo came to seek shelter from the storms of winter, and here the Indians hunted them and prepared their year's supply of pemmican. If the newcomers were not to starve they must seek the same shelter and the same food-supply, and so too must the members of the second party, which, as McDonnell knew, was to leave Scotland that year. So while some of his men were building Fort Douglas, near the forks of the Red and the Assiniboine, he and others of his party built Fort Daer on a point of land close to the junction of the Pembina and Red rivers, and near the present town of Pembina.

Meantime, Lord Selkirk had been active in reorganizing the affairs of the Company and in having his agents prepare the second party. This second party, which included some of the permanent settlers and more servants, sailed from Stromness under Owen Keveny on June 24th, 1812. The opposition of the North-West Company appeared in strenuous efforts made to hinder the work of recruiting, and many wild, exaggerated stories of the new world were circulated. Having better fortune than that of the previous year, this party was able to set out from York on August 26th. They travelled in three boats, there being seventy-one persons in all, and reached Red

River on October 27th. There they found they must go at once to Pembina to spend the winter.

" The Indians agreed to carry their children," says Ross in his *Red River Settlement*, " but all the rest, both men and women, had to trudge on foot ; while all their little superfluities were parted with by way of recompense to their guides. . . . The journey from Pembina exhibited a strange perversion of things ; the savage in aristocratic independence was completely equipped and mounted on a fine horse, while the children of civilization, degraded and humbled, were compelled to walk after him on foot." But, as Ross goes on to say, " to the Scotch immigrants who were completely in their power, they were everything they could wish, mild, generous, trustworthy."

The new settlers had their first experience in hunting buffalo, which were that year very plentiful near Fort Daer, and the women learned how to make pemmican, which was to be for so long a staple food among them.

In May of the following year the colonists all came back to the more fertile land at the Forks, as the site of Winnipeg was then known, and began the heavy task of breaking the land, sowing the crops, and building themselves rude homes in the wilderness. They had no tools but hoes wherewith to break the tough prairie soil, for no one had thought to send ploughs or harrows. Moreover, these settlers had for the most part been fishermen, not farmers. Nature too failed them. Ross speaks of this summer as one of " peace with hunger." Fish were scarce, and even the small fruits failed, so that the main dependence for food was the prairie turnip, which is a variety of the pea family. There was also a weed, known as fat-hen, of which large quantities were gathered. But, even with the poor tools at their disposal, they found that the land was very fertile. It is on record that four quarts of wheat produced twelve bushels, so it was not altogether in a hopeless mood that, hearing that the next party of settlers would not arrive until the following year, they determined to go again to Pembina, saving every grain of the precious wheat for seed.

Ross records the outstanding feature of that winter thus : " notwithstanding the extreme kindness shown by the French half-breeds to the Scotch settlers last winter, they now kept aloof and regarded our people with a jealous eye. Ignorant and awkward as the settlers were in such pursuits, they had nevertheless to think and act for themselves, slaving all winter in deep snow to preserve life."

This deep snow kept the buffalo from coming in from the plains ; the settlers were not able to travel on snow-shoes as were the Métis ; and the hardships they endured in searching out the Indian camps in order to get the buffalo meat, and in dragging it on sledges back to Fort Daer, were such as to discourage the hardiest. " They returned to the Forks in the spring," says one chronicler, " resolved never to go to Pembina again under any circumstances."

But hard and disheartening as was the lot of the first and second parties, it was after all not nearly so discouraging as the misfortunes which befell the third. By this time there had been many evictions and the trouble of Lord Selkirk's agents was not to get a party, but to choose out of seven hundred applicants the hundred who were all that could be taken. That the number was thus limited was due in great part to another of those acts which showed clearly that Lord Selkirk's plans had not the support of the Hudson's Bay Company men actually engaged in the fur trade. They had failed to build boats at York, and word had been sent that no more than a hundred persons could be transported to the colony. Again the agents of the North-West Company sought to hinder the sailing of the vessels. In the end the party got away on June 28th in two ships, the *Eddystone* carrying the men who were going out in the Hudson Bay's Company service and the *Prince of Wales* the colonists. Typhoid fever broke out on the *Prince of Wales* during the voyage, and several of the colonists died and were buried at sea. When the ship arrived at Churchill many were so ill as to be helpless. With a

disregard of duty and orders rare in the Company's service
the Captain of the *Prince of Wales*, Turner by name, refused to carry his passengers to York, to which port they
were to have been taken, and sailed away, leaving them
on the rocks at Churchill, without shelter and without
food except such as the Factor at Fort Prince of Wales
chose to give them.

The Company clerks made their way overland to York,
but there was nothing for the settlers to do but to winter
at Churchill. Fifteen weary miles they went up the
Churchill River to a wooded spot and there built a rough
encampment. It was October before it was finished,
and a month later before they were free of the fever.
Supplies of every kind were scarce, for the Factor, Auld,
was by no means generously inclined towards them.
A thirty-mile trip was necessary in order to bring any
supplies from the fort, and when the abundance of par-
tridges seemed to assure them a supply of fresh food Auld
took from them the flint locks of their guns. Hostile
to them from first to last, Auld spoke of the Highlanders
as " civilized caffres," and called the young leader,
Archibald McDonald, " proud, stupid, and foolish."

No hardships could daunt these courageous Scots.
With the first breath of spring it was decided that the
strongest should push on to York Factory to get an early
start to the Red River. Accordingly, on April 6th, a
procession of 21 men and 20 women set out on that
150-mile walk in what was still winter weather. We
read with a thrill that in the middle of the long procession there marched a Highland piper playing to keep
their spirits up. The strongest of the men went ahead
with the sledges to beat a path for the women, while two
or three brought up the rear to prevent straggling.
Even the unfriendly Auld testified that none hung behind
on the march except the small party of Angus MacKay,
his wife, and three friends, who stayed behind that the
son of the MacKays might be born on the lonely trail.
In the same order in which they had left Churchill those
gallant forerunners of all the brave adventurers who have

come to make their homes on the western plains, marched into camp at York Factory. A month later and they were off on the 750-mile journey to their new home. They arrived at Red River, June 21st, 1814, and began to build their cabins and to break what ground they could, having still no proper tools.

To all appearances Miles McDonnell, the Governor of Assiniboia, had established control of the territory. He had issued a proclamation forbidding traders to take any more pemmican from the district than would serve to carry them to the next post, and even for that they must apply for a licence. Now, pemmican was the staple food of the men travelling through the territory on the trading expeditions, and the Red River country was not only the centre of its production but also the best distributing point for the Nor'-Westers. They, therefore, were alarmed and indignant at the action of the Governor and, the Métis being in sympathy with them, they continued quietly to have their men hunt the buffalo and make and store pemmican for their traders. Carrying things with a high hand, McDonnell went out to the North-West post, Assiniboine House, seized the pemmican stored there, put part of it in the Hudson's Bay Company post across the river, and brought the rest down to Fort Douglas for his own settlers, right past Fort Gibraltar, the North-West post at Red River. Many threats of further hostilities came from both sides, but in the end a compromise was reached and the North-West winter partners went off to the meeting at Fort William, while the settlers hoped for peace.

The Nor'-Westers had, of course, been opposed from the beginning to the whole project of the settlement, and the action of the Governor had confirmed their worst fears of interference with their trading operations. It has to be remembered that just before the coming of the first settlers they had found themselves apparently on the eve of complete success in their fight with the Hudson's Bay Company. In the year 1811 more furs were taken by Nor'-Westers to Montreal out of Hudson

Bay territory than were shipped to England from all of the Hudson's Bay Company posts. Not only did they fear the interference with the fur trade which the settlement would certainly cause, but they feared also the loss of profitable trade with the Indians. The Hudson's Bay Company was able to bring goods from England much cheaper than the North-West Company could transport them from Montreal, and thus was able to undersell its rival. John Pritchard, who lived through all these troubles, having been early in the country as a North-West man, expressed it thus in a sworn statement. He wrote that he had :

" always conceived this to be the reason of the hostility manifested by the North-West Company against the establishment of a colony in the quarter either by the grantees of the Hudson's Bay Company or by any others, although the Indians are desirous of it because until a colony shall be established there the great number of servants employed by the North-West will enable them to keep out of the country all traders and all supplies except their own, whereas, after the establishment of a settlement, the supplies not raised in the colony itself must necessarily be brought from England and not through Canada ; and a liberal trade would thereupon be the consequence, to the great benefit of the Indian."

The Nor'-Westers have left us under no doubt as to their feelings and their intentions towards the new adventure. One quotation from a letter written by Simon McGillivray to the winter partners of the Company as early as 1812 will suffice to show their hostilities. " It will require some time, and, I fear, cause much expense to us as well as to himself before he is driven to abandon the project ; and yet he must be driven to abandon it, for his success would strike at the very existence of our trade."

Excitement ran high at the annual meeting at Fort William that summer of 1814, and plans were laid to destroy the colony. " You see myself and our mutual friend Cameron," wrote Alexander Macdonnell on his

way back to the West, " so far on our way to commence
hostilities against the enemy in Red River. . . . Something serious will undoubtedly take place. Nothing but
the complete downfall of the colony will satisfy some by
fair or foul means. A most desirable object if it can be
accomplished ; so here is at them with all my heart and
energy." When to the state of mind of the Nor'-Westers
is added the fact that the Hudson's Bay Company men in
Canada liked very little either the new and more business-
like methods of Lord Selkirk in connection with the fur
trade, or the settlement idea, it will be easily seen that the
colonists had many enemies and few friends.

It was not long before the colonists were in doubt as
to just who were their friends. The Nor'-Westers,
immediately upon their return from the Fort William
meeting, claimed jurisdiction over the whole territory.
They arrested and sent away the sheriff. They hunted
the buffalo and stored pemmican. Finally they arrested
the Governor himself. All this time they were giving
parties and presents to the settlers. Luxuries and
wines, such as had not been seen in the interior before,
were carried up from Fort William. It was whispered
to the settlers that they would never be happy and
secure at Red River, but that there was in Upper Canada
another and a better land of promise to which the North-
West Company would have them conveyed free of charge
and in which they would each be given 200 acres of land.
Any wages Lord Selkirk might owe them the Company
would pay, and, if three-quarters of the settlers would
accept the offer, they should have free food for a year.
With the offer threats were judiciously blended. Finally,
the Governor surrendered to the North-West agents, and
in June 1815 all but thirteen families who remained
loyal to Lord Selkirk, were carried to Upper Canada.
Forced to leave Red River, these thirteen families set out
sadly for Lake Winnipeg. Fort Douglas and all the
houses were burnt to the ground. "I am happy to
inform you," wrote Simon McGillivray, " that the colony
has all been knocked on the head by the N. W.

Company." But Simon McGillivray was not quite right. John McLean, and three other men, resisting all persuasions and threats, remained at the Forks. They cared for the tiny crops which had not been destroyed, and began at once the work of rebuilding Fort Douglas.

Another party of settlers, this time under Robert Semple, the new Governor of Assiniboia, was already on its way and arrived at York Factory in August. Lord Selkirk had by now established an organization at Montreal, and from that city came Colin Robertson with a party of twenty men. He brought back the thirteen families from Jack River (Fig. 6), beyond the head of Lake Winnipeg, whither they had gone, and on November 3rd the Semple party joined them at the Forks. There was great rejoicing that day. There had been a beautiful harvest. Buffalo were plentiful. " The Colours were hoisted," wrote Semple to Lord Selkirk, " the guns were fired, at night we laughed and drank and danced, and now the serious calculations of the Colony commence." There being no houses at the Forks, the whole colony had once more to enact the weary journey down to Pembina, and to spend the winter there. They returned in the spring full of hope and began to till the soil.

The Nor'-Westers spent the winter preparing to deal still more harshly with the colony, which had proved not to be so completely knocked on the head as Simon McGillivray had believed. This time they roused the Métis to take their part. A leader of the Métis, Cuthbert Grant, called Warden of the Plains, organized them, and in the early summer, after a winter of struggle, in the course of which Governor Semple had seized and dismantled Fort Gibraltar, they began to come towards the settlement.

Their arrival precipitated a tragedy on June 19th, 1816, which is known as the Battle of Seven Oaks. Sixty men, under Grant, mounted on prairie horses, were coming down the Portage highway—the same road as Portage Avenue in Winnipeg—that evening. When they were within four miles of Fort Douglas they turned off to the

north-east. The look-out at the fort having seen them,
the alarm was given, and Governor Semple and his men,
to about the number of thirty, marched north along the
colony road, which corresponded to Main Street in
Winnipeg, thus travelling almost parallel to the Métis.
When he came closer, Semple, seeing that there were more
men than he had thought, sent back to the fort for
reinforcements, but went on without waiting for them.

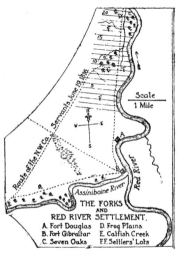

Fig. 7.—Plan of Red River Settlement showing the lines of
march of the Métis under Cuthbert Grant, and the men of the
settlement under Governor Semple, from the papers of the
Manitoba Historical and Scientific Society.

Soon he found himself confronted by a half-moon of
Métis, who were still moving in the same direction as
he was, that is, away from Fort Douglas. Before long
the Métis turned ; one of their number, Boucher, rode
up to the Governor, who seems to have engaged in angry
talk with him. It is one of the matters of dispute who
fired the first shot ; but, that shot having been fired,
there was a general engagement, and in a few moments
Governor Semple and all his party were either killed or

From a painting ascribed to Raeburn at St. Mary's Isle, Scotland.

LORD SELKIRK.

wounded. The Métis killed on the spot several of the wounded, including Governor Semple, barbarously mutilating some of them. Twenty-one were left dead, the others taken prisoners. The settlers who had sought refuge in Fort Douglas surrendered, and all the property was delivered to Cuthbert Grant, who took possession in the name of the North-West Company. The settlers, in despair, set out again for Lake Winnipeg, and once more it seemed that the colony must be at an end. The North-West partner, Alexander Macdonnell, who had organized all this attack, received the news at Portage la Prairie with what has been described as " almost incredible exultation," while it is on record that " the gentlemen present all shouted with joy."

From the beginning it had been the intention of Lord Selkirk to come himself to the colony at the head of a large party of settlers. Year after year he had been obliged to postpone his coming, but in the winter of 1815, following the burning of the colony, he had come out to Montreal. There, finding it impossible to get from the Canadian Government the soldiers for whom he had authority from the Secretary of State in Great Britain, he had engaged some members of two disbanded regiments of German and Swiss mercenary soldiers, known as de Meurons, from the name of their commander. Accompanied by these soldiers, he was actually on his way to Red River when, at Sault Ste. Marie, he heard of the Seven Oaks affray. Changing his plans, he went to the North-West post at Fort William and there carried things with a high hand, a course of action which was to lead him into much trouble in the courts of Ontario, where his friends were few and the friends of the North-West Company many and powerful.

The North-West Company was still in possession of Fort Douglas. Lord Selkirk determined to retake it and sent his de Meurons forward in the winter time. By the last day of the year they had reached Fort Daer, and, having taken it, moved on to the Forks and took Fort Douglas. In June Lord Selkirk himself arrived at the settlement, where he spent four months with the colonists, who had once more been escorted back from Norway House. In those four months he made a deep impression on them as a man both wise and generous. R. G. MacBeth, writing of the recollections of his father, who was one of those settlers, says, " They spoke of his distinguished appearance, of the gentleness of his manner, the softness of his voice, and the whole fascinating personality of the man, which drew around him the Indians, who called him " The Silver Chief." During this time the settlers were confirmed in the possession of their land, their obligation to pay for it being cancelled. Lots were set aside for a church, and a school, and a burial ground, —now occupied by St. John's Cathedral, and College, and Cemetery, in Winnipeg—public roads, bridges, and a mill site were decided upon, and arrangements made for an experimental farm. Lord Selkirk also made a treaty with the Indians—the Saulteaus and the Crees. Led by Peguis, who must always be held in honour as a true friend to the early settlers, they agreed to give Lord Selkirk a strip on each side of the Red and Assiniboine rivers as far back as a white horse could be seen on the prairie on a clear day, or, as another expression put it, as far as light could be seen under a horse across the prairie. This meant a distance of two miles, and the original farms were that length and from four to five chains wide along the river bank. " So correct and unerring was his judgment," writes Alexander Ross, " that nothing he planned at this early date could in after years be altered to advantage."

It was the only visit which Lord Selkirk was able to pay to his colony. He left it in the autumn and returned, via the United States, to Montreal, to meet that series of trials and lawsuits which, in the end, wore him out. How bitter the animosity to him was, and how pervasive the influence of his enemies, may be judged by a letter written by the wife of the Chief Justice of Upper Canada about her husband, who had presided at some of the Selkirk trials. " He is now enveloped in papers and much engaged in reading the documents before the Parliament relative to the contest between the North-West Company and the Earl of Selkirk. It has fallen to his lot to prove the want of dependence on his Lordship's veracity." In such courts it is not surprising that not a single person was ever brought to justice for the killing of the colonists at Red River. Alexander Ross recounts, however, that all of those taking part in the actual killing died a violent or sudden death.

Lord Selkirk went back to England in the fall of 1818, intending to return shortly, Lady Selkirk remaining in Montreal to wait for him. But while in Montreal he had contracted tuberculosis, and his far-sighted and unselfish plans for his new world colony were defeated by his death in France in April 1820, at the comparatively early age of forty-nine.

Meanwhile the settlers had had in 1817 a bountiful harvest, the wheat yielding forty-fold, the barley giving fifty-six bushels for one, and potatoes 145 for one. But to remain at the Forks for the winter meant to consume all and to have nothing for seed. So to Pembina once more they went. There they had a winter of great hardship, having to go in search of the buffalo to the open plains in weather thirty-five to forty degrees below zero. The following year there was every sign of a good crop when, suddenly, in July, the grasshoppers came and destroyed everything. That summer, too, the colonists were saddened by the forcible carrying off by the North-West Company of James Sutherland, who, in the absence of a minister, had been appointed to marry and bury until a minister should come. He had been much beloved and was sorely missed. Just as the hopes of a crop were blasted came a party of French Canadians in charge of Father Provencher and Father Dumoulin, drawn hither by an appeal made by Lord Selkirk when in Montreal. Together they all went at once to Pembina, where the French Canadians remained. In the spring the others returned only to find the grasshoppers hatching from the eggs left in the ground the year before, and the crop again a complete failure. Once more, in spite of all determinations not to do so, they had to winter at Pembina, but by now they had developed into good hunters and were making, says Ross, "rapid strides towards a savage life."

That winter several men went south to get seed. They bought 250 bushels at ten shillings a bushel, and brought it back in flat-bottomed boats, arriving in June 1820, incidentally showing that navigation between the settlement and the States was possible, for the same boats which ascended the Mississippi descended the Red. This wheat, for which Lord Selkirk's estate paid, cost, by the time it reached Red River, about $5,000. Though it arrived late, " yet it came to sufficient perfection for seed," writes Ross, " so that from that day to this (1851), in spite of grasshoppers and other evils, Red River has not been without seed for grain." The care and labour expended upon the land, which they still worked without proper tools, is shown by a story told by John Pritchard, grandfather of Archbishop Matheson. In this year he had one bushel of seed wheat. With his own hands he dug his field with a spade and then he and his sons sowed that bushel of wheat, kernel by kernel, reaping therefrom the astonishing total of seventy-four bushels.

The affair of Seven Oaks had startled the Governments of both Canada and Great Britain into thinking about this western country which still seemed to them little worth attention. Commissioners Coltman and Fletcher were sent out from Canada to make enquiries. It happened that the agreement under which the North-West Company was organized was due to expire in 1822. Some of the wintering partners were discontented with their profits ; Lord Selkirk was removed ; his family were weary of the vexations attending their efforts ; the continuance of the struggle would obviously be fatal to both parties. There were, therefore, conditions which made it possible for Edward Ellice of the North-West Company to bring about an amalgamation of his company with the Hudson's Bay Company in 1821. The lands granted

SIR GEORGE SIMPSON, WHO RULED WESTERN CANADA
FOR FORTY YEARS.

to Lord Selkirk still remained in the possession of his family.

In 1820 there had arrived at the settlement Rev. John West, the first Protestant clergyman to reach Manitoba. It was a great disappointment to the Scottish settlers that he was not a Presbyterian, but an Anglican, and unable to speak " the gaelic." Mr. West began at once to build a school house, in one end of which he held services, while the other end served for a home for the schoolmaster, Mr. Harbidge. Three years later some of the French Canadian families returned to the settlement from Pembina, and having secured land in St. Boniface began, under the direction of Father Provencher, who was shortly after made a Bishop, to build a church and a school. The population of the settlement now began to grow. It had been increased in 1821 by the arrival of some Swiss mechanics, who had followed an agent of Lord Selkirk from their homes in the towns of Switzerland, down the Rhine, across the Atlantic, to Hudson Bay, and thence to the settlement, being some five months on the way. They settled near the de Meurons, who had been given land both in Point Douglas and immediately across the river, so that they could be quickly called together for the defence of the colony. The Swiss, however, were discouraged by the hardships, especially by the necessity, which still rested upon some of the settlers, of going to Pembina each year in order to save the crop for seed. Gradually they left the settlement and settled down on the Mississippi, where some of their descendants may be found at the town of Galena.

The amalgamation of the two companies resulted in a large increase in the settlement. One company did not require so many men as two, and the employees were retired in large numbers. They were given an opportunity to get land at the settlement, and many, liking now the free life of the new world, chose to settle there rather than return to their old homes. Donald Gunn says that the number of families thus coming to make their homes in Red River in the years 1822 and 1823 was so large as to

outnumber entirely the Scottish settlers, and, according
to Ross, there were then about 1,500 people living in the
settlement.

Life now began to take on a more settled character.
The experimental farm which Lord Selkirk had planned
when in the colony failed, with a loss to the Selkirk estate
of something like $10,000. The effort to establish a
winter road to Hudson Bay also proved a costly failure.
But the project of the Buffalo Wool Company drew
practically all the settlement together in the first common
business undertaking. Organized by Governor Simpson
and under the patronage of Lady Selkirk, this company
was to manufacture wool out of the buffalo hides, which
were, apparently, to be picked up on the prairie at no cost
at all. "All Red River was at work," says Ross,
"high wages gave a high tone to the undertaking."
But high wages meant high costs, and the wool, which
cost $12.50 to manufacture in Red River, could not be
sold in London for more than $1.08. Back to the spades
and the hoes went the colonists. But they had this much
good fortune out of the venture, that the work for the
Company, which cost in the end over $30,000, had put
some ready money into their pockets, and so, when
enterprising Americans brought a few cattle down the
Red River, they were able to buy them even at the high
prices asked. These were the first cattle to come into the
settlement, except one bull and two milch cows which the
North-West Company had brought down to their post.
Subsequent lots were eagerly bought up, though never
again did they bring such high prices as the first time,
when good milch cows sold as high as $150 and oxen
trained to work were $90 each. About this time, in the
summer of 1825, ploughs made their advent in the settlement. Wood for them was, of course, at hand, but the
iron had to be brought by the settlers from York Factory
at a cost of 25 cents per pound for the iron, and six
cents per pound for carriage. Once at the settlement it
cost $20 for the blacksmith's work, so that to become the
owner of a plough was not an easy accomplishment.

It was also shortly after the union of the two companies that the far-famed Red River cart, first made in 1801, made its appearance. The old canoe men of the North-West Company were now no longer required, since the traffic all came and went from Hudson Bay, and gradually they changed themselves into hunters. Living at first on the Saskatchewan, they afterwards came down to Red River and, being men of some means, possessed horses for which they wanted carts. These carts were made out of the wood at hand without any iron at all, and each man who used one carried in his cart the simple tools required for their manufacture—an axe, a handsaw, an auger, a chisel, and a crooked knife—so that, wherever he might be, the cart could be repaired.

Such trading as was done in the settlement was done at Lord Selkirk's stores entirely by barter and exchange. Quite early the settlers had a grievance as to the way in which accounts were kept and as to overcharges which they claimed were often made. Shortly after Lord Selkirk's death, Mr. Halkett, one of his executors, came out to inspect the colony and made an adjustment of all debts, recommending on his return that all trading should henceforth be done through the Hudson's Bay Company. The Company's bills of exchange became henceforth the recognized medium of trade; though there was some money in the colony and much business continued to be done by barter.

"The year 1825," Ross records, "was one of great enterprise among the colonists. No less than 42 houses had been built within a few months. Strings of fencing were made, enclosures formed, and a stirring industry manifested itself on every side." But the promise had a rude setback in "the disastrous year 1826, one of the most fatal both as to life and property that ever befell Red River." The fall was cold, the early snows ruined the hunting, the hunters, mostly Métis, suffered incredible hardships, many being frozen to death. But the settlers themselves felt no alarm until a strong south wind made the snows melt rapidly. On May 2nd the

Red River rose "nine feet perpendicular" in twenty-four hours. Three days later all the settlers abandoned their homes, taking what furniture they could out through the roofs and driving their cattle to higher ground. For twenty days the waters continued to rise, till they covered the ground to a depth of sixteen feet. Not a house was left standing. All thought this must be the end of the colony. On May 22nd the men were holding a council to consider where they should seek a new home, when word was brought that the waters were no longer rising. It was June 15th before any of the settlers could approach their former homes, and wheat could not be sown until the third week of the month.

During this trying time the de Meurons reverted to their wartime standards and carried off both the furniture and the cattle of the settlers, often selling the latter back to them as beef at the high prices which the threatened famine permitted them to extort. When the flood had abated, those of the Swiss who still remained, and the de Meurons, who were now in great disfavour, could not face the task of rebuilding their homes, and decided forthwith to emigrate to the United States. "The Hudson's Bay Company," says Ross, "glad to see them go, furnished assistance, and 243 individuals left for the United States on June 24th."

But for the Scots there was no more talk of a new home. With dauntless courage they "resumed work on their cheerless farms, now as bare and naked as the day they came to the country." Fire, flood, famine, warfare, the grasshoppers, and a host of smaller hardships, they had gallantly withstood. The turning point had come. They were to prove to the world that this far northern country—the so-called polar regions—was not only inhabitable but attractive enough to overcome many handicaps. They not only decided that this part of the North American continent was to be inhabited by a civilized society ; they had indirectly made certain that it was to be part of the British world. Their own courage, their own dauntless fortitude, had brought them to this, but it nevertheless remains true that the British West owes its beginning to the foresight and courage of Lord Selkirk, of whom Sir Walter Scott wrote, " I never knew a man in my life of more generous and disinterested disposition, or one whose talents and perseverance were better fitted to bring great and national schemes to a successful conclusion."

CHAPTER IV

AN ISLAND COLONY

" There is a spot on this continent which travellers do not visit and from which civilization seems in a measure shut out. Deserts, almost trackless, divide it on all sides from the habitations of cultivated men ; no railroads, or steamers, or telegraph wires, or lines of stages make their way thither ; to reach it, or, once there, to escape from it, is an exploit of which one may almost boast. Receiving no impressions from without, it reflects none. It sends forth neither newspapers, nor books, nor correspondents' letters ; no paragraph in any newspaper records its weal or woe ; it is not even marked on the maps or mentioned in the gazetteers. Yet Red River Settlement, for that is the name of this unknown spot, contains a population of 6,000 souls, eleven places of public worship, profusely supplied with clergy (including two bishops), a citadel of formidable strength and large size, several large two-storey stone houses, with modern conveniences, a dozen mills, ever so many model farms stocked with fine cattle, and provided with all the modern implements of agriculture, one or two manufacturing establishments, a court house with a recorder of $4,000 a year, a governor, a staff, and an imposing body of mounted police. There is more than one good library there, and several good cellars ; a man may dine there according to Soyer, drive a two-forty in a dashing cariole over the crisp snow, dance the latest Cellarius polka redowa with ladies of any shade of colour from the pure bronze to the mere white, discuss the principles of human society and the theory of popular governments as learnedly as the thing could be done at Washington or Cincinnati."

Such was the description of Red River Settlement written by one who came overland from the United States, and published in one of the foremost American magazines in the autumn of 1856. Though it is a description of what was observed in one particular year, it serves equally well for a picture of life as it was in the colony from the time when the ravages of the flood of 1826 were repaired, down almost to the year 1860, when the causes which were to bring about a rapid change began to make themselves felt. Sir George Simpson, who became Governor of Rupert's Land when the two companies, North-West and Hudson's Bay, were amalgamated under the ancient name of Hudson's Bay Company, ruled in Red River, as he did in all Western Canada. He might write of Lord Selkirk, " his was a pure spirit of colonization," but he had no mind to further that colonization project in the pursuit of which Lord Selkirk had sacrificed both his health and his fortune. His interest was the great fur trade of the Company, as it was the interest of the Governor and committee in the London offices.

" Herein," says Chester Martin, " lay the grave significance of the coalition for Red River Settlement. The interests of the fur trade once more predominated. The indifference of the old Hudson's Bay Company directorate was no longer concealed ; Nor'-Westers continued the most rancorous hostility to the settlement. Colonization at Red River was left for two generations stranded above the current upon which Selkirk had hoped to launch it."

Thus Red River remained an island of settlement in the great North-west. Only once did it receive any European immigration. Twenty families of Lincolnshire farmers came out, but they remained only a few years, finding the hardships and privations too great to be borne. For the rest, the colony grew beyond the rate of natural increase by the addition of the men of the Company, who found it a haven wherein to make homes for themselves and their families, often of half Indian blood. Three years after the flood of 1826 there came from James Bay sixty families of the Company's people. By the time another year had passed, there were in the colony 204 houses, all of them new, and in the next twenty years these increased slowly to 745. By the time the end of this isolation period was in sight, the population of the settlement, which had been about 1,500 at the time of the flood, had increased to about

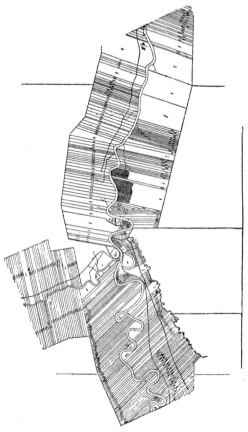

Fig. 8.—Plan of lots along the Red and Assiniboine rivers taken from an old Hudson's Bay Company map. The varying directions of streets in Winnipeg arise from this survey. The triangle in the centre is the site of the modern business section. Some of the old trails and creeks may also be seen.

6,000, made up of " Englishmen, Irishmen, Scotchmen, Canadians, French Canadians, Americans, English half-

LANDING AT YORK FACTORY.
Once a year a Hudson's Bay Company's ship arrived at York Factory.

breeds, Canadian half-breeds and Indians," as Milton and Cheadle described them. The English and the Scottish settlers gradually took up all the land between the two forts of the colony—Upper and Lower Fort Garry, especially on the west side of the river. They also settled along the banks of the Assiniboine in the districts known as St. James and Headingly. The French Canadians and the Métis came from different parts of Rupert's Land to live on the east bank of the Red River in St. Boniface, on the west bank of the Red above the Assiniboine and on the Assiniboine River itself beyond the English-speaking settlements. The usual allotment of land had a varying narrow frontage on the river and a depth of two miles, with a stretch of another two miles beyond used in common as hay lands.

The great chronicler of this period is Alexander Ross, who, coming to the settlement from the Hudson's Bay Company service in 1825, received a large grant of land, which he called Colony Gardens, and became sheriff and postmaster, and a leading man in the community.

Speaking of these first years he says:

" The better to advance each other's interest, as well as for mutual support, all sects and creeds associated together indiscriminately and were united like the members of the same family in peace, charity and good fellowship. This state of things continued till the Churchmen began to feel uneasy and the Catholic grew jealous so that projects were set on foot to separate the tares from the wheat. Whatever reasons might be urged for the division in a religious point of view, it was, politically considered, an ill-judged step. Yet the measure was carried and the separation took place. From these original causes party spirit and political strife have been gaining ground ever since. The Canadians became jealous of the Scotch, the French of both ; and their separate interests as agriculturalists, voyageurs or hunters had little tendency to unite them. At length, indeed, the Canadians and half-breeds came to a good understanding with each other, leaving then but two parties, the Scotch and the French. Between these, although there is, and always has been, a fair share of mutual good feeling, anything like cordiality in a common sentiment seemed impossible, and they remain till this day politically divided."

By " this day " Ross means sometime about 1851, when he was writing his journal.

It is easy to imagine the political life of the settlement against this background. For almost ten years after the flood the colony remained in the possession of the Selkirk family, directed for them by a governor. Difficulties in the administration arising, the Company bought out the interests of the estate for $425,000, though it is estimated that the settlement first and last cost the Selkirks over $1,000,000. Thereupon a council was set up to aid the Governor of Assiniboia, as the district was still called, but, as the council was mainly composed of the Hudson's Bay Company senior employees, and the Governor was often the Chief Factor at Fort Garry, there were many murmurings. These came from both the French and the Scotch, their leaders desiring some voice in the government of the colony. In 1837 the Company applied to the British Parliament for an extension of the twenty-year licence it had been given at the time of the amalgamation, and its rights were extended until 1859. By the time that year approached, it had become quite clear that some form of government in which the settlers should have a share would have to be set up.

The Hudson's Bay Company had, after the reorganization, adopted some of the plans of the Nor'-Westers. The control remained in a governor, who with a deputy governor and five directors made up the London committee. But there was now established in Rupert's Land a new official, called the Governor of Rupert's Land, who resided sometimes in Montreal and sometimes in the Company's territories. At the head of the fur trade were twenty-five Chief Factors and twenty-eight Chief Traders, who now became sharers in the profits of the fur trade to the extent of 40 per cent. These men also made up the council of the Governor of Rupert's Land. The annual meeting place was changed from Fort William to Norway House

(Fig. 6), and to that point every year went as many of these officers as could reach it. There they consulted with the Governor and selected men to fill the vacancies in the council, Chief Factors being chosen from the Chief Traders, and the latter from among the junior commissioned officers of the Company. Norway House was made the central distributing point and Fort Garry the administrative centre of the trade of the whole North-west.

Under the Governor of Rupert's Land was the Governor of Assiniboia, assisted by his council. In the early days there seem to have been few laws and little crime. But, as difficulties increased, the Company thought it better to have legal advice and brought out from Montreal a lawyer, Adam Thom, to be Recorder of Rupert's Land and trial by jury was now established. Their choice proved to be an unfortunate one. It would have been hard enough in any case for a company appointee. It was harder because Mr. Thom was known to be bitterly anti-French. He began by refusing to allow French to be spoken in his court, and by giving arbitrary decisions which the London committee sometimes felt forced to disallow. His lack of judgment served the Company ill, and in the end he was deposed, his place being taken by other men from the outside, who, though appointed by the Company, commended themselves to the settlers as being fair and just. Gradually magistrates were appointed for the different parishes ; local and general courts grew up ; and a more formal system of administration of justice came into being.

The authority of the Company was furthur strengthened by the arrival, quite unexpectedly, in September 1846 of a force of nearly 400 soldiers, the reason of their coming being that the British Government feared that the trouble with the United States over the Oregon boundary might extend itself to Red River. They had, however, the effect of quieting threatened opposition to the Company, especially as their colonel became Governor of Assiniboia. When, two years later, they retired, their places were taken by a body of pensioners under Major

Caldwell, who was also Governor. Though these pensioners remained seven years, they seem to have had little effect on the colony, which they left in 1855, to be succeeded two years later by a company of Royal Canadian Rifles, which stayed only three years, its presence being the last attempt of the Hudson's Bay Company to protect its rights by military force.

It was, however, in the matter of trade that the Company and the settlers came into sharpest conflict. The charter of the Company gave them the exclusive right of trade with the Indians, and this right Sir George Simpson, backed by the London committee, was determined to maintain. It was a right which the settlers did not think just and which they, therefore, did not feel many scruples about ignoring. The Hudson's Bay Company had taken over from the Selkirk estate the business of supplying goods to the settlers, and quite early in this period had added to their store at Upper Fort Garry another store twenty miles down the river at the Lower, or Stone, Fort, which had been built in 1831. Very soon private traders came to dispute this business. But it was not so much the trade with the settlers that the private traders wished to share as the riches of the fur trade. Here the Company came into conflict not only with the traders but with the Métis. Hunting the buffalo for the Company, the Métis came to hunt it for themselves. Hunting the buffalo, they came to hunt other fur-bearing animals also or, if not themselves to hunt, to trade with the Indians for them. At first the Company seems to have kept on pretty good terms with the Métis, purchasing all the pemmican, whether needed or not, and thus getting the furs. But, as the traders became more numerous and the demands of the Métis more exacting, as it began to be possible to deal with traders on the outskirts of civilization in the United States, more and more the Company's rights were disregarded. "By 1847," says Ross, "there were no fewer than 102 English traders in the settlement, and nearly as many more from the United States." Many of those

In the North.

Archdeacon Cochrane's Indian Village on the Red River.

were doing business on a very small scale. " Almost every door is now a shop door," says Ross. But some of them were doing a substantial business, and, among these, the leaders were James Sinclair and Andrew McDermot. The Company prohibited the export of furs, and many stringent regulations were passed which Recorder Thom enforced. When James Sinclair wished to export tallow, the only possible article of export other than the forbidden furs, the Company suddenly refused to bring his supplies from England, thus making it impossible to carry on his business. Just when things were becoming very tense and the settlers and traders were petitioning the Home Government against the Company, came an outbreak of influenza, followed by measles, and then by the " bloody flux," which attacked both Indians and whites. For six weeks the deaths averaged seven a day and the resulting sorrow put an end to much of the hostility. Then the soldiers came to Red River, and for a couple of years the agitation against the Company was much less aggressive.

The cause of the free traders was supported heartily in London by Alexander K. Isbister, a native of Red River, whose name is honoured in Manitoba because of his generous gifts of scholarships to the University. It was, however, an event in the settlement itself which brought the issue to a climax. A Métis, William Sayer, with three other traders, was arrested for illicit trading in furs and brought to trial in the spring of 1849. On his behalf, and stirred up largely by Louis Riel, a miller on the Seine River and father of the Louis Riel of later troubles, the Métis assembled and some 400 or 500 of them surrounded the court house on the day of the trial. Though Sayer admitted his guilt Recorder Thom was told by Sinclair, who was acting for Sayer, that, if the prisoner were not released without punishment the Métis would take the law into their own hands. Sayer was found guilty but released without punishment and the Métis returned to St. Boniface shouting, " Le commerce est libre—vive la liberté." Though the legal rights of

6

the Company remained as they had been before, the traders had, through public support, won the right to trade as they would.

But, if Governor Simpson set his face against further colonization and sought by all the means in his power to uphold the trading rights of the Hudson's Bay Company, he was in many ways generous towards the colonists already settled at Red River. He made many attempts to increase their prosperity and well being. Two experimental farms were undertaken at great cost, only to meet with failure ; people to teach brickmaking and spinning were brought out, the first with no success, the latter with much, since it is recorded that by 1837 practically all the inhabitants were wearing homespun garments. The great difficulty, now that crops were being produced, was to find a market. The Governor met that by promising to buy in the colony the Company's supplies, which were still being brought from England, only to have his effort defeated by the poor quality of some of the produce.

The same result met his effort to promote the growth of flax and hemp, for which the soil of Red River was thought peculiarly suitable. Full of interest too are the many speculative efforts undertaken in which the Governor seems always to have been ready to aid. The story of one of these illustrates well the mixture of bad luck and bad management which seems to have ruined all these enterprises, the cost of which was largely borne by the Company. A company was organized to introduce sheep-raising into the colony. As much as $60,000 capital was raised, though it was organized only seven years after the flood, and two men were sent south to Missouri to buy the sheep and drive them back to Red River. The people in Missouri, believing that these representatives required thousands of sheep, where in reality only hundreds were needed, put up the price to $2.50 a head. This so angered Rae, the leader of the expedition, that, though the price was afterwards lowered, he refused to have anything to do with the Missouri sheep raisers, and pushed on 450 miles farther to Kentucky, where he bought 1,471 sheep at practically the same price he was offered in Missouri. His real difficulties came when he began to drive the sheep to Red River. He had to pay for pasturage every night. Finding at one point that the sheep were suffering from heat, he ordered the fleece cut, after having made a bargain for its sale. The buyers were unable to pay cash for the entire amount, and, again angered, Rae had all the wool burned rather than accept from the settlers, who badly needed the wool, the price they were able to pay. All along the way his sheep died from exposure and hard driving. As they fell ill, he would order his men to cut their throats and press on, till even his men revolted from the slaughter. "From St. Peter's to Red River," wrote Ross, "the road was marked for future travellers by 1,220 carcasses." Only 251 of the sheep ever reached the settlement. The Governor refunded the money subscribed in the colony, but it is not surprising that he wrote, "Red River is like a Lybian Tiger; the more we try to tame it, the more savage it becomes; so it is with Red River; for every step I try to bring it forward, disappointment drives it back two."

But though speculations might fail, all the time the colony was going steadily forward through the quiet steadfast efforts of the settlers, who were developing their farms and improving their condition. For a long time small wooden houses, about twenty or thirty feet long, with two rooms, contented the people. Gradually there came stone foundations, shingle roofs, partitions and doors, plastered walls, and windows, first of parchment and later of glass. The wooden houses too became improved, and, towards the end of the period were of two stories. "Taste, as well as convenience," says Ross, "began to receive its due share of consideration. The luxury of glass windows, and a lock on the doors, things hitherto scarcely known in Red River, have become fashionable, indeed almost general." Barns were built, more land enclosed and cultivated, implements procured, and stock increased and improved. Iron was still hard to come by and furniture was for the most part made without it.

R. G. MacBeth records that his grandfather surrendered his sword that pegs might be made out of it for the spinning wheels of the women.

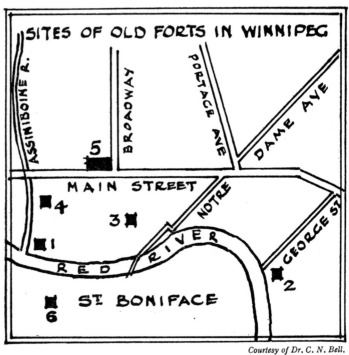

Courtesy of Dr. C. N. Bell.

Fig. 9.

1. Mythical Fort Maurepas, 1737,
   Fort Rouge, 1738,
   Fort Legardeur de St. Pierre,
   Fort Bruce and Boyer, 1780,
   Fort Alex. Henry, 1803,
   Fort Gibraltar (original), 1807–16.
2. Fort Douglas, 1812.
3. Fidler's Fort (H. B. Co.) 1818.
4. Fort Garry the 1st (rebuilt Fort Gibraltar, 1822–35).
5. Fort Garry 2nd,, 1835–82.
6. Traditional Post of H. B. Co., 1780.

THE "SELKIRKERS" AT
ST. PAUL IN 1860.

Picturesque Canada.

AT THE PORTAGE.

The use of stone was encouraged by the Company, which in 1830 had built the first stone building in the colony—a powder magazine at Upper Fort Garry. The following year Lower Fort Garry was commenced, but was not finished for four years. It was built in the same form as it is to-day, except that several of the buildings have been torn down. Four years after it was begun, the Company began the erection of the Upper Fort Garry, the gate of which is still standing behind the Manitoba Club in Winnipeg. It was farther back from the Red River than the early Fort Gibraltar, which was rebuilt and renamed by Governor Simpson just after the coalition. The old buildings of the earlier fort were used by the Company until 1852, when they seem to have been swept into the river by the flood.

Windmills had been established at various points for grinding the wheat, for which at first the settlers had been obliged to use hand mills, which they called querns, some brought from Scotland but more fashioned out of such stones as were available. Food and clothing were plentiful, and practically all the Scottish settlers had saved a little money. Ross makes a little picture of conditions.

" Abundance on every side testifies to their industry and economy and this within doors and without in the same profusion. No want of blankets here on the beds ; the children well clothed and houses warm and comfortable. The barns teeming with grain, the stables with cattle and all classes wearing more or less of their own manufacture. Everything is exactly as it ought to be. Every man minds his own business ; every woman may be found in her kitchen."

" ' I have travelled much and seen many countries, but under all circumstances I have seen no part of the world where the poor man enjoys as many privileges and is more happy and independent than in Red River,' was the verdict of a visitor to the colony."

The supply of pemmican, still needed both for the colonists and for the fur trade all through this period and after it, was obtained exactly as it had been when the settlers first came to Red River. Twice a year, early in June and again in the latter part of August, the hunters gathered themselves and their families, their horses, their oxen and Red River carts, and their dogs and started off for the plains. They left the settlement in straggling fashion, but once out to the west, or the south, they set up a form of organization which they maintained until their return. Camp was always made in the shape of a great circle formed by the Red River carts, into the centre of which were driven the cattle and the horses and within which the hunters and their families placed their tents. Very definite rules were laid down with heavy penalties, among which was one that no buffalo were to be hunted on Sunday. When they came within reach of the buffalo no one was allowed to fire a gun until all were ready. Then, mounted on their swift ponies, at a given signal the men started in a body, loading and firing as they went, the hunters carrying the bullets in their mouths. They did not stop to identify the buffalo they killed until the shooting was ended by the flight of such buffalo as had not already been slaughtered. But when the hunt was over, each man could tell exactly where were the buffalo he shot and how they would be found lying on the plain. At once the work of cutting up the buffalo and making the pemmican was commenced, but as one of the rules was that no camp should remain more than three days in the same place, there were many animals left for the wolves. Indeed, often many more were left than the wolves could manage, and the extinction of the buffalo was threatened.

Some idea of the number of people engaged in these hunts may be gained from the record of the summer hunt of 1840 : 620 hunters went out, having in all 1,210 Red River carts ; with them went 650 women, 360 boys and girls, 655 horses, 586 oxen and 542 dogs. One, who accompanied them, records how he watched 400 hunters start at the word of command, and return bringing into camp the tongues of 1,475 buffalos. This particular hunt resulted in over a million pounds of pemmican. The price paid was twopence a pound, and the custom of the Company was to buy all that the hunters wished to sell. They and their friends consumed vast quantities in feasts, and it was a commonplace that the return of the hunters meant a large increase in wages, since, while there was plenty to eat, the Métis were unwilling to work. Not long after the return the hunters would be once more impoverished and would have to secure an advance from the Company to carry them to the time of the next hunt. Ross sets down that in twenty-five years he had not known a plain hunter " able to clear his way or liquidate his expenses, far less to save a shilling by the chase."

Paul Kane, the Canadian artist, who crossed the continent for the purpose of depicting the life of the Indians, and who painted many vivid pictures of them, gives in his journal a graphic description of such a hunt in Southern Manitoba.

" Everything being adjusted, we all walked our horses towards the herd. By the time we had gone about two hundred yards the herd perceived us, and started off in the opposite direction at the top of their speed. We now put our horses to the full gallop and in twenty minutes were in their midst. There could not have been less than four or five thousand in our immediate vicinity, all bulls, not a single cow amongst them.

" The scene now became one of intense excitement : the huge bulls thundering over the plains in headlong confusion whilst the fearless hunters rode recklessly in their midst, keeping up an incessant fire at but a few yards' distance from their victims. Upon the fall of each buffalo the successful hunter merely threw some article of his apparel, often carried by him solely for that purpose, to denote his own prey, and then rushed on to another. These marks are scarcely ever disputed, but, should a doubt arise as to the ownership, the carcass is equally divided among the claimants. The chase continued only about one hour, and extended over an area of from five to six square miles, where might be seen the dead and dying buffaloes to the number of five hundred."

The other chief mode of earning a livelihood for the

Métis and the French Canadians was in the transport service of the Company. Until the very last years of this period there was practically no communication with the outside world, except through the Company ship, which came every year to York Factory. On it came the mails and supplies for a whole year, the Company and individuals alike having to send their orders on the ship of the year before. All these goods, whether for themselves or for private traders, were brought down in the Company's boats and by a wonderful system of brigades, as they were called, distributed even to the posts near the Arctic. All this carriage was performed by inland or York boats, each of which had eight rowers and a steersman, and carried about three and a half tons of freight prepared in packages of 100 pounds each. A brigade was composed of from four to eight of such boats, and, during the summer, these brigades were constantly on the move carrying in supplies and bringing back furs. Passage of strong rapids had to be made by unloading the boats and carrying them and their freight around ; lesser rapids could be managed by men on shore pulling the boats through. Sometimes across lakes it was possible to lessen the toil by hoisting sail, but for the most part the men rowed. Of all the brigades, the Portage la Loche brigade was the greatest. This portage was on the height of land dividing the waters which flow into the Arctic Ocean from those running into Hudson Bay, and to it went the men from the South and East to meet the men from the far North and West. This brigade usually left Red River in June and went first to Norway House, to which it carried agricultural produce from the colony. At Norway House it loaded the English goods which had been brought up from the bay the fall before, and then set out across Lake Winnipeg, up the Saskatchewan River, past Forts Cumberland and Isle à la Crosse to the Portage. Returning, the brigade went to Norway House and from there to York Factory carrying furs. If the annual ship had not yet arrived, it waited and brought back the freight for Red River. On this trip, if everything was favourable, the men would be away from the settlement about four months. For this labour the Company paid them at the rates of $175 to a guide, $100 to a steersman, $90 to the bowsmen and $80 to the middlemen. These men are said to have had a riotous time spending their wages on their return, but, what with advances made to them by the Company when they enrolled for work in December, with further advances made to the men themselves while on the trip and to their families for supplies, there was often little to spend. Of the boatman's toil, Father Lacombe has written, "without having seen it one could form no idea of the hardships, the cruel fatigues of these boatmen."

In other ways the colony made marked progress. Both the Anglican and the Catholic church had laid their foundations in the early troubled days of the settlement. No more than the Scottish settlers were they daunted by the flood. Rev. Mr. West, the first Protestant clergyman, had returned in 1823, but he was quickly followed by Rev. D. T. Jones and then by William, afterwards Archdeacon Cochrane, an indefatigable worker and a great leader. From the school house built by Mr. West came rapidly a new church, the Upper Church, near where St. John's Cathedral now is, then, six miles further down the river, the Middle Church, or St. Paul's, as it came to be called ; and afterwards the Lower Church, which, later, was St. Andrew's. Archdeacon Cochrane, eager to bring Christianity and civilization to the Indians, after several years of ardent effort, persuaded some of them to take up a settled pastoral life at St. Peter's, where he built the first mission church for the Indians in the North-west. In his journal of October 1835 he records his joy in his work.

"Now from the opposite side of the river, I see the village standing along the crescent bay ; twenty-three little white-washed cottages are shining through the trees each with its column of smoke curling to the sky, and each with its stacks of wheat and barley. . . . In the centre stands the school house where sixty merry children ' just let loose from school ' are leaping, running or wrestling, and all is life and hopefulness."

Another ten years, and Archdeacon Cochrane was involved in the great work of building the stone church which still stands at St. Andrews and which was finished in time to be consecrated by Bishop Anderson, the first Bishop of Rupert's Land, who arrived in the colony in 1849. Not ready yet to rest from his labours, Archdeacon Cochrane went in the fifties to establish another Indian settlement at Portage la Prairie. To that place followed him against the wishes of the Governor some families from the Red River Settlement. Thus began the first development of Manitoba to the west of the Red River valley.

The Roman Catholic Church had also developed its mission begun in the earlier days at St. Boniface. It had established missions at St. François Xavier, at a point on the Winnipeg River about 200 miles away, and on Lake Manitoba. In 1844 the Grey Nuns arrived and opened in St. Boniface the first convent, and a year later came Frère Taché, who was shortly afterwards ordained a priest by Bishop Provencher. Before the end of the period he had become the Bishop of St. Boniface. The Oblate Order, established in Canada in 1841, devoted itself with untiring zeal to mission work among the Indians. " To obtain anything like a correct view of the extent of the field of labour occupied in Rupert's Land by the Catholic priesthood," says Hargrave, " Red River Settlement must sink far into the background and the attention be turned towards the vast uninhabited wastes of the interior, where the savages whose only homes are in their tents, lead a migratory life."

As early as 1840 the Company had invited the Wesleyan Society to establish missions in the North-west, and Rev. James Evans, famous as the inventor of the written Cree language, came out as superintendent of these missions, which were established at several points. Two of them were in Manitoba, but none in Red River until after this period.

All this time the Scottish settlers had been bitterly lamenting the fact that the promise that they should have a minister of their own faith had never been carried out. They had made many and strenuous efforts to interest the Company without moving it from its decision to aid only the Anglican church in Red River. They had then applied to the Church of Scotland with no effect. It was not until the matter came into the hands of the Presbyterians of Canada that it finally received serious attention, with the result that, in the fall of 1851, there arrived in Red River Rev. John Black, the first Presbyterian minister. Full of delight, his congregation had made haste to prepare for him a home at Kildonan of such proportions that on September 28th, 300 of the Selkirk settlers gathered for service " in the Manse." The choice of the Canadian church had been wise, for John Black proved a great religious leader for his people, while his preaching was of a quality to satisfy the considerable degree of education to which many of the settlers had now attained.

Schools had developed rapidly in close alliance with the churches. We have seen how a schoolmaster accompanied Rev. John West, and how Bishop Provencher began early the establishment of schools in St. Boniface. Very shortly after the flood of 1826, the wife of Rev. D. T. Jones established a school " for the gentlemen sons and daughters of Hudson's Bay Company Factors," while a little later John Pritchard opened a school for the same purpose across the river in what is now East Kildonan, afterwards amalgamating it with St. John's school which was the beginning of St. John's College in Winnipeg. Though some of the Company's officers were sending their children to school in England, and some to Canada, and some even to the United States, there were also early established schools for the higher education of girls with which, following the time of Mrs. Jones, are associated the names of several English women, notably of Mrs. Mills and Miss Davis.

Everywhere, as parishes were established, schools were

attached to them and the records go to show that there were many children constantly attending, and that at night the adults took advantage of them. It was when the Grey Nuns came that the Catholic church began to expand the schools under their direction, the first convent opening with eighty pupils. Gradually an orphanage was established, St. Boniface College developed, and parochial schools, opened as outside churches, were built. Perhaps the first of those was the school established by

WOMEN'S CANADIAN CLUB, WINNIPEG.
Fig. 10.—Miss Davis' Academy, still standing on the road to St. Andrew's Locks.

Angelique Nolin at St. Eustache, which, however, was abandoned in 1843.

Not until 1849 did the Presbyterian community have a school of its own. In that year John Inkster opened a school, which for fifteen years met in a log house on what was then known as Frog Plains but is now Kildonan. Another name associated with educational efforts in the settlement is that of Donald Gunn, historian of the early years of the Settlement, who for a time conducted a commercial school to fit the sons of Company officers to go into the service.

THE LOUISE BRIDGE.

H. S. Seaman, Esq.

FIRST HOME OF DONALD STEWART
IN WESTBURNE, 1872.

A SOD HOUSE—THE FIRST HOME OF
MANY SETTLERS.

The mention of Donald Gunn naturally calls to mind another educational force in the settlement, that of the Red River Library of which he had charge. This was kept in his house at St. Andrews, then much the most popular part of the settlement. Its nucleus was 500 volumes bequeathed by Peter Fidler, which, with a grant of £50 from the Company, was turned over to the library when it was officially inaugurated on September 30th, 1848. It was at the home of Donald Gunn also that the many scientific men visiting the North-west towards the end of this period found aid in their enquiries, and for several years he acted as the correspondent of the Smithsonian Institute.

It is related, also, that music was much loved by the people of those early times, though they gratified their desire for it with some difficulty. Such pianos as there were in the colony, and they were very few, had to be sent all the way from England, making the journey from Hudson Bay in a York boat. The violin was the chief instrument and such was its general use all through the Company service, as well as in Red River, that every year there was brought out a consignment of violin strings as part of the regular supplies.

Amusements, too, were of a simple character, though as early as 1848, the regiment gave a ball at which white kid gloves made their first appearance. The two great holidays were May 24th and New Year's Day. Horse-racing was the great summer feature. Transferred to the winter, this became carioling. Every young man sought to have a fine horse, and the showing off of it, with its ornamented harness and its fine cariols or cutter, was the occasion of great contests. Weddings were the centre of fun in the winter time. They were made the occasion of feasting and dancing which began the day before the wedding, and frequently lasted four or five days. The surprise party was another favourite form of amusement and there were quieter forms, such as quilting bees, and the parties where knocking barley, or carding wool, was the entertainment. The older folk, among the Scottish people, found much satisfaction before the arrival of Dr. Black in the mid-week meeting, where kindly Anglican clergy often conducted a prayer service with no prayer book at all after the Scottish form. On New Year's Day everyone kept open house for all, even the Indians living near the settlement, and on this night at Fort Garry, and at all the Company's posts, festivities were finished with a dance given by the resident factor.

The peaceful current of life in this period was rudely interrupted by the flood of 1852 when once again the river overran its banks and became a torrent more than six miles wide. Beginning to rise on May 7th, the waters continued to increase until the 22nd, which by a curious coincidence was the same day on which, in the last great flood, the waters had reached their crest. By the 12th, half the colony was under water and all the fencing and loose property had disappeared down the river. "Dwelling houses and barns," says a chronicler of the time, " were floating in all directions like sloop under sail, with cats, dogs, and poultry in them. . . . The very mice, snakes, and squirrels could not find a hiding place above or below ground."

This flood was particularly distressing to the Scottish settlers, because in the enthusiasm over the arrival of their minister the fall before, they had already gathered timbers, stone and lime for the building of their church. All the lime and many of the timbers disappeared beneath the flood, but neither they, nor their pastor, would be prevented from holding service. Leading them back to high ground he set up a stone for pulpit and preached his regular Sunday sermon. That stone has since been built into the Winnipeg church which bears his name. The year after the flood they gathered again the necessary materials and built the church now known as Old Kildonan Church.

The destruction caused by the flood was less serious than that caused in 1826, if only because there was so much more land under cultivation, so many more cattle, and so much larger a quantity of grain. There were

also many more people living on higher ground or able
to reach it.   As in 1826, there was but one man drowned.
But the kind of damage done was nevertheless most
distressing, as is revealed by an entry in Bishop Anderson's
journal.   Under date of May 26th he writes : " Went
down to the house in the morning ; gratified to find only
twenty inches of water instead of forty in our rooms.   The
deposit of mud under the water made our movements
more difficult. . . . It seemed like a recurrence of the
plague of Egypt, as the frogs had entered our chambers
with the water—no pleasant sight to behold."

But not even floods could turn the Bishop from his
work, for that same day he brought up for examination
Thomas Cochrane, the son of the Archdeacon, who, by
another coincidence, had been born at the time of the
last flood.   Ten days later, the flood being sufficiently
abated to hold service in St. Andrew's church, he ordained
Thomas Cochrane to the ministry.   Altogether during
this flood 3,500 people left their homes and took to the
open plains, and the loss to property was estimated at
$100,000.   On June 12th, exactly one month after the
flood had driven them out, the people were able to go
back to their homes and begin the work of restoring or
rebuilding.

In 1853 there came the first open sign that the long
time of isolation was drawing to a close.   Until that year
all the communication with the world outside was by
means of two mails a year.   One went by the Company's
annual ship to the old country ; the other by the winter
packet to Montreal.   But, though Red River might be
a lone island of settlement in the vast area that is now
Western Canada, to the south men and women were
pouring into the new territory of Minnesota.   When in
the summer of that year, following hard upon the track
of settlement, the United States set up its most northerly
post office at Fort Ripley, to the north-west of St. Paul,
the people at Red River organized a monthly mail service
to and from the fort and so for the first time came into
what was, for them, frequent touch with the world outside.

Now the more adventurous among the Red River traders began to go to the rapidly growing city of St. Paul to sell their furs and buy goods to sell again in the settlement. The Hudson's Bay Company, too, felt the coming of new times. Heretofore all its supplies had come by the annual ship to York Factory. But, in 1859, finding their old system insufficient for the growing trade, it experi-

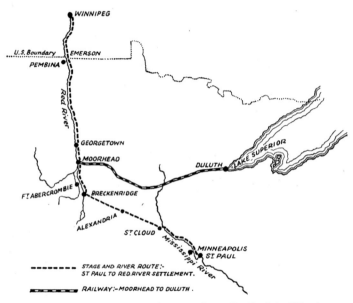

Fig. 11.—Map showing the route from St. Paul to Winnipeg taken by early traders and settlers.

mented by bringing a consignment of goods to Red River via Chicago and St. Paul. Once established, this trade route expanded rapidly until at its high point as many as 1,500 ox-carts were kept busy from spring until autumn on the rough trail between St. Paul and Fort Garry.

Change followed rapidly upon change. Two young newspaper men from Toronto, William Buckingham and William Coldwell, bringing their printing press and their

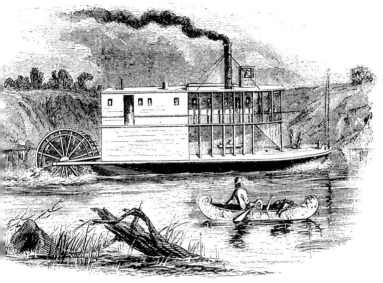

"ANSON NORTHUP," AFTERWARDS THE "PIONEER," ON THE RED RIVER.

type by those same ox-carts, published three days before Christmas in 1859 the first number of the first newspaper in Western Canada. They called it the *Nor'-Wester*, and it appeared once a fortnight. In that summer, to the delight and astonishment of the settlers, a small flat-bottomed boat, formerly the *Anson Northup*, but now rechristened the *Pioneer*, had made a few trips up and down the river from Fort Garry to Georgetown at the head of navigation on the Red River. This little town, named for Sir George Simpson, may still be seen on maps of Minnesota a few miles above the present town of Moorhead. With the regular monthly mail, a regular trade route to St. Paul, a newspaper and a steamboat carrying both goods and passengers to and from the great world outside, the days of the island colony were ended. The settlement at the forks of the Red and Assiniboine was beginning to see itself as the spearhead of all that progress which has since come to the western plains. What a difference still divided it from the Winnipeg of to-day may be seen from the following picture of the men of Red River drawn by an American writer just at this time of change.

" For the last two months our streets in St. Paul have been filled with the wild, picturesque groups of our northern neigh-bours, the Pembinese and the Selkirkers. We see their strange accoutred ox-trains, shaggy ponies and wolfish-looking dogs ; but there is something in the air of their free firm step and bold, yet graceful, abandon of carriage, with their nobility of stature, that awakens at first glance an interest in their story. That they have a story you can read in their bronzed features and the long floating chevelure that waves around their shoulders. Their dark coarse coats glittering with a savage profusion of buttons of polished brass ; their long waving sashes of the brightest red, and jaunty little caps half Tartar half French ; even their loose trousers of English corduroy, or some dark woollen stuff, if not of elk or bison skin, down to the quaint and dingy moccasins where-with they clothe their feet, savour of the wild, wondrous and romantic. Such, indeed, their story is. No novel ever written upon the scenes of far western wilds and hunter life could equal the thrilling wildness and strange truth of their brief history."

7

CHAPTER V

THE END OF COMPANY RULE

WHILE all these changes were taking place in Red River, in the world outside there was developing a new attitude towards the Settlement and towards the Company which ruled it. Canada—then, it will be remembered, only the present provinces of Ontario and Quebec—was beginning to think about her great hinterland. Confederation plans were in the air, and, if British Columbia were to be brought into the Dominion, some way to communicate with her across British territory had to be found. Moreover, Canadians, having won responsible government for themselves, were ready to give sympathetic hearing to the complaints against Company rule drifting down from settlers in Assiniboia. The Hudson's Bay Company's licence was due to expire in 1859 and within and without the settlement there seems to have been general agreement that it ought not to be renewed. In 1857 the Canadian Parliament took action by petitioning the British House of Commons. As a result a committee of the British Parliament was ordered " to consider the state of those British possessions in America which are under the administration of the Hudson's Bay Company or over which they possess a license of trade." Knowing the value of those western plains to-day, we smile to read that a great deal of evidence was submitted to show how completely inaccessible this country was, how little fertile land it contained, and, generally, how altogether undesirable it was. There was also much evidence on the other side. The interests of Canada were watched over by Chief Justice Draper, who seems to have had a vision of what was to come.

" I hope," he said to the committee, " you will not laugh at me as very visionary, but I hope to see the time, or that my children may see the time, when there is a railway going all the way across that country and ending at the Pacific ; and so far as an individual opinion goes, I entertain no doubt that the time will arrive when that will be accomplished."

The men who listened to him must have been astonished and thrilled by the rapidity with which that vision became realized. Twenty-eight years later, Donald A. Smith drove the last spike in the Canadian Pacific Railway.

The British committee did not take long to make up its mind. The districts along the Red and Assiniboine rivers, it said, were likely to be needed soon for settlement. " Arrangements should be made by which these districts may be ceded to Canada upon equitable principles, and within the districts thus annexed to her the authority of the Hudson's Bay Company would of course entirely cease."

Just as the committee was completing its work, the Canadian Government was taking the first steps to prove that there could be convenient communication with Red River over Canadian territory. It sent out an exploring expedition. Part of it, under S. J. Dawson, an engineer, was to survey a road from Lake Superior to Fort Garry ; the other part, under Professor H. Y. Hind, was to report on the nature of the country and the character of its vegetation and soil. Mr. Hind published a report which was widely discussed and drew much attention to the west. That it was not all favourable attention may be seen from an article in the *London Illustrated News* of October 2nd, 1858 :

" The present state of society and the condition of the people is not encouraging. The European and Canadian elements have been gradually diminishing for years, and the half-breed population is apparently growing closer to the habits and tastes of their Indian ancestry.

" The majority of the population are gradually becoming poorer and approaching nearer the Indian state—a result which seems to spring from the hitherto almost hopeless circumstances under which husbandry has been conducted, and a quiet unostentatious suppression of every kind of industry which might lead to the selection of permanent homes by the half-breed and Indian hunters."

Nor was R. M. Ballantyne, who wrote this article, alone in his unfavourable opinion. Just about the same time there was published the report of the Palliser expedition, which had been sent out by the British Government to examine the fitness of these western prairies for settlement and development. Its author said:

"I cannot recommend the Imperial Government to countenance or lend any support to any scheme for constructing, or, it may be said, forcing a thoroughfare by this line of route, either by land or by water, as there would be no immediate advantage commensurate with the required sacrifice of capital ; nor can I advise such heavy expenditure as would necessarily attend the construction of any exclusively British line of road between Canada and the Red River Settlement. . . . The time has now forever gone by for effecting such an object and the unfortunate choice of an astronomical boundary has completely isolated the central American possessions of Great Britain from Canada in the east."

Here, surely, is proof that the prophetic gift should be exercised with great restraint.

In the light of these statements it is, perhaps, not surprising that Canada did not at once make the arrangement for taking over Red River Settlement outlined in the British Committee's report. For another ten years the Hudson's Bay Company remained the ruling force in the colony, though, under all the new conditions, its authority gradually weakened. The energetic Canadians and Americans pushing into the territory wished to share in its government. The *Nor'-Wester*, with which were soon associated James Ross, the most brilliant and assertive of the Selkirk descendants of that day, and Dr. Schultz, perhaps the most aggressive and enterprising of the newcomers, became a centre of opposition to company rule. When the regiment of Royal Canadian

Rifles was taken back to Quebec over the long journey via York Factory and Hudson Strait, the Company was left without any means of exercising power other than its natural privilege.

It was unfortunate for the Company and for the people of the settlement, too, that in 1860, Sir George Simpson, who had been for forty years the Governor of the Company in Canada, died. Of his administration it is impossible to speak too highly. His place was taken by Governor Dallas, who came to Red River from British Columbia. Even the Company's own men called him " the Greenhorn," so it is not surprising to find that he did not maintain the authority of his office. He was succeeded by William Mactavish, already Governor of Assiniboia, and the last of the Hudson's Bay Company men to hold sway over the plains and mountains of Western Canada.

The news that the directors of the Hudson's Bay Company had sold the assets of the old Company to a new concern known as the Finance Corporation, which began to trade in the shares, did not help to maintain the loyalty of the Company's men, the more so as the chief factors and traders felt themselves injured in that they had not been consulted, nor even informed, that the sale was about to take place. Sharing the profits of the fur trade ever since the days of the amalgamation of the two warring Companies, they had come to look on themselves as actual partners.

" And now," says Hargrave, " a feeling of stupefaction, quickly succeeded by one of deep indignation, may be said to have stolen over the senses of the holders of commissions in the fur trade. . . . The *Nor'-Wester* was cruel enough to insult their misery by an assurance, which carried with it an irresistible conviction of the truth, that they had all been sold like ' dumb driven cattle.' "

While there was all this restlessness in the air, the affairs of the settlement were making steady progress. In the summer of 1862, the little *Pioneer* gave way to the

large *International*.   This steamboat, which was 200 feet
long and 30 wide, arrived for the first time on May 26th,
having taken seven days to make the trip from Georgetown.   She brought with her 200 passengers, of whom
no fewer than 160 were young Canadians, "who had
come with the intention of pioneering an overland route
across the continent to Cariboo," to which point discoveries of gold were luring them.   That same summer
brought the scientific party of Lord Milton and Dr.
Cheadle, whose book tells the stirring tale of the fate of
those young pioneers.

But, seen from this distance, much the most important
event of that eventful summer was the actual beginning
of the village of Winnipeg.   Just where the fur-runners'
trail coming down the Assiniboine to Fort Garry crossed
the trail running down the Red River—in present-day
Winnipeg the corner of Main Street and Portage Avenue
—Henry McKenny, a half-brother and partner of Dr.
Schultz, built a store.   With much amusement and even
with jeers, the people from the fort and the settlers from
Point Douglas and points farther down the Red, watched
this building go up.   It was much too far from the river,
they said, and in the spring the land was so low, it was
nothing but a swamp.   Further cause for ridicule was
found in the shape of the building, which being long and
high—a second storey was to serve as a stopping place—
had to be shored up with timbers against the prairie
winds.   Noah's Ark was the name given to it, and it was
predicted that its owner would have need for the boat
which usually accompanied the toy ark of the day.   But
Henry McKenny had caught his own glimpse of the future
and was not to be laughed out of his plans.   Before long
he was followed by others and the first land boom of
Winnipeg was on.   Hargrave says that land around
this spot rose "from $1.85 an acre to $125 a square
chain," which means in our money from $1.85 to $1,250
an acre.   It even, in a few cases, went as high as $2,000
an acre.   Yet through all this betokened movement and
change, the growth was very slow.   When Rev. George

Dominion of Canada Archives.

The corner of Portage Avenue and Main Street, Winnipeg, about 1870. The building on the right is on the site of the Bank of Montreal.

Young arrived five years later to begin the ministry of the Methodist church, he drew a picture of the village that then was.

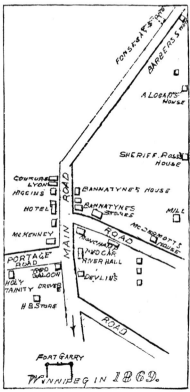

Fig. 12.—The accompanying sketch, made by Rev. Dr. George Bryce for the Manitoba Historical and Scientific Society, shows the principal roads and buildings in the village of Winnipeg just at the time when the rule of the Hudson's Bay Company over Western Canada was coming to an end.   Sheriff Ross's house and the mill were close to the river.

"But what a sorry sight was presented by that long thought-of-town of Winnipeg on the day we entered it.   What a mass of soft, black, slippery and sticky mud was everywhere spread out before us.   Streets with neither side walks nor crossings, with now and then a good sized pit of mire for the traveller to avoid or flounder through as best he could, a few small stores with poor goods and high prices; a few small dwellings with no 'rooms to let,' nor space for boarders. Neither church or school in sight or prospect; population about 100 instead of the 1000 we expected—such was Winnipeg on July 4th, 1868."

This village of Winnipeg, as it soon came to be called, was a quite unimportant part of the settlement. The centre of life and population was still at St. Andrews, the centre of Company rule at Fort Garry. Up and down the Red River were the homes of the settlers, and out the Assiniboine River as far as Portage la Prairie, then the remotest western settlement, were here and there groups of farmers drawing a comfortable living out of the prairie soil.

That living was not to be won without facing dangers, as well as hardships, as was sharply brought home to the settlers in the time of the Indian rising in Minnesota and Dakota. The Company and the settlers, by their just and tactful treatment, had kept the Indians in friendly relationship, but south of the boundary conditions were not so happy. There, there was no Company with a tradition of government, which, in the main, made for good treatment. Settlers came in with a rapidity entirely unknown in the Red River. The state of Minnesota, alone, within a ten-year period increased its population from 10,000 to 200,000. Such pressure of incoming peoples left little time or energy for the consideration of the claims of the original inhabitants. They were somewhat ruthlessly pushed out of the way. When the United States was engrossed in the Civil War, the Sioux Indians, smarting under a sense of wrong, broke out into open warfare and massacred the settlers. The trade route between Georgetown and Pembina was closed, and great fears were entertained for the safety of the people in Red River Settlement. Two or three times bands of Sioux—one numbering 3,000 souls—came to Fort Garry seeking first of all food, and then protection from their enemies. They recalled to the Company's officers that they had always been friendly to the British. Such aid as the settlers and the Company could spare was given to them and they were finally induced to make their peace with the American authorities.

Hardly was the colony clear of its fear of Indian assaults, when in 1864 the old enemies of the Selkirk settlers, the grasshoppers, again descended upon it. For four successive years they did damage to the crops, laying each year eggs which developed the following summer. By 1868, as in the time of the Pharaohs, " they covered the face of the whole earth, so that the land was darkened, and they did eat every herb of the land, and all the fruit of the trees. And there remained not any green thing in the trees, nor in the herbs of the field throughout all the land."

Blown along by the winds these grasshoppers struck the walls of the fort and of buildings until they lay in heaps three feet high. Decaying in the sun they made a horrible stench, so that they had to be carried off in wheelbarrows and burned in great heaps. Clothes could not be hung out to dry nor windows opened, for the grasshoppers ate all they touched. One of the pioneer women, still living in Winnipeg in 1928, described how she came that summer to Winnipeg—a little girl of eight years. No houses were to be bought or rented and she had the fun of living in a tent on the river bank. She recalls that when finally her parents found a home in the second storey of a log house on Notre Dame Avenue East, the grasshoppers came in through the spaces between the logs so fast that her mother swept them up several times a day and burned them.

Scanty harvest the three or four years before had exhausted all reserves and famine faced the settlers.

" As the season advanced," says Hargrave, " prospects grew darker, the buffalo hunt had been during the summer a complete failure and no improvement took place in the autumn. The numerous settlers who had gone to pass the winter on the lake fishing grounds returned to the settlement with the disastrous intelligence that the fisheries had failed ; and to complete the universal helplessness the rabbit and the pheasant had entirely disappeared. Thus all the sources from which the colony draws its usual provisions had been cut off."

In its extremity Red River for the first time appealed to the outside world. The response was immediate and generous. The Company gave $8,000 and from England, the United States and Canada came nearly another $40,000. With co-operation within and help from without, the settlement pulled through until the next harvest, but how remote the settlement still seemed, even when this response was being made, is shown by a letter written by Rev. Dr. George M. Grant, of Halifax, afterwards President of Queen's University. " I could have collected the money quite as easily, and the givers would have given quite as intelligently, had the sufferers been in Central Abyssinia."

" Yet there were not wanting statesmen with the eye of faith to look into the future," wrote Sir George Parkin, " and George Brown and Sir John Macdonald were at one in feeling that the great heritage, so long monopolized by the Hudson's Bay Company, must belong to Canada, and that half the continent was too large a reserve for the scattered agents of a trading company and a few thousand Indians." Once the union was an accomplished fact they did not hesitate. The year following saw commissioners from the Canadian Government in London making arrangements for the transfer of the rights of the Hudson's Bay Company. For a payment of $1,500,000, which the British Government lent to Canada, the Company surrendered its rights in Rupert's Land, thus going far beyond the recommendations made by the British Committee ten years before. Of all the vast area, seven times as large as the four provinces already in the Confederation, the Company was left with only one-twentieth of the fertile land and a reserve of 500 acres around each post. It has been estimated that during the 200 years of its rule the Company had taken out of the country more than $100,000,000 worth of furs—a fabulous sum in those days. Out of its reserve land, much of which is

DAVID LOUIS RIEL.

as yet unsold, the Company is still realizing considerable sums.

Now that Canada had secured the western territory desired, and the people of the settlement were to be free from the rule of the Company, it must have seemed that the way was clear for a new development. For a long time the people in Red River had been wanting a share in the government. In the year of Confederation a determined effort had been made to get for Dr. Schultz a seat on the Council of Assiniboia, then always composed of the Company's friends. In the same year, the settlers of Portage la Prairie who were outside the borders of Assiniboia, had tried to set up a government of their own which they wished to call The Republic of Manitoba. Grave disapproval on the part of the British Government soon put an end to that movement, but it did not end the wish of the people to get from under the rule of the Company. The allegiance of the chief traders and factors, already weakened by the first sale to the Finance Corporation, was still further lessened as the news drifted in that the directors had once more, without any consultation with the men who braved the dangers and starvations of the fur trade, agreed to surrender the Company's rights. A little good fortune and all would have been well. But misunderstandings and bad fortune attended almost every step. Donald Gunn makes a note of "the faculty for making mistakes with the very best intentions in the world which in turn attacks almost every person connected with the Red River about this time."

The first of these mistakes was made by the Canadian Government. Before its commissioners had even set out for London to make the final arrangements, it sent a survey party, under the direction of John A. Snow, to make a road from Fort Garry to the Lake of the Woods on the route surveyed ten years before by the Dawson party. Now at this time the Canadian Government had no right in Assiniboia. The people of Red River might be united in their desire to put an end to Company rule, but they were by no means united in a wish to join with the new Canadian Confederation. Certainly one group—the newer Canadian settlers—wished that, but another group quite as definitely wished to annex at any rate the settled portion to the United States, while a third thought it would be best to become a British colony having no connection at all with Canada. So, with the coming of the Snow party, an outcry arose against the Canadian Government for assuming that it already owned the territory. The plea that the party had been sent to give relief to those suffering from the famine was not taken very seriously, since only a small number of men of the country were employed. It was a further piece of bad fortune that members of the party became involved in a scheme to buy Indian rights in the land, since this alarmed and offended many of the settlers ; and the publication by the *Toronto Globe* of letters written by a member of the survey party, in which people in Red River were severely and unkindly criticized, added further to the indignation.

With the passing of the strain of months of famine, things might still have worked out smoothly had not the Hon. William MacDougall, then Minister of Public Works in the Macdonald Cabinet, decided that he would begin at once to make a survey of the lands which the Canadian commissioners in London were arranging to have transferred to Canada. It was expected that the whole matter would be concluded by the end of the year, and Mr. MacDougall apparently thought there was need for haste in preparing the land for new settlement. He consulted no one as to the wisdom of the step, and he explained to no one what was to be done, and the reasons for it. News drifted slowly into Red River. Alarm and suspicion grew. The men of the Company, still the most influential element in the colony, were in no mood to help the Canadian Government out of the difficulties it had itself created. By the time the second survey party, headed by Colonel J. S. Dennis, appeared in Red River everyone was in a highly nervous and suspicious state.

As the plans for the survey developed, it became clear

that it was proposed to re-survey the country in a manner altogether different from that with which the settlers and Métis were familiar. The Company had laid out the Settlement on lines similar to those of the survey of Lower Canada—long narrow lots each having a river frontage. The surveyors proposed to ignore this system and to establish the more economic square sections now in general use. They failed to make it clear that it was not the intention to disturb those already in possession of homes and farms, and among the Métis, who made up the great majority of the population, the fear spread that their lands and homes were to be taken from them.

In *The Canadian Dominion*, by Charles R. Marshall, is a passage outlining well the conditions as they were at this moment in Red River.

" To appreciate the history of the Red River revolt it is necessary to observe the exceptional variety and intricacy of the interests that were involved. Never was there such a mixture of elements in such a little pot before. . . .

" First, must be named the difference of race dividing the little community into natural rivalries. Next, the difference of religion separating the people into two antagonistic parties. Then must be considered the separate interests of the powerful Hudson's Bay Trading Company with its own policy to pursue and its great profits to make, an association surrounded, of course, with enemies as every monopoly is sure to be. With all this, however, it must be remembered that the isolated conditions, which the people here all shared, tended strongly to unite all interests against the outside world of foreigners. But to assist the complication we must take into account the divergent interests of a number of energetic American residents and their sympathizers, within and without the settlement, who, covertly or openly, advised a policy of annexation to the United States. Add still the influence of a restless but imbecile Fenian party, whose aim was to establish an independent republic from which they might make war upon Canada and Great Britain. The imbroglio is not yet complete. It is no secret that the government at Ottawa were themselves divided as to the policy to be adopted in Manitoba. The Quebec party were naturally for increasing their own influence, perpetuating the Catholic religion and strengthening

French interests in the new country. The Ontario party were
equally determined to prevent the growth of a second Quebec in
the Dominion and set themselves in unreasoning haste to secure
Protestant and English supremacy."

Colonel Dennis was not long in perceiving that adverse
forces were at work in Red River, and that a survey,
which was bound to run lines across lots and, in some
cases, through the barns and homes of people already
living along the rivers, could not be made without causing
serious trouble. He so reported to Ottawa. But
MacDougall was determined to carry out his plans and
Colonel Dennis, was ordered to proceed. He had no
more than begun actual work when, on October 11th,
1869, a party of French Métis, led by Louis Riel,
interrupted the survey and threatened violence if the
work were not at once stopped. It seems now that it
might have been simple to explain that, whatever sort
of survey might be made, there was no intention of
interfering with land as it was already held. But the
Canadian Government, by its disregard of all protests,
had alienated any support it might have been able to
win. " These gentlemen," said Governor Mactavish on
his return from a trip to Ottawa, " are of the opinion
that they know a great deal more about this country
than we do." " Monseigneur Taché," wrote Sir George
Parkin, " the Roman Catholic Bishop of the district and
the idol of the half-breeds, on his way to the Vatican
council, turned aside to warn Sir George Cartier of
impending trouble and was, so it is said, greeted with
a contemptuous laugh." Nor did it lessen the mis-
fortune that Governor Mactavish was taken ill on his
return and was thereafter unable to grapple with the
difficulties ; nor that at the United States border and
in the city of St. Paul were influential groups who did
not mean to lose the trade of Assiniboia if, by any means
of their devising, they could draw that settlement into
the United States. By this time most of the Hudson's
Bay Company's goods were coming into the settlement

by the American route and a flourishing trade with St. Paul had grown up.

The appointment of Mr. MacDougall himself as Governor of the new North-west Territories did not tend to ease the situation, and he did not improve matters by taking with him, when he set out for Red River, five gentlemen from Eastern Canada, who, it was rumoured, would take the principal posts in the new Government. To a people who had been clamouring for a share in the Government this could not be pleasing. It was thought that the Queen's proclamation taking over the country would be issued about December 1st, and Mr. MacDougall was directed by the Government at Ottawa to proceed to Red River and there await that event.

By the end of October, when Mr. MacDougall and his party arrived at the boundary, Louis Riel was the centre of a large party of French Métis, who were determined to keep the new Governor out of the colony until he agreed to the terms which they desired to make. Riel was the son of that popular miller of the Seine who had been prominent twenty years before during the time of the Sayer trial. He was also the grandson of Marie Lajimonière, the first white woman to come to Red River to make a home. Better educated than most of his party, high spirited and popular, he became the accepted leader, although when the National Committee of the Métis of Red River was organized, John Bruce was made the President and Riel the secretary. A letter was sent by this committee to Pembina to await the arrival of the new Governor. It ordered him not to attempt to enter the North-west Territories without the consent of the committee. As a more practical way of making sure that their orders were obeyed, Riel and his party built a barricade across the highway at the Rivière Sale, near the present St. Norbert.

Mr. MacDougall was not disposed to take the letter or the news of the barricade very seriously. He came on to the Hudson's Bay Company post, which was just inside the Territories, as Western Canada was then called. There he remained, but he sent Captain Cameron of his party, a son-in-law of Sir Charles Tupper, on to Red River. At the barricade Captain Cameron was turned back and, two or three days later, Riel sent a party of armed men who forcibly escorted the new Governor and his party back to Pembina, warning them to remain outside the Territories.   For some months he remained there, hoping to be able to come to Fort Garry, and then returned to Ottawa.

Even before the arrival of Governor MacDougall, Colonel Dennis, acting as his agent, had made an effort to see if a force could be raised from among the English and Scotch residents to oppose the French Métis.   His report represents the settlers as saying :

" We have not been consulted in any way as a people. . . . The character of the new government has been settled in Canada. . . . We are prepared to accept it respectfully and to become good subjects.   But when you present to us the issue of a conflict with the French party, with whom we have hitherto lived in friendship, . . . we feel disinclined to enter upon it, and think that the Dominion should assume the responsibility of establishing among us what it, and it alone, has decided upon."

So little of any desire to support the Dominion Government or to oppose the Métis was there, that when, on the morning of November 3rd, Riel and his men presented themselves at Fort Garry, saying they had come to guard it, they were able to take possession without any other protest than that of Dr. Cowan, the Company officer in charge.   Once in possession of the fort, Riel and his party assumed, step by step, the position that they were the constituted authority, able and ready to negotiate terms with the Government at Ottawa for the future government of the country.   Though he had to imprison the editor of the *Nor'-Wester* to get it done, Riel issued a proclamation inviting each parish in the settlement to send delegates to a convention to discuss the situation. Governor Mactavish made a vain effort to stem the tide. He too issued a proclamation reminding everyone that

After a Painting by Paul Kane

The Stovel Company, Winnipeg.

UPPER FORT GARRY AS PAUL KANE SAW IT.

The bridge in the foreground was over the creek which crossed Main Street in front of the present City Hall.

the Government of the country was legally still in the hands of the Hudson's Bay Company. But Riel was in possession at the fort. The parishes chose their representatives. The usual bad luck, however, surrounded the convention. The delegates fell to wrangling and nothing was accomplished. Into this situation came another proclamation, this time from Mr. MacDougall, still waiting at the boundary. December 1st had been the day originally set for the transfer to Canada of the Hudson's Bay Company rights. On that day, and without knowing whether the matter had been concluded, —and in fact it had not—he issued a proclamation calling on all residents to submit to the Queen's Government and appointing Colonel Dennis to the high-sounding position of Conservator of the Peace. As such he was to arm, equip, and provision a force to disperse the insurgent Métis.

The immediate effect was to rally all the Métis around Riel and his associates John Bruce, Ambrose Lepine, and W. B. O'Donaghue. A bill of rights was issued by their party a few days later which, as even Colonel Dennis reported, contained nothing unreasonable. Riel seized the offices of the newspapers, now two in number, the *Nor'-Wester* and the *Pioneer*, issuing on the same day the first number of his own paper, the *New Nation*. He cleared all the stores in the Settlement of arms and ammunition. Reckoning correctly, as it turned out, that the old settlers would not resort to arms, he then turned his attention towards a party of Canadians about fifty in number, who, in order to protect the Government stores and other supplies in a warehouse belonging to Dr. Schultz and directly behind his own house near the corner of Main Street and Notre Dame Avenue east, had armed themselves and were on guard inside the warehouse. They were summoned to give up their arms and surrender. Believing that they had a promise from Riel that they would simply be marched to the fort and then released, they finally surrendered. They were, indeed, marched to the fort but, in place of being released, the

8

men of the party were closely confined under conditions of much hardship. The women were given rooms in the Governor's quarters.

G. D. McVicar, who was one of the prisoners, has left a description of the conditions they found at the fort.

" On arriving at Fort Garry, we were received by volleys of musketry and imprisoned in three rooms. In these rooms we were packed so close that we had to break the windows to keep from suffocation. In one there was a bed and a table and in that room the poor fellows found themselves in the morning in a condition something like the following : seven on the bed, two under it, two under the table and the remaining space literally packed with human beings. One man slept all night hanging on the bed post. We were fed on pemmican and tea. After this, thirty-eight, myself included, were moved to Fort Garry gaol, the worst indignity of all. The place is close, small and unhealthy—a narrow hall and six cells, six by nine and filthy in the extreme."

With this opposition safely out of the way, Riel issued another proclamation renouncing all allegiance to the Company and declaring the Provisional Government the only established authority. It was now known that Canada had not yet taken over the rights of the Hudson's Bay Company, and so it was easy for Riel to override any other opposition that remained. People supposed to be sympathetic to the Canadians already in gaol were arrested ; the Company's books and funds and the Government supplies were seized, and towards the end of the year Riel became head of the Provisional Government, in name as he had been in fact, Bruce dropping into the background. " You may depend upon it," wrote Colonel Dennis, who escaped in disguise, " these people are fully in possession for the winter."

Up to this moment Riel had kept a cool head, moving cautiously from point to point and succeeding in keeping the English-speaking settlers, except the Canadians, out of any open opposition. From now on there appears a different Riel. Bishop Taché, at a later time, attributed to him " an insensate pride and an unquenchable thirst for power." These characteristics now began to appear. By them he antagonized, one by one, the men whose counsels might have helped to bring his insurrection to a peaceful termination. " If he had at once," wrote Major Boulton, " opened the prison doors, and let all his unfortunate victims out and allowed the people, without intimidation, to elect their delegates to the new convention, an honourable career might have been open to him. But this was not his course ; there was a want of moral stamina and diseased vanity in the man that had proved his ruin."

By this time the Canadian Government had begun to realize the danger of serious trouble. Mr. Donald A. Smith, Chief Officer of the Hudson's Bay Company at Montreal, was appointed a special commissioner to go to Red River and try to bring about a peaceful solution of the difficulties. Upon his arrival at Fort Garry, Riel demanded that Commissioner Smith take the oath of allegiance to his Government, and, when that was refused, the Commissioner was detained within the fort, though Riel did not venture to confine him with the other prisoners in the gaol. Day by day the leading men of the colony visited him, and as the Commissioner outlined to them his plans, now known to be conciliatory and even generous, little by little the opposition of the English-speaking settlers to Riel strengthened, the allegiance of the French-speaking settlers weakened. Mr. Smith had left his formal instructions at Pembina for safe keeping. Before long he was able to send Richard Hardisty, his brother-in-law, for them. On that journey Hardisty was guarded by a party of fifty French Métis who had begun to distrust Riel's good faith. Once in possession of his official papers, Commissioner Smith called a public meeting within the fort. On January 19th, with the mercury at 20 below zero, over a thousand people stood for hours in the courtyard listening to his statements. Riel having constituted himself interpreter, was able to delay proceedings, but the audience insisted on hearing all the papers, even though they had to adjourn the meeting at dark and return the next day. Commissioner Smith was most adroit and successful in his presentation. At the end of that meeting there was for the first time in anxious months in Red River cheering and a general feeling of goodwill. It was agreed that a convention of forty people in all, twenty from the English and twenty from the French parishes, should meet and "decide what would be best for the welfare of the country."

This convention, after arguing for days, finally agreed to recognize the Provisional Government which Riel and his Métis had set up, and Riel took the oath again as its President. In return for this concession Riel promised to release all the political prisoners. The Hudson's Bay Company, the British Government, and the Canadian Government found scant comfort in this arrangement, but at Red River the compromise was received with enthusiasm. "The utmost good feeling prevailed," writes Begg. "French and English shook hands, and for the first time in many months a spirit of unity between the two classes of settlers appeared."

The enthusiasm was soon dampened, for Riel did not keep his promise to free all the prisoners. Only two, Dr. Cowan and A. G. B. Bannatyne, were actually released, though twelve others were let out on parole. Distrust of Riel grew. Rumours of bad treatment of prisoners caused general uneasiness. A party of about seventy-five men, led by Major Boulton, lightly armed and equipped, marched down from Portage la Prairie in bitter winter weather. At Kildonan they found food and shelter prepared for them, and more than 300 men armed ready to join them. Thereupon Riel released all the prisoners. The hotter spirits were for marching on the Fort, but wiser counsels prevailed, and the Portage men, their arms stacked on sleds, started on the return journey. They followed a trail which brought them near the Fort, and, as they passed, Riel's men came out and arrested forty-eight of them. Their leader, Major Boulton, was put into chains and sentenced to be shot. Only by the pleadings of Commissioner Smith and by those of all the influential people in the colony, including Mr. and Mrs. John Sutherland, whose son had just been shot by a half-crazy Métis, was Major Boulton's life spared. A condition of Riel's consent was that Commissioner Smith should undertake to get the English-speaking settlers to share in the election which was to take place within a week.

A less happy fate awaited the next man upon whom Riel's anger fell. Thomas Scott, who had been taken prisoner with the other Canadians in Dr. Schultz's warehouse, had, like Dr. Schultz himself, escaped from gaol. Unlike Dr. Schultz, who was now making his way to Ontario, Scott had gone to Portage la Prairie and had returned with the armed party to help the other prisoners. He was among the members of the party who were arrested on their way home, and thus for the second time he fell into Riel's hands. Between the two men there was already bad blood. After the merest pretence of a trial, on March 3rd, Scott was condemned to be shot at noon the next day. Perhaps believing still, as he had said earlier in the day, that " they merely intended to frighten him," Scott was led outside the fort and shot by a firing party of six men, one of whom discharged his pistol at the unfortunate man as he lay moving on the ground. Even after Scott's death Riel was ruthless. His friends were not allowed to have his body, and the place and manner of his burial remain unknown. These very circumstances added fuel to the fire of indignation which now inflamed the public mind against Riel.

" The death of Scott," says Begg, " struck horror into the minds of all classes in the Settlement." It also struck horror into the minds of the Protestant population of Ontario, who, because Scott was an Orangeman, saw in his execution a cold-blooded murder instigated by religious differences. Immediately Ontario was swept by a demand that armed forces should be sent to put down Riel and the Métis, and the mediation of the Quebec representatives in the Cabinet availed nothing. It was agreed with the British Government that an armed force supported by both Governments should be sent, and preparations were at once begun.

Five days after the shooting of Thomas Scott, Bishop Taché returned to the Settlement. The moderation of his counsels was soon felt. The newly elected council, which had not yet met, though the English-speaking settlers had kept faith about going to the polls, was called together. Commissioner Smith was allowed to leave for Eastern Canada and the delegates, already chosen to negotiate on behalf of the Provisional Government, set out for Ottawa. In the earlier stages the negotiations at Ottawa were beclouded by the storm of indignation against Riel sweeping Ontario and two of the delegates were arrested. But larger views prevailed. By May 1st terms had been arranged. Instead of forming part of the North-west Territories, the old district of Assiniboia was to be the nucleus of a new province to be called Manitoba. On May 12th, 1870, the Manitoba Act, setting up the constitution of this province, and providing for its entry into the Dominion as a fully organized province, passed the Dominion Parliament.

Back in Red River the Provisional Government was still in existence, and Riel was powerful enough to win from the Hudson's Bay Company a loan of $15,000, the use of the Company's stores to the amount of another $20,000, and an agreement that the whole of the Company in the North-west should recognize the Provisional Government. But as news of what was happening at Ottawa reached the settlement, Riel's friends began to waver, and he, himself, to change his attitude. In April he pulled down the flag of the Provisional Government and hoisted the Union Jack. He even celebrated the Queen's birthday. But the desertion of the Métis continued. Riel finally found himself left with only a corporal's guard in the fort.

While the Métis were quietly returning to their homes a force of 400 men under the command of Colonel Wolseley was on the way to Red River, coming by steamer to Fort

William. Surmounting all but impossible difficulties of transport on the journey, via the Kaministiquia River, Rainy Lake, and the Lake of the Woods to the Winnipeg River, the advance party, composed of the British part of the force, reached Point Douglas on the morning of August 24th. From that point they marched, hoping to surprise Riel, through pouring rain and deep mud, up to the Fort. They entered it unopposed. Forsaken by all save a handful of followers Riel had fled, his uneaten breakfast still upon the table. As the troops marched down the trail, which in present-day Winnipeg is Main Street, they saw, flying from a building close to the corner of Portage and Main, used for Canadian Government offices and supplies, a home-made Union Jack, which Mrs. Crowson, still living in 1928 and well able to tell the story of that exciting morning, had sat up all night to make at the behest of the jubilant Canadians. They might also have seen across the river Riel and his two friends—O'Donaghue and Lepine—who, having cut the cable of the ferry on which they had crossed the river, watched the progress of the soldiers whose entry into Fort Garry marked the final passing of the Provisional Government.

Three days later the Ontario force arrived. For a few days the Company still held rule at Fort Garry, Donald A. Smith, who had returned, taking charge. In co-operation with Colonel Wolseley, confidence was quickly restored, and when a few days later still the Lieutenant-Governor of the new Province of Manitoba, Adams G. Archibald, arrived from the east by canoe, the last line of the story of the Hudson's Bay Company rule in the North-west had been written. Thereafter its part was to be that of an economic rather than of a political power.

CHAPTER VI

LAYING THE FOUNDATIONS

" THE one point of view having peculiar interest to the stranger is gained by turning west or southwestward. Far as the eye can see, there is stretched out before you an ocean of grass whose vast immensity grows upon you more and more the longer you gaze upon it. Gallop out alone in the evening a few miles towards the southwest, and the least impressionable of mortals will experience a novel sensation. A feeling of indescribably buoyant freedom seems to tingle through every nerve, making the old feel young again. Old age and decrepitude belong to civilization and the abodes of men. We can even associate it in our minds with the mountains whose rocks themselves appear as monuments of preceding centuries ; and the withered and fallen trees in ancient forests seem akin to it ; but upon the boundless prairie, with no trace of man in sight, nature looks so fresh and smiling that youth alone is in consonance with it."

So wrote Colonel Wolseley, in Blackwood's famous Magazine, not long after his return from the Red River Expedition. Though he remained only a few days at Fort Garry, his discerning eye caught the lure which was to bring thousands of men and women from the East to write further chapters in that romance which is the history of Manitoba.

When, on the morning of September 2nd, 1870, Adams G. Archibald, the new Lieutenant-Governor, drew up in his canoe at Fort Garry, he was met by Commissioner Donald A. Smith, whose words of greeting, " I yield up my responsibilities with pleasure," brought the response, " I don't anticipate much pleasure on my own account."

" From the first," writes Begg, " his task was a difficult one, in attempting to affiliate two distinct classes neither one of which could be thoroughly conciliated without giving offence to the other." . . . For the moment he was well received. " The appearance and manner of the new Governor of Manitoba," said the *Manitoba News Letter*, " go a great way towards impressing those with whom he may come in contact that he is thoroughly capable of bringing about that much to be desired peace and quietness which the province has been yearning for."

In a letter written to Sir George Cartier the day after his arrival, Mr. Archibald expressed his relief that at least one of the outstanding problems would not have to be dealt with immediately, since Riel and his companions had fled from the country and were now in the United States. " It is perhaps the best solution," he wrote. " While feeling runs so high here, as it does at present, an attempt at arrest would have been met by resistance and in the end we would perhaps have had to call out the military, and we would have had a world of trouble, which the absence of these people enables us to escape."

It was only a partial escape, for, from the side of the settlers and of the Canadian soldiers who spent that first winter at Fort Garry, came many demands for action against those concerned in the death of Scott. There were encounters too between them and the French Métis, in which, as Governor Archibald reported, " men were so beaten and outraged that they feel as if they were living in a state of slavery." Eleazar Goulet, who had been with Riel in Fort Garry, was drowned as he sought to escape from an angry crowd in Winnipeg by swimming across the Red River to St. Boniface.

So far as was possible the Governor turned a deaf ear to the complaints from both sides and proceeded with the business of establishing parliamentary government and civil administration in Manitoba. The first requisite was a census in order that proper voters' lists might be prepared for the election of members from the twenty-four constituencies into which the province was divided. The result of this census was to show that Manitoba was beginning its career as a province with a population of

11,963 persons.   Of these 1,563 were white ; 1,553 were Indians ; and 9,848 were Métis, either English or French. Of the white population slightly less than one-half had been born in the North-west.   294 were Canadians, as the people who came from the eastern part of Canada were then and for long afterward called ; 69 had come from the United States ; 412 were from Great Britain or Ireland ; 15 had come from France ; and 28 were from other countries.

Immediately after the completion of the census, the election took place.   On December 30th, the following members of the first legislative assembly were returned :

Baie St. Paul	Joseph Dubuc
Headingly	John Taylor
High Bluff	John Norquay
Kildonan	John Sutherland
Lake Manitoba	Angus McKay
Popular Point	David Spence
Portage la Prairie	Frederick O. Bird
St. Agathe	George Klyne
St. Andrews, North	Alfred Boyd
St. Andrews, South	E. H. G. G. Hay
St. Anne	John McTavish
St. Boniface, East	Marc A. Girard
St. Boniface, West	Louis Schmidt
St. Charles	Henry J. H. Clarke
St. Clements	Thomas Bunn
St. François Xavier, East	Pascal Breland
St. François Xavier, West	Joseph Royal
St. James	Edwin Bourke
St. Norbert, North	Joseph Lamay
St. Norbert, South	Pierre de Lorme
St. Paul	Curtis J. Bird, M.D.
St. Peters	Thomas Howard
St. Vital	Andrew Beauchemin
Winnipeg	Donald A. Smith

How different the distribution f the population was then from what it is now, a little study of the list will show.

Almost   immediately   the   Cabinet   was   chosen   with

Henry James Clarke as Attorney-General ; Marc Amable Girard, Treasurer ;   Alfred Boyd, Minister of Public Works and Agriculture ;   Thomas Howard, Provincial Secretary ;   and James McKay, without portfolio.   Mr. Boyd held office for a few months only, resigning to make way for John Norquay, who was to play a large part in the development of the province and who remains the only native son of Manitoba who has achieved the office of Premier, as he is still one of the most highly regarded of all the men who have held that office.

In order to secure what it had been felt would be a safeguard for the rights of the minority, the Manitoba Act had provided for a second chamber in the provincial Parliament.   It was to be called the Legislature Council and its members were to be named by the Lieutenant-Governor.   Accordingly, Mr. Archibald now chose as the first members François Dauphinais, Hon. Donald Gunn, Solomon Hamelin, Colin Inkster, John Harrison O'Donnell, M.D., Francis Ogletree, and James McKay who became speaker.   It was not long, however, before it was felt that the province would be as well off without this second chamber and five years later it voted itself out of office. Colin Inkster, who was shortly after appointed sheriff, and who continued to give service to Manitoba in that office for fifty-one years, and Dr. Bird are the only survivors of all the men who made up that first Parliament.

The machinery of government being completed, a home for Parliament was secured by renting from A. G. B. Bannatyne part of his residence, the largest in the community.   It stood back from Main Street, close to where the main office of the Bank of Commerce now stands, and served as Parliament House for two years until it was destroyed by fire.   The opening ceremony, to which the Governor drove from the Fort along Main Street, accompanied by a guard of one hundred men, " had a completeness and dignity," says the *Manitoban* of that week, " which were creditable to our young province."   The thing that surprised the newcomers, reports an eyewitness, was to find so many well-dressed ladies.

Gravely the new Legislators settled down to the business of making laws for Manitoba.   After a session of six weeks they had forty-three bills ready to receive the assent of the Lieutenant-Governor.   Among them were acts for the establishment of courts, and of a system of education ; for the incorporation of the colleges of St. Boniface and St. John's and of the professions of law and medicine.   Thus the machinery of government was set in motion, rather, it should be noted, by the adoption of practices which had grown up in Great Britain or the older provinces than by the development of the institutions of the old Assiniboia where the Company officials had been supreme.

On April 26th, 1871, there came floating down the Red River on a scow which they had made up at Abercrombie in Minnesota, eight men described by J. W. Dafoe as " the first ripple of that mighty flood which was later to transform the prairie."   They and others who speedily followed them, as well as many of the discharged soldiers, who had made up their minds to remain in the west, were eager for land, but as yet there was no machinery by which they might secure it.   The rebellion had interrupted the work of the surveyors and all plans for the allotment of land had come to an abrupt ending.   The spring of 1871 brought a general land hunger and, when the Dominion Government passed an order-in-council that actual settle-ment would be recognized when the surveys were made, it was taken to mean that anyone who staked out a claim would have the right to hold it against all comers.   At once the *Manitoban* was filled with notices of claims that had been staked and notice boards dotted the prairie even to the walls of Fort Garry.

In the summer, however, the surveyors came, bringing with them definite plans of a survey into the block system. Allowances were to be made for the narrow lots which had already been laid out along the Red and Assiniboine rivers.   In these river lots lies the explanation of the peculiarities of the plan of the city of Winnipeg.   In the fall of the same year Gilbert McMicken, who had been ap-pointed Receiver-General and Dominion Lands Agent, arrived to open the Government Savings Bank and the Dominion Lands Office, announcing that he had come to "administer with impartial justice the Manitoba Act as it affects public lands in spirit and to the letter."

Thereafter it was possible, and indeed necessary, to secure land under legal terms, but those very terms worked great hardship to one element in the population. Under the agreement for the transfer from the Hudson's Bay Company the Government had set aside for distributing among the Métis 1,400,000 acres of land. This meant that each head of a family was to have 160 acres plus a patent for his house and its land, plus an allowance for each child. But, since the surveys were not made, there was no way of making the allotments. In this impasse the Métis were given scrip for their share of the land. The terms under which this land was to be allotted were modified so as to be less and less agreeable to them. They found the demands of life in the rapidly expanding community very different from those of life on the plains as the servants of the Company, and, as the scrip was transferable, they sold it freely and retreated gradually from the more settled areas. The average price at that time for the scrip of an individual was about $15. Through these sales thousands of acres passed into the hands of speculators.

It was not only the Métis who felt unhappy about their lands. Almost immediately after the arrival of Governor Archibald, the Indians, fearful that their claims might be forgotten, had asked him to make a treaty with them. This the Governor had promised should be done sometime in the following year. Accordingly, in the summer of 1871, the new Indian Commissioner, W. M. Simpson, began the business of making treaties with the Indians for the surrender of the land to the Dominion Government. In this work he had the able assistance of the Lieutenant-Governor, himself, and of Hon. James McKay, whose influence with the Indians was very great as was his actual knowledge of their ways of thinking and living. The first treaty was that made with the Indians of Manitoba. It provided for each band a reserve of sufficient size to allow land for each family in the proportion of 160 acres for a family of five. Each head of a family of five was also to receive an annual allowance of $15. In addition each person was to receive a present of $3, and certain gifts of ploughs, harrows, animals and clothing were to be made as each family settled upon its land. For the Indians living in Manitoba the reserves were placed at St. Peter's at the mouth of the Red River, on the Roseau River, at Fort Alexander on the Winnipeg River, and about twenty miles above Portage la Prairie on the south side of the Assiniboine River—four reserves in all.

All this time there continued to be a feeling of uneasiness owing to Riel, and of dissatisfaction that no one had been punished for the shooting of Thomas Scott. Further cause of unrest came in the news that the Fenian forces in the United States might make an attempt against Manitoba. Though there was now a tri-weekly mail, news still travelled slowly and accurate information was hard to get. From August until October 3rd, when the Lieutenant-Governor issued a proclamation calling upon the residents to enroll themselves against the invader, there were rumours and counter-rumours and general uneasiness throughout the province. Riel had slipped back across the border and councils of the Métis were held at St. Norbert. The English-speaking people feared that the Métis, known to be uneasy about their lands, would join the Fenian invaders. Undoubtedly the Fenians themselves, using O'Donaghue, Riel's old lieutenant, as their agent, sought to bring this about. Though the matter is not clear, there is reason for believing that the Métis did not have any intention of allying themselves with the American disturbers.

The raid itself proved an insignificant affair, partly owing to the good offices of United States Consul Taylor. Captain Wheaton, of the American troops at the border, having orders to prevent any raid, acted promptly on warning given by Consul Taylor. He arrested O'Donaghue and the other leaders, when they, with a party about forty in number, took possession of the Hudson's Bay Company post at Pembina on the morning of October 9th. The day after, in response to the call of the Lieutenant-Governor, men of Winnipeg and Kildonan were marching towards Pembina in rain and deep mud. At St. Boniface Riel was organizing companies of Métis for the defence of the province. On the following Sunday Governor Archibald went to St. Boniface, reviewed the 350 Métis there enrolled, and publicly thanked and shook hands with Riel and Lepine.

The result of this act must have stunned the Governor. The English-speaking people, many of them still bitter that no vengeance had followed the death of Scott, refused to believe that the Métis had acted in good faith. The cry was raised that the Lieutenant-Governor had recognized rebels and murderers. The common opinion was that the Métis had not enrolled until after they had news of the defeat of the raid. The Lieutenant-Governor, himself, believed that the Métis had been won to support the Government. "I am perfectly satisfied," he wrote, "that the prevailing impression among the French, as among the English, was that there was to be a fresh raid and that the action of the French was not based on the idea that the affair was over."

Indignation rose to fever heat in Ontario. An order-in-council was passed at Ottawa calling for an expedition of 200 men. These were speedily enrolled and reached Winnipeg six weeks later. The Government of Ontario offered $5,000 for the arrest of those concerned in the killing of Scott. The County Council of Middlesex, from which Scott had come, offered a reward.

Among the French also excitement ran high. Resistance to arrest was advocated. Governor Archibald saw the fruits of his careful policy of conciliation ruined by his injudicious act of shaking hands with Riel and Lepine. "The difficulty is not among the people of the country," wrote Archibald to Sir George Cartier, "but among the small bands of lawless men, idlers and roughs, who infest the taverns of Winnipeg. These men have no influence except for mischief, but they might light a flame it would be hard to extinguish. For a few days I felt the danger was extreme. The only possible way to avoid a serious outbreak was to get rid of the two men whose presence in the country formed the pretext for the action of the roughs at Winnipeg."

With the aid of Archbishop Taché, and by the payment of a large sum of money, these two men were persuaded to leave the country. A few months later, Governor Archibald resigned to become Lieutenant-Governor of Nova Scotia. His time in Manitoba had been full of vexations and difficulties, but his desire to give his best service to the province was generally recognized. He carried with him when he left, an address of appreciation which was signed by over 1,800 citizens, including many of the leaders of public opinion. He was succeeded in Manitoba by Alexander Morris, who had been the first Chief Justice of the Province.

Not yet was the trouble over. Returning to the country, Lepine was arrested, tried and convicted of murder. He was sentenced to be hanged, but this sentence was commuted by Lord Dufferin to one of two years' imprisonment. Riel, in the meantime, had been elected for the constituency of Provencher, had attempted to take his seat at Ottawa, had been declared an outlaw and had again fled from the country. The whole question of amnesty for the French Métis who had taken part in the insurrection, which had been in dispute all this time, was finally settled by a resolution carried in the Dominion Parliament recommending general amnesty for all except Riel and Lepine. These two were banished for five years. Riel passed out of Canadian history for ten years and quiet was restored in Manitoba.

The atmosphere of romance which the student of the history of Manitoba continually meets, is rarely more pervasive than in the story of the days when the country was first being opened up to settlement. There are many angles from which it may be viewed but, perhaps, none which throws it into a clearer light than that of the development of transportation, by which the oncoming seekers for free land and for the country of youthful hope and enterprise were to be brought to the prairies. In 1870 there was neither stage line nor steamboat running regularly to or from Winnipeg. The individual traveller had to depend entirely on his own efforts. Usually he came either on one of the irregular trips of the H.B.C. steamer in the summer, or by Red River cart, or by driving in his own wagon. All freight save that belonging to the Company had to come by the brigades of Red River carts which plied between Fort Garry and St. Cloud or Abercrombie in Minnesota where the railroad ended. But, in the summer of 1872, J. J. Hill put the steamer *Selkirk* on the river to make regular trips between Moorhead and Winnipeg. His competition made the H.B.C. turn their boats into general freight and passenger carriers, and so rapidly did the boat traffic in the Red River expand that, when the railway reached St. Boniface six years later, there were fifteen regular steamers. Along with the steamboat service there was developed a regular stage to Abercrombie, at first triweekly and then daily. Soon there came also a triweekly stage to Portage la Prairie and following closely upon that, a regular mail service from Winnipeg to the Saskatchewan.

Steamboats were called into service too for traffic to the west. Flat-bottomed, stern-wheeled boats were taken to the north end of Lake Winnipeg, pulled over the rapids at the mouth of the Saskatchewan River and then used as freight carriers up and down that river. On the Assiniboine River, where now there is no navigation, there was then a regular service to the west. In 1877 the *Prince Rupert*, a steam tug drawing three barges, made its way successfully to Portage la Prairie. Soon this vessel and other boats were travelling to Brandon. From this there developed a regular service on the Assiniboine, which, by the end of two years, had reached even to Fort Ellice, a distance of more than 200 miles from Winnipeg.

9

Most of the settlers came by way of the United States. A few came by the Dawson route, that water and road route which the Canadian Government, in its eagerness to have an all-Canadian way of approach to the west, had opened from Thunder Bay to Red River. Efforts were made to maintain a regular service over this route but in the end it had to be abandoned, having cost the country the sum—large for those days—of almost $1,300,000.

In the years following Confederation, not only here, but in all parts of Canada, there was much discussion of a railway which should link the east and the west together over Canadian soil. The Government of Sir John A. Macdonald was resolved to have this railway built by means of grants to a private company, but, in the midst of the negotiations, the revelation of what is known as the Pacific Scandal, turned them out of office. The succeeding Government of Alexander Mackenzie was less optimistic as to the immediate future of Canada, and, therefore, more cautious in the matter of building railways. But that Manitoba should have some connection with the eastern provinces, through Canadian territory, was felt to be imperative, and so the Government began to build a combination water and rail transport route between Winnipeg and Lake Superior. This plan proved impracticable and had to be abandoned. A railway was then built from Winnipeg to Lake Superior as a Government undertaking which was afterwards transferred to the Canadian Pacific Railway and incorporated in its line.

But in the meantime, in order to give Manitoba more immediate rail connection with the outside world, the Government undertook to build a railway between Winnipeg and Pembina to meet the American railway advancing to that point. Though the first sod was turned in 1874, financial difficulties delayed the work in the United States. It was not until Donald A. Smith and George Stephen, with their American allies, James J. Hill and Norman W. Kittson, took hold of the project that the road in both countries was pushed to completion. Lady Dufferin, wife of the Governor-General, drove the first spike of the Manitoba road on her visit to Winnipeg in the fall of 1877, and on December 9th, 1878, the long-expected first train finally arrived in Winnipeg, or, to be exact, at St. Boniface, for as yet there was no bridge across the Red River. From no regular connection of any kind with the outside world to a completed railway service, measures the progress made by Manitoba in its first eight years as a province.

Events continued to move quickly. The tide of political fortunes brought back to power the administration of Sir John A. Macdonald and the project of building a transcontinental railway by means of grants of land and money to a company was pushed ahead. This company was headed, in fact, by George Stephen and Donald A. Smith, though the latter's name does not appear because of a personal feud with Sir John, and became the Canadian Pacific Railway Company. At once Manitoba was filled with intense excitement. By which route would the railway pass, was the question of the hour. It was known that the engineers had recommended that it should cross the Red River at Selkirk and go westward through the narrows of Lake Manitoba, making its way to the Yellowhead Pass for the crossing of the Rocky Mountains. But this was to side-track Winnipeg and to carry the line north of most of the settled area. Every little settlement on any possible route at once saw itself a metropolis of the future. East Selkirk laid out a town site and several buildings were put up in anticipation of the great city which was to be there. Portage la Prairie, Emerson, Minnedosa, West Lynne, Rapid City, Grand Valley, all saw themselves as great centres. Accounts of mass meetings filled the newspapers. Numberless delegations went to Ottawa. In Winnipeg, business men, seeing their future threatened, bestirred themselves to get the railway to cross the river at their city. A year or two before, the City Council had refused any financial aid towards the building of a railway bridge across the river. Now it was glad to offer $200,000 for the erection of the Louise

Bridge, if only the railway would cross at that point.   In the end public opinion outweighed the judgment of the engineers, and the railway took the southern route. But not until the uncertainty and excitement had turned almost everyone who had, or who could get, any land, into a speculator.

Settlement had followed on every improvement in transportation, and the Manitoba of 1880 was very different from the Manitoba of 1870.   Augustus Mills, who came with Lord Wolseley, has left it on record, through Dr. Bryce, that he and a friend, shortly after their arrival, climbed to the top of the tallest building in the village of Winnipeg at the corner of Portage and Main.   From that vantage point they counted all the buildings they could see.   Omitting Fort Garry they found there were 33. In the summer following, there arose one day at the dinner table in the Davis House an argument as to just how many people there were living in Winnipeg.   That afternoon, in order to settle the question, Mrs. D. M. Walker, but recently arrived from Ontario to join her husband, who had come with the Wolseley expedition, went from house to house counting the people.   She found that there were 276.   By 1880 the little village of thirty-three buildings and between two and three hundred people, had become a flourishing city of almost 8,000.   Alexander Begg tells a graphic story of that decade in his *Ten Years in Winnipeg*.   In the beginning of the period he is able to describe in leisurely and detailed fashion the businesses carried on by A. G. B. Bannatyne, John Higgins, W. H. Lyon, Dr. Schultz, H. S. Donaldson, Robert Patterson, E. L. Barber, W. G. Fonseca, G. Gingras, George Emmerling, Onis Monchamp, William Drever, J. H. Ashdown, Brian Devlin, Charles Garret, Archibald Wright and the Hudson's Bay Company which now found it worth while to have a store in the village as well as the larger one at the fort.   Even his detailed description required in all only a few pages.   But when he comes to the end of that ten years, forty-five pages are required in which to give the formal advertisements of the firms then doing business.

Bulman Brothers.

The first Legislature of Manitoba and the first
Parliament Building, 1870.

It was a time of many changes, of quick ups and downs, as even the slightest reading of the records of the time will show.

Turning over the newspapers of that period stirs the imagination and gives the reader something of the thrill of the excitement with which the old-timers of the day must have watched the changes rushing upon them. In the very first year, 1870, the opening of the Dominion Lands Office and Savings Bank ; and the change from Hudson's Bay bills to the money of Canada. In the following year, the election of the first school trustees, Stewart Mulvey, W. G. Fonseca and Archibald Wright, and the opening of the first public school—a log building in Douglas Point with W. F. Luxton as the first teacher and an enrolment of fifty pupils with an average attendance of twenty-five ; the first life insurance company—from the United States ; the first baker, who soon did a flourishing business ; the first carriage factory ; the first saw-mill ; the first election to the Dominion Parliament resulting in the return of Donald A. Smith for Selkirk, the constituency which included Winnipeg, and of Pierre de Lorme and Dr. Schultz ; the visit of the American editors representing the great dailies of the United States ; the opening of Manitoba College in Kildonan with young George Bryce, just arrived from Toronto, to aid Dr. Black in the teaching ; the opening of the first Grace Church under the charge of Rev. George Young ; the first telegraph communication with Eastern Canada ; the influx of newcomers so great that one of the Bannatyne buildings had to be converted hastily into an immigration shed ; the summing-up at the end of the year of all the new buildings—places of business and homes—led by the new store which J. H. Ashdown was building on the site of the present one, and the fine new home of A. G. B. Bannatyne.

With the coming of another year the exciting news that the Hudson's Bay Company was about to sell lots in its reserve, all with the canny demand that buildings of a certain value should be put on them before the end of another year ; the opening of the new ferry at Point Douglas where some day, it was thought, the railroad bridge would be, as indeed it is ; the arrival of that first steamboat for general traffic ; the opening of the first chartered bank, the Merchants ; the first brick factory ; the first furniture factory ; the first jewellery store ; the first billiard room, with six tables, of which it is recorded " as a mark of energy on the part of the proprietors that they laid a sidewalk at their own expense from Main Street to their doorway " ; the opening of Wesleyan Institute on the Grace Church property ; the publication on November 9th of the first number of the *Manitoba Free Press*, the only one of the four papers then in existence to survive ; at the end of the year election riots, when the Chief of Police was wounded and two newspaper offices destroyed. With another year came agitation about the incorporation of Winnipeg as a city, hotly opposed by some who feared increased taxes ; the organization of the Board of Trade, or rather of two Boards of Trade, until the warring parties settled their differences ; the vain effort to get waterworks to replace the water ox-carts of the summer and the blocks of ice of the winter ; the first street lamp in front of the Davis House on Main Street ; the setting up in business of the first barber, " a Tonsorial Artist from New York," as he proclaimed himself ; A. G. B. Bannatyne following the fashion of older cities by putting large shop windows in his store ; the last Indian Dog Feast ; the building of Osborne Barracks ; the beginning of the Canada Pacific Hotel, which stood where the Fort Garry apartments now are. As the pages turn over one can fairly hear the hum of talk over all these changes.

This year of 1873 must always be a landmark, for, on November 8th, the opposition of the Legislature and the unwillingness of some of the citizens having been overcome, the act was passed making Winnipeg an incorporated city. It was, however, not until January of the following year that the first election was held and the organization of the city government completed.

Seven candidates contested for the honour of being the city's first mayor, Frank E. Cornish being successful. Councillors were also elected, Thomas Scott, Archibald Wright, Andrew Strang, Herbert Swinford, James McLenaghan, W. B. Thibideau, Robert Mulvey, James H. Ashdown, John Higgins, W. G. Fonseca, and Alexander Logan, who later became mayor, the only native of the province to have held that honour. In the new town land values were seen to be rising. Lots in the McDermott Estate which, two years before, were sold for $50, were now selling at $400. A. W. Burrows, uncle of Lieutenant-Governor Burrows, with shrewd enterprise, was interesting Easterners in Winnipeg by selling them lots in the new city. Business too was increasing. The number of buildings rose to 903 and the imports were in this year of the city $1,979,000 as compared with $918,000 the year before. In the midst of all this excitement, there arrived to take charge of the new Knox Church—on Portage Avenue at the corner of Fort Street—a man who was to play an invaluable part in the development of Manitoba, and indeed of the whole North-west—the Rev. James Robertson. Manitoba College, now with a professor of theology in the person of Dr. Thomas Hart, moved into the city quarters on Main Street near Point Douglas. All through the late summer the grasshoppers were abroad in the land and the crops suffered greatly.

The Sisters of the Holy Name in this year established in Winnipeg on Notre Dame Avenue east near the river a convent and school which grew into St. Mary's Academy. In doing so they took over the small log building on the site of the Frontenac Hotel in which, for the preceding five years, the Grey Nuns had had a small school, and Mass had been said every Sunday. This year also saw the building of the first St. Mary's Church placed on the site of the present church. The original building may still be seen on Carlton Street, where it now serves as the shelter for the Sisters of Providence. The upper storey was used as a church, the lower one was the residence for eight years of the great Catholic missionary to the Indians, Father Lacombe, who was for that time rector of this parish.

Another year and Winnipeg was selling its first bonds, and having a serious argument in the Council over which of the three banks should do its business. Social events opened with the first skating carnival. Summer brought the first steam ferry between St. Boniface and Winnipeg, an event of great magnitude, as life was then. The Winnipeg Council undertook the laying of the first sewers and found itself called to an account by an indignant mass meeting of citizens, assembled at the corner of Portage and Main, demanding to know why the contract had been given to the highest bidder. In this year too, in spite of the almost total failure of all garden and field crops through the last serious plague of grasshoppers, a new city hall was undertaken, after the floor of the room in which the Council was meeting threatened to give way. There was much discussion as to the effect upon the new building of the creek which ran through the present site of the Royal Bank building. This creek crossed Main Street, and over it had been built a new bridge, called Brown's Bridge, after the first city clerk. A thrifty council made use of the creek, and its bed served for the cellars of the new city hall which stood just in front of the present one. From this year too dates the General Hospital built on the present site, which was donated by Andrew McDermot, and the opening of the First Baptist Church. There was also much excitement over a horse bred by the Archbishop and bought by some American dealers which won the large prize of $1,200 in a 2.40 race at Chicago. Once again there came in quietly a man who was to do great service in the city; the Anglican Church, having decided to make Winnipeg a regular preaching station, built Trinity Church and called Rev. O. Fortin to the rectorship of the new parish.

One of the outstanding events in the whole history of Manitoba marks out the year 1876 as one to be remembered. On October 21st the first shipment of wheat was sent to Eastern Canada, the first tiny trickle of an ever-increasing stream. It was carried by steamboat and rail to Duluth and from that point made its way by the Great Lakes to Toronto. There were in the whole shipment, which was consigned by Higgins & Young to Steel Brothers, 412 sacks or 857 bushels. It brought a price of eighty cents a bushel, and the freight to Toronto cost thirty-five cents a bushel. This wheat was sent for the purpose of distribution as seed among the farms of Ontario, a demand having arisen because the millers had declared " Manitoba Hard " to be the best wheat they could get for milling purposes.

One by one in quick succession followed the " mammoth mill " of the Hudson's Bay Company grinding 1,350 bushels every twenty-four hours ; the dedication of the new Grace Church, with its stained-glass windows brought all the way from Toronto ; the sale for $15,000 of that property at the corner of Portage and Main which Henry McKenny had bought for the first building in Winnipeg at a cost of $250 ; the hunting of wolves for sport just outside the city limits ; the organization of the first curling club, and the playing of the first curling match, forerunner of all the bonspiels, by two rinks, skipped by A. G. B. Bannatyne and A. McMicken, for a prize of a barrel of oatmeal, which was sent to the hospital ; the organization of the Winnipeg Literary and Dramatic Society, and the Non-Pareil Dancing Club ; two new schools, one in the centre and one in the north ward ; two ladies preaching in the notorious Red Saloon while the proprietor stood by to see that they got a respectful hearing ; the first excursion to Lake Winnipeg on the Manitoba ; the first regatta on the Red River ; all the excitement of preparing for Lord and Lady Dufferin with R. A. Davis, at the same time Premier of the province and manager of the Davis House, at the head of the com-mittee ; the Lieutenant-Governor's ball, for which a new ballroom was added to the house in Old Fort Garry ; the citizen's ball attended by 300, " His Excellency remarking on entering the room that he had witnessed more expensive decorations but nothing more beautiful " ; the organization by the combination of the existing colleges of the University of Manitoba under the influence of Governor Morris with Archbishop Machray as its first Chancellor ; the coming of the first locomotive, " The Countess of Dufferin," brought down the river on a flat boat and now resting in the park opposite the Canadian Pacific Railway station in Winnipeg ; a quarter of a million dollars spent in buildings in Winnipeg in one year, 300,000 letters mailed through the Winnipeg post office in the same year ; crowds of immigrants so large that the barracks must now be used to shelter them ; the great election contest between Donald A. Smith and ex-Lieutenant-Governor Morris ; the organization of a company of infantry, the beginning of the 90th Rifles ; the Premiership of John Norquay ; the arrival of the first train on December 7th, 1878, coming from Pembina ; establishment of regular train schedules—thirty-one hours to St. Paul, three days to Toronto ; the fight over the $200,000 for the Louise Bridge ; the building of the Queen's Hotel, which still stands near to the corner of Portage and Main as a memento of the enterprise of that day ; the arrival at the foot of Bannatyne Street of the sail boat *Jessie McKenny*, bringing up the river over the St. Andrew's rapid a cargo of lumber sent by the two young adventurers in this business, Walkey and Burrows, to Brown and Rutherford ; the coming of the first car of fruit, though five years before a heated caravan wagon had brought the first California fruit ever to reach the city ; the visits of legions of newspaper men eager to write about the new country ; and this in the midst of streets of mud against which the bits of sidewalks in front of stores were no protection ; of poorly built houses which could not be kept warm against the intense cold ; of women keeping house and bringing up their families in the midst of what appear now impossible hardships, though their memories seem all to be of a time of peace and plenty and happiness, while affairs moved in a swiftly flowing tide towards that day of days, July 26th, 1881, when the Canadian Pacific Railway, crossing the Louise Bridge, finally entered Winnipeg. Then the dreams of the city as a great centre on a road running from coast to coast all across Canadian soil came within sight of fulfilment.

Out in the province there was expansion too, though not on the same swift scale as in Winnipeg during this decade. There still was lacking that accessible market for wheat, which later was to bring growth so rapidly. But each improvement in transportation had its effect, and to the west and south-west, and then to the north-west, went newcomers settling at first along the water-courses and the hoped-for lines of railway, and later on the open prairie. When it became certain that the trans-continental railway would be built, settlers came in increasing numbers, with the result that, at the end of the first decade, the population had grown from 12,000 of the first census to 62,660. The census revealed, even at that date, a surprising number of new Canadians. There were 8,652 Germans, 773 Icelanders, 250 Scandi-navians and 24 Russians and Poles. Out beyond Manitoba in the North-west Territories were 56,000 people, of whom about 4,000 were whites. The needs of all the population, as well as of the survey and trading and railway-con-struction parties, were largely supplied from Winnipeg and formed part of the foundation upon which its expansion was based.

Thus within the small frontier city and in the territory beyond the stage was set for the most spectacular event in the history of Winnipeg—" The Boom." There are still living in Manitoba many people who went through that experience of extraordinary speculation in land in 1881–82, who may be induced to re-live the excitement and glamour of those months, when fortunes were made overnight ; when on each successful speculation still more successful ones were pyramided. Romantic stories abound. Everyone joined in the scramble for wealth he had not earned. Land was sold like any commodity

—butter and eggs, or boots and shoes. Soon the real-estate offices were unable to handle the business. Auction sales at which were offered sometimes whole townsites of places whose names are now unknown, were held on street corners. Hill, in his *History of Manitoba*, says that in Portage la Prairie alone there were no less than thirty offices whose exclusive business was the buying and selling of lots.

"To a calm and considerate mind," he writes, "the situation was certainly unique. A craze seemed to have come over the mass of the people. Legitimate business in many cases was thrown aside and buying and selling lots became the one aim and object of life. Carpenters, painters, tailors and tradesmen of all kinds threw aside their tools to open real estate offices, loaf around the hotels, drink whiskey and smoke cigars."

No settlement was too small to share in the excitement; no place too remote or unknown to have its lots eagerly bought. Prince Arthur's landing was advertised as "The New Chicago," Manchester was described as "the future great manufacturing town of the North-west;" Minnedosa was called "the railway centre of the North-west," and on the strength of this $500,000 worth of property changed hands in two months; High Bluff was advertised as the "best chance of the season."

Through the winter of 1881–82 the speculation was at its height; small investors pooled their savings to, handle property at enormous prices. When ready money was scarce notes were often substituted. Nothing was lacking to draw the speculators on and on to the bitter end. The newspapers of those days make breathless reading with their tales of prices which ran higher in Winnipeg than they were in Chicago, then a city of half a million people.

If it was the enterprise of A. W. Burrows in selling Manitoba lots in Eastern Canada which marks the definite beginning of the boom, it was the offering of lots in Edmonton, aided by the fact that the flood of the spring of 1882 kept new people from coming in for several weeks,

Western Canada Illustrated.

PARLIAMENT BUILDINGS AND GOVERNMENT HOUSE— AFTER
" THE BOOM."

H. S. Seaman, Esq.

ST. BONIFACE IN 1880.

which marks its collapse.   Edmonton was then the outer-most fringe of the new advance.   It was also a well-known Hudson's Bay Company post.   In some way the idea of buying lots there caught the fancy of people in Winnipeg.   Money was saved for purchase as the rumour fled that these lots would be offered.   On April 12th the auction sale was advertised for Friday the 14th.   Edmonton was described in large type as the country of " Gold, Coal, Timber, Mineral and Wheat.   Bounded on the South by the grazing land of the Bow River District, on the North by the Peace River and on the West at a distance of seventy miles by an uninterrupted forest of spruce Timber."

On the fatal Friday these spaciously bounded lots were eagerly bought and at high prices.   On the day after they were as eagerly offered for sale.   One who lived through this time describes the doorways and windows of all offices and some stores as liberally decorated with the sign " Edmonton Lots for Sale."   But there were no buyers.   Turning over the newspaper one sees how rapid was the decline.   Four days later the Free Press contracted the size of its paper because of the decline of advertisements.   Two weeks later there was an effort to whip the boom into new life with the return from the United States of a popular auctioneer.   Real-estate agents went on offering their properties, but their advertisements were no longer convincing.   The boom was past recovery.

When life resumed its normal way it was found that, while some wise men had quietly taken their profits, the majority were left with land worth little and obligations which formed for years an intolerable burden.   In many cases the burden could not be borne.   A syndicate of five men owned a four-mile strip west from the Red River including Fort Rouge and Crescentwood.   Unable to pay their taxes they gave up their land.   Seven thousand dollars would have cleared the hundreds of acres in the western and northern parts of the city owned by a single citizen.   But $7,000 was an impossible sum, and his land too was surrendered. Winnipeg entered into a period of depression and retardation which lasted for years and was shared in a greater or less degree by the whole province. During the boom, in the words of one who lived through it, " Twenty gold pieces were just nothing " ; so after it, in the words of another, " The fortunate man was he who could produce a real ten-dollar bill." Most people had nothing. " A singular fact," says Hill, " was that only a small percentage, say five per cent., of those engaged in it improved their financial position ; seventy-five per cent. of the land gambled in returned with all the payments made thereon to its original owners."

Yet the results were not altogether bad. Much building and expanding of services was done under the impetus of the boom, and this remained. There was a new Court House, a new Parliament Buildings and Government House, a total in all of $5,000,000 of new building. There were also street railways, lighting by gas, the telephone, and improved waterworks. The population of Winnipeg doubled in 1881 and the civic assessment trebled. Not all of this gain was lost, but, as one writer expresses it :

" The general effects were pernicious and uninspiring. Credit was shaken. The violent reaction from a fictitious opulence by speculation to the sounder but more toilsome thrift by agriculture, industry and commerce, dimmed for many years the well-founded promise of prosperity. The establishment abroad of provincial credit was slow and difficult long after the city of Winnipeg had recovered from its depression and the province had regained its accustomed confidence in the future."

CHAPTER VII

RIGHTS AND REMEDIES

It was in a moment of intense strife that the province of Manitoba entered the Dominion of Canada. It was in the mood of fighting for what she considered her rights that she continued that relationship for many years. Even yet the echoes of that mood linger, since Manitoba is still seeking [1] for the control of those natural resources which were withheld from her when the province was created out of the old district of Assiniboia. That Manitoba and all the western prairies had been purchased by the Dominion Government from the Hudson's Bay Company for $1,500,000 was the feeling at Ottawa. Out of the lands, and forests, and mines, and water powers, of that little known land the Dominion Government proposed to recoup that expenditure.

Before Manitoba was a year old the agitation for what were always spoken of as "better terms" began. It was found that the work of creating a province had to be carried on with what seemed an impossibly small area of between 13,000 and 14,000 square miles, and with a niggardly financial allowance from the Dominion Government representing the entire income. Out of its $67,000 a year Manitoba voted in the first year $20,000 for building roads and bridges. The most rigid economies were practised in the effort to make the best possible use of the subsidy. But as settlers came in, more and more roads and bridges had to be built, and more and more there was a demand, not to be denied, for schools for the children of the new-comers.

As soon as he was installed in office in 1879, and had

[1] It is gratifying to record that in the summer of 1928 an agreement was made between the Dominion and Manitoba Governments for the transfer of the control of the natural resources to the province.

met his Legislature, Premier John Norquay, taking with him the Provincial Secretary, Hon. J. Royal, made a trip to Ottawa to lay the disabilities of the province before the Federal Government. This, the first of many pilgrimages, was not very successful. A small addition to the financial allowance was made, but the right to control her own lands, or to grant charters for the building of railways, was sternly denied. A year later saw the Premier back in Ottawa, and this time he secured an extension of the boundaries, though any control of lands and any right to build railways was still denied. " Until we are in the enjoyment of privileges accorded to other provinces," said the Premier at a banquet tendered to him on his return, " it is not in the nature of things that there should be that accord and harmony between this province and the rest which is so desirable in the interests of all."

The extension of the boundaries in 1881, which increased the area of Manitoba to almost 74,000 square miles, did little to establish the longed-for accord. The western boundary was fixed where it is now, but the eastern boundary was a mythical line described as the westerly boundary of Ontario. The Governments of the Dominion and of Ontario were at the moment engaged in a dispute as to where that boundary line should run, the Dominion Government having refused to accept the award of three arbitrators appointed to settle the vexed question. According to the Federal Government this boundary was a line running north and south through Port Arthur ; according to the contention of Ontario, it followed the line which is the present easterly boundary of Manitoba at the southerly end. Though Manitoba was not eager to assume any responsibility until the dispute should be settled, the presence in the disputed area of large crews of men, engaged in building the railway from Lake Superior to Winnipeg, created a very difficult situation. Traffic in liquors had been forbidden along the line of railway construction, but the demand for liquor brought into play many of the schemes of the bootleggers of a later day.

" The whole region was literally flooded with liquor," says Begg. " It was estimated that at least 800 gallons per month was disposed of on the section between White Mouth River and Lake Wabigon during the winter and spring of 1881. The liquor was taken from Winnipeg concealed in oatmeal, beans and coal oil barrels to some convenient point from which it was distributed by dog train in winter, and by canoe in summer, all along the line."

In the effort to control the situation there arose a rivalry among the law officers and magistrates of the Ontario and Manitoba Governments. No one knew exactly whose job it was in any given case, and when after the incorporation of Rat Portage, as Kenora was then called, the Manitoba Government, accepting the Dominion's boundary line, set up a court at that centre, a situation developed which reads more like a comic opera than a bit of real life. The Manitoba jail was broken open by the rival police and afterwards set on fire. The different magistrates and police officers arrested one another. The way of the enforcer of law was more difficult than that of the law breaker. On the same day there were elections for the Legislatures of Manitoba and Ontario, the people thus having the unique opportunity of voting for members of two Legislatures. After the election the trouble increased until finally the Ontario authorities arrested and held in jail the Manitoba Chief of Police. Finally a compromise was arranged and the whole boundary question submitted to the Privy Council, which, in 1884, decided in favour of the Ontario contention.

But of all the matters in dispute concerning " better terms," which were continually sought by Manitoba, none roused such bitterness as that one spoken of as " Disallowance." This arose out of the refusal of the Dominion Government to permit Manitoba to grant charters for the building of railways within her own borders. Though the Government of Manitoba had made many efforts, it had failed entirely to induce the Dominion Government to modify its position.

As settlers began to take up land in the more distant

10

parts of the province, it seemed obvious that they must have railways ; railways which would carry supplies into the settlers ; railways which would carry the wheat which those settlers raised on the western plains down to the markets of Eastern Canada. From the days of the Selkirk settlers the problem had remained the same. Wheat might be grown in plenty, but there was no way to get it easily to the place where it was wanted, and lacking this way the wheat was valueless. The Provincial Government received many offers to build the needed railways, and charters were granted, only to be " disallowed " by the Dominion Government. On February 17th, 1881, the contract to build the Canadian Pacific Railway was definitely concluded between the Federal Government and " the Syndicate." Under its terms, in addition to $25,000,000, 25,000,000 acres of land, and the railway already built, valued at $37,000,000, the contract also gave the company a monopoly of railway building south of its main line for the next twenty years. The satisfaction of having railway communication with Eastern Canada assured was much tempered by fear of this monopoly. It was further lessened by the method under which the railway company was to take its millions of acres. Alternate sections along both sides of the railway, a mile long and twenty-four miles deep, were to belong to the company and to be free of all taxation, unless sold, for twenty years after the grant. It did not take long for the men who were guiding the destinies of Manitoba to see that this grant would make settlement difficult, and the " landlock " of the Canadian Pacific Railway became another grievance preventing that much-to-be-desired accord between the Provincial and Dominion Governments.

For the moment, however, all eyes were fixed on the railway problem as the most urgent. Three charters granted by the Provincial Government in 1882 were disallowed.

" The intelligence of this sweeping act of disallowance was an unpleasant surprise to Manitoba," says Begg, " and created a storm of indignation among the impulsive of the population, who were ignorant of, or chose to ignore, the ' monopoly clause,' as it was beginning to be called, of the Canadian Pacific Railway contract. Indignation meetings were held at Emerson, Portage la Prairie, Brandon, and West Lynne at which resolutions were passed and suggestions made as to the proper mode of procedure in combating the disallowance policy."

There was no disposition at all to take into account the great adventure upon which the men who had undertaken to build the Canadian Pacific Railway had embarked, nor to realize the ease with which railways could be built from the United States into Canadian territory and the eagerness of the United States to absorb as much as might be of the trade of this western country. Through the country to the south, nearly all the supplies and settlers were still coming. Not even the builders of the transcontinental line themselves foresaw at this time the great future which was to be the justification of their venture. In those days it seemed vital to guard at least the first years of this effort to bind Canada together, undertaken in the first instance as the price of the adherence of British Columbia to the Dominion.

These considerations weighed little in a country suffering from the collapse of the boom, from bad frosts, and generally from grievances, which, it believed, kept back the tide of settlement now beginning to ebb. As one writer has described it, the country was in a continual state of insurrection. The Government of Premier Norquay, allied by party ties with the Government of Sir John A. Macdonald, could find no way to induce the Dominion Government to abate the grievances, and was forced to join the outcry against their political friends. Even the rapid completion of the Canadian Pacific Railway and the arrival of the first transcontinental train on July 1st, 1886, bringing Sir John himself for his only visit to the West, caused no lessening of the feeling that Manitoba must determine her own railway development.

The Norquay Government finally yielded to the public clamour, now such as no Government could withstand and live. It re-enacted some of the charters which had been disallowed. It also undertook the building of the Red River Valley Railway from Winnipeg to West Lynne across the river from Emerson. This road would parallel on the west side of the river the Pembina branch of the Canadian Pacific Railway coming down on the east side. The Canadian Pacific Railway threatened to remove its shops from Winnipeg. Rumours ran that troops were to be sent to prevent the construction of the new road. Money could not be secured abroad for the enterprise, so it was subscribed by the citizens. But political considerations in the opposition party over-rode their desire for the railway. The terms of the contract, the general conduct of the Norquay administration, were bitterly attacked. " Deserted at the crisis by those upon whose support he had relied, and crushed between a reckless party opinion in Manitoba and the exigencies of his party at Ottawa, Norquay resigned," writes J. W. Dafoe, " in an attempt to divert from the party responsibility, which was indeed scarcely his own." Two weeks later the Liberal opposition, under the leadership of Thomas Greenway, had organized a government. " Discredited as a politician ; deserted and derided by those who had fawned upon him in the days of his popularity ; abandoned and condemned by the swarm of tuft hunters, who had waxed fat and impudent through his careless good nature," says Begg, " John Norquay resigned office, proud in the consciousness of his own integrity, and retaining the respect and esteem of those who knew him best."

John Norquay left the Government a poor man, as he had entered it, but he also left it a broken-hearted man. His death two years later removed one of the most attractive figures in the history of Manitoba at the early age of forty-five. " His weakness," said the *Free Press* at the time of his death, " lay in the bigness of heart which could never constrain itself to say no to a friend."

Just a few weeks before the death of John Norquay, A. G. B. Bannatyne, another attractive figure in the story of Manitoba, died, also universally mourned. He was the merchant prince of his day, succeeding in that rôle his father-in-law, Andrew McDermot. Generous with his money and with disinterested service, he exercised a great influence, always in the direction of conciliation and co-operation, down to the day of his death, though disappointment over financial losses following the boom narrowed his activities towards the end of his life.

Public opinion was now at that pitch in Manitoba when the will of the people could no longer be thwarted. Bombarded by expressions of opinion from all sides, including the conservative association of Winnipeg, visited by Hon. J. C. Aikins, just then finishing his term as Lieutenant-Governor, the Macdonald Government at last gave to its political opponents that which it had denied to its friends. A compromise was arranged with the Canadian Pacific Railway whereby it gave up its monopoly rights and received in exchange the guarantee of the interest on $15,000,000 worth of new bonds, by means of which it was able to quicken its rate of construction, already amazingly rapid.

But the railway struggles in Manitoba were not yet over. The Greenway Government, now having a majority of twenty-eight in a house of thirty-eight, turned its attention to that Red River Valley Railway with which the late Government had sought to break the monopoly. It refused an offer for its purchase from the Canadian Pacific and entered into negotiations with the Northern Pacific Railway. As a result the Northern Pacific and Manitoba Railway was organized to take over this Red River Valley Railway, complete it, and also build lines from Morris to Brandon and from Winnipeg to Portage la Prairie. But to build these lines it was necessary to cross the Canadian Pacific Railway. This the company, indignant that all its offers to purchase had been refused in favour of an American company, determinedly opposed. In support of its position there was the "General Railway Act of Canada," but the citizens of Winnipeg saw in this refusal nothing but another exercise of that monopoly, which, they believed, they had just overturned. When Joseph Martin, who was the Attorney-General of the province, ordered the workmen to continue laying the tracks by which it was proposed to make the first crossing of the Canadian Pacific six miles west of the city, he had the entire population of Winnipeg and the province with him. To turn over the pages of the newspapers for the months of October and November of 1888 is to live again the excitement, which ran for weeks at fever heat. The Canadian Pacific, under the direction of William Van Horne in his office in the city and William Whyte in his private car attached to a live engine on the track—a private telegraph line connected them—made it clear that there would be no crossing except by forcible means. Public opinion made it equally clear that force would be attempted, if necessary. On Friday, October 20th, Dr. Schultz, Lieutenant-Governor since the preceding July, issued authority to swear in special constables. It was thought that the track layers would reach the Canadian Pacific line the next afternoon, and scores of men rushed to be sworn in. They were headed by the most substantial citizens of Winnipeg ; in the lists one may read the names of John Galt, J. H. Brock, J. H. Ashdown, R. W. Jameson, and F. C. Wade. An engine and three cars waiting on the tracks at Water Street the next day were filled to overflowing long before the time to start, while up and down the platform walked still other scores of men begging to be sworn in.

There was an anti-climax at Fort Whyte, as the point where the opposing forces were to meet was at once named, for when the train crowded with eager citizens arrived, it was found that the track layers were still so far off as to make it impossible that they would reach the Canadian Pacific line that night. The crowd returned to Winnipeg, but the following days revisited the scene of the expected conflict. Then the Canadian Pacific fenced off its property. It further barred the way by dumping an engine in the path of the track layers, and it applied to the court for an injunction. In Winnipeg the volunteer constables kept in close touch with the Government officials, while from all over the province came offers of help from farmers, who had hoped that the new railway might get through that fall in time to help in carrying out the wheat crop, now too large for the Canadian Pacific Railway to handle alone.

On the night of October 24th, guarded by the special constables, the Government's track layers tore up enough of the Canadian Pacific tracks to put in a diamond permitting the new railway to cross. This done they returned to the city leaving a guard of twenty-two men in charge. But the next morning General Superintendent Whyte with fifty men dispersed these guards, tore up the diamond, restored the Canadian Pacific rails and brought the diamond in triumph to the city. Then the storm broke loose ; the mayor called a public meeting at which, says an eye witness, every chair was smashed. The Canadian Pacific put a guard of 200 men at its tracks and kept a train moving slowly up and down over the proposed place of crossing. No chances were to be taken, it seemed. Meals were carried out to the men ; colonist cars were sent out in which they might sleep ; and on Sunday G. H. Campbell, who was assisting Whyte, gathering up some hymn books, went out and held a religious service at the track side.

There were three places at which Canadian Pacific track was to be crossed. Morris, Portage la Prairie, and Fort Whyte. At all these places guards were maintained, though the main fight was at Fort Whyte. For days the struggle went on while the early snows of winter came. In the city the company's lawyers, Aikins and Culver, lost the injunction case before Judge Killam and won it before Chief Justice Taylor, J. S. Ewart, W. E. Perdue, now Chief Justice, and the Attorney-General, appearing for the province. The case was then carried to the Supreme Court of Canada.

While the decision was awaited, the Canadian Pacific Railway train with its guards and the Government train with its special constables faced each other across the disputed line. "At the point where the two trains almost touched," wrote a *Free Press* reporter, "a fire was burning in the ditch along the Canadian Pacific, while sitting on one side of it was the company's watchman, and on the other sat four or five of the Government police. Although warming themselves at the same fire, no communication passed between them. Thus they sat through the long hours of the night in the falling snow." At least once in the time of waiting the Government forces scored a success. On the night of November 3rd they managed to elude all the vigilance of the Canadian Pacific and laid across the track planks over which the rails were carried. The situation was fast becoming impossible and a sort of truce was arranged until the Supreme Court should give judgment. "It is to the credit of all concerned that despite this intense feeling, no rash act was committed," says Hill. "One rash shot fired would certainly have called for a reply, and no one could tell where the matter would have ended." When the decision of the Supreme Court was given it sustained the position of the Manitoba Government. With this decision the interference of the Federal Government with the railway development in Manitoba, which had for so long kept the public mind inflamed, came to an end, and the era of competitive railway building was inaugurated.

In the midst of the struggle over disallowance, the people of Manitoba had had to turn aside to a fight of a very different kind. The outbreak of the second Riel Rebellion, though it took place in the North-west Territories—the Saskatchewan of to-day—and, though the incidents belong to the story of that province rather than to the story of Manitoba, rudely interrupted life here and breathed fresh vigour into old controversies.

With the oncoming of fresh settlement from the east, with the withdrawal of the buffalo farther and farther west, many of the Métis, who had formerly lived in

Manitoba had trekked west and had established themselves in the valley of the Saskatchewan River. As the hunt ceased to offer them a livelihood, they settled upon the land, and in so doing laid out their lots after the system they had known in Manitoba, that is, in the long narrow lots with a river frontage. The surveyors who were sent afterwards into this part of the prairies to prepare for settlement had their definite instructions to follow the block system. They executed these instructions with a complete lack of discretion and tact, and thoroughly alarmed the Métis, who believed themselves in danger of losing their new homes and lands. " In some instances," says Begg, " the block system of survey placed as many as ten settlers on one section and cut off three-quarters of each of their original claims. . . . Added to this, new settlers were pushing their way into the country, taking up choice locations wherever they could find them, and the old cry of 1869–70 was revived that the lands of the half-breeds were to be taken from them."

There was also much dissatisfaction over the settlement of outstanding Métis claims to scrip land and over the delay in issuing patents to land which had been selected. The Métis had been for years agitating to have some recognition of their holdings. In the beginning they had the sympathy of the English-speaking settlers. There seems every reason to think that a little care might have prevented open conflict. But that care and consideration, effective though it was in the instances to which it was applied, was not generally exercised by the Dominion Government's representatives, and in their distress and alarm the Métis invited Louis Riel to return and champion their cause.

Riel was then living at St. Peter's Mission in Montana, where he was teaching school. The term of banishment for which he had been sentenced after the 1870 rebellion had expired, and he was free to return. The invitations were pressing. He resigned his school and arrived in the Saskatchewan country in the summer of 1884. At first he tried moderate, lawful methods. A " Bill of Rights " was drawn up, and for almost a year petitions went down to Ottawa, all to receive the same reply of silence. Gradually Riel turned to the idea of rebellion. He spent three months encouraging his people to take up arms, and in March of 1885 he formed a provisional government, placed himself at the head of an armed force, raided some stores and took several prisoners. Mounted police under Major Crozier hurrying to the scene fell into a trap of Riel's devising, with the result that Riel was able to achieve what seemed a considerable victory in the battle of Duck Lake.

" It was at once felt by both government and people," wrote Major Boulton, who came from his home in Russell to play a prominent part in this rebellion as he had in the first one, " that the half-breed rising in the North-west, if allowed to assume important dimensions and become an Indian rising, would cause great disaster to the commercial interests of the country, and throw its prospects back for many years by retarding immigration, which is so essential to its development."

General Middleton, then commanding the Canadian forces, was sent at once to Winnipeg to take such steps as might seem necessary. Before he reached Winnipeg, word of the Duck Lake disaster had come through and General Middleton at once called for troops. The call was quickly answered by the 90th Rifles, which Colonel Kennedy had just organized, by a field battery under Major Jarvis, and by a troop of cavalry under Captain Knight. But the share of Manitoba did not end there. Many retired military men came forward. Major Boulton raised a force of mounted men out in the province. Colonel Scott raised a regiment known as the 91st Battalion and Lieutenant-Colonel Osborne Smith another known as the Winnipeg Light Infantry. From Ontario and Quebec and the maritime provinces came regulars and militia, and the campaign went steadily forward until it was ended by the capture of Big Bear on July 3rd, 1885. Riel was already a captive. Before the end of the month he was being tried in Regina, and in the following November he paid the price of his adventures on the scaffold. His body was brought back to his family and lies buried close to the cathedral of St. Boniface.

Three months of fighting, with the loss of thirty-six killed and over one hundred wounded, the excitement which this caused in every community in Canada from which men had gone to fight, the interest with which the trials of Riel and of the Indians and Métis, who were tried at the same time —eight Indians were hanged and between fifty and sixty Indians and Métis got varying sentences—all combined to stir into fresh life that sense of contest between the English- and French-speaking peoples of the West which, as Alexander Ross had noted years before in his journal, "caused them to remain politically disunited." In Manitoba there was not lacking an issue upon which this revived interest in matters of discord might centre. Membership in the first Legislature had been based upon a scheme of twenty-four constituencies, twelve of them English-speaking and twelve of them French. Under the influence of the idea that this province would be one with a population equally divided between the peoples of the two races and languages, the Manitoba Act had declared, " either the English or the French language may be used by any person in the debates of the houses of the Legislature and both languages shall be used in the respective records and journals of those houses." Similarly either language might be used in the proceedings of the Courts.

In the same way a system of education was planned to suit a population, which was dual in religion as well as language. One of the first acts of the first Legislature had been to create a board of education upon the lines of the Quebec system having two sections, one Catholic, one Protestant. Each of the twenty-four constituencies was made into a school district, and each section of the board thus had twelve districts under its supervision. The law directed that such money grants as the province might make towards education should also be equally divided. When the first board was appointed by the Government it was found to consist of eight clergymen and four lay-men—Archbishop Taché, Rev. Joseph Lavoie, Rev. George Dugas, Rev. Joseph Allard, Pierre de Lorme, and Joseph Dubuc, afterwards Chief Justice, made up the Catholic section ; the Protestant section was composed of Bishop Machray, Rev. Dr. Black, Rev. Cyprian Pinkham, Rev. George Young, John Norquay, and Dr. Bird.

The incoming of great numbers of settlers from Ontario, nearly all of them English-speaking and Protestant, soon changed the condition, which had existed when the province was first organized. The proportion of French-speaking citizens fell rapidly, and with that fall there was a lessening of the weight and influence of their opinions. By the time the election of 1878 was over, it was seen that the French representation had fallen from one-half to one-third. After the election of the next year, it had further declined to one-sixth. Five years after the establishment of the first school system there were 30 Protestant schools, with 1,600 children and only 22 Catholic schools, with 1,134 children. It was, therefore, easy to convince the English-speaking citizens that there was an obvious unfairness in the equal division of the provincial grant for education. By 1881 the situation of the French politically having been further weakened through a serious quarrel between Premier Norquay and his French fol-lowers, the Legislature found it possible to make an important change. The school grant was now to be divided between the Protestant and Catholic sections of the board in proportion to the number of children between the ages of five and fifteen who were residing in the districts where schools were in operation. Otherwise, with some slight modifications, the system went on as before.

The old charges of disloyalty and rebellion, heard so loudly after 1870, were revived with even greater strength after the rebellion of 1885. Along with this revival went the fervour of the fight over disallowance, and the in-creasing determination, fed by both struggles that Mani-toba should, in her own house, do as she pleased. A visit in August of 1889 from D'Alton McCarthy, M.P. of Toronto, offered the occasion for focusing all the dissatisfaction. In a speech made at Portage la Prairie, at a banquet tendered him by the Orangemen, he urged the people of Manitoba to unite in demanding the abolition of the French language and the Catholic schools. Joseph Martin, the Attorney-General, electrified the audience by seconding all that the visitor had said, declaring that either he would soon cease signing documents in the French language, or he would cease to be Attorney-General. The echoes of the agitation aroused by those speeches are still resounding in Manitoba.

Their immediate effect was to bring about the two things which D'Alton McCarthy had urged. Two months later, without any warning, the official *Gazette* was issued in English only. The Legislature, by a vote of four to one, defeated the motion of censure offered by the French members. It was felt at once that it was only a matter of a brief time until the Government would seek the abolition of the Catholic schools. From that moment, until the school bill was actually introduced in January 1890, agitation and strife reached into the remotest corner of Manitoba. " The Roman Catholic minority," says one writer on this period, " surprised by the suddenness and ruthless scope of the Government measures, opposed the change with a bitterness born of the unavailing struggle for their hard won privileges. . . . With equal bitterness the Protestants insisted upon the right of the majority."

Manitoba was now a province of 150,000 people. It was urged that it was nonsense to say that it should be bound by terms made at Ottawa without the knowledge of even the 12,000 people who lived in Manitoba in 1870, for Archbishop Taché, in the midst of the struggle, produced a secret agreement with the Ottawa Government made at that time, that Manitoba should have separate schools after the Quebec model. The Protestant case was further strengthened by the fact that in 1889 the Protestant schools were receiving on the average $142 each annually, while the Catholic schools were getting on the average $226, and had accumulated a surplus of $13,000.

When the legislature met, the Government was ready with its bill. The old system was to be swept away. In its place was to be set up a department of education which was to have charge of all public schools. It was to have the assistance of an advisory board, partly appointed by the Government and partly by educational bodies. This board was to deal particularly with academic matters. It was to have charge of all text-books and of the important matter of religious exercises. The public schools, it was declared, were now to be non-sectarian. No other religious exercises than those which the advisory board, having this condition in mind, might allow, were to be tolerated. All the school districts of the province were to come under this act. Education in the public schools of the province was to be free, and all property was to be taxed for their support. There was not, however, any clause compelling all children to go to these schools. There was not even a clause compelling them to go to school at all. But to be a public school sharing in the public money, a school had to come under the new department of education, thus submitting to the conditions of the new law.

The debate on this legislation was singularly bitter— " the most prolonged and bitter ever witnessed in the Manitoba legislature," says Begg. But the Government pressed steadily on, and there seems to have been little doubt of the result from the first. Statements made by the Attorney-General expressed the prevailing temper. " If the constitution were against their abolition public opinion was against their maintenance. Nine-tenths of the people were united in the abolition of separate schools." The opinion of the Attorney-General was mirrored in the final vote, which stood more than two to one for the Public School Act.

But the passing of the act by the Manitoba legislature was but one stage in a controversy which continued with violence for the next seven years, and which, in the end, came to occupy the centre of political life in the whole Dominion. For the moment the scene of the conflict transferred itself to the law courts. The Catholics were faced with a condition in which they must pay taxes to support schools to which they would not send their children, since their religious convictions and the teachings of their church would not permit a separation between education and religious instruction. Dr. Barrett, a Catholic tax-payer in Winnipeg, appealed to the courts against the act on the ground that it was not within the power of the province to take from the Catholic citizens their own schools. With varying fortunes the case passed through the Canadian courts and reached the Privy Council.

Now the Manitoba Act, under which the constitution of the province had been set up, had declared that the legislature might not pass any law which would prejudicially affect the rights of any class of persons which they had, either by law or by practice, in connection with denominational schools at the time of joining the Confederation. But all the evidence before the court showed that prior to Confederation there had been no public schools. Archbishop Taché's statement which, even in the heat of the moment, was accepted by everyone as an exact statement of the facts, set out that there had been only church schools, both Protestant and Catholic. To this statement the Privy Council gave great weight. It was on this fact that its decision turned. That decision declared that, since there had been no system of public schools, there was nothing which had been taken away, and that the Catholic citizens still had every right which they had had prior to Confederation.

Failure having met this effort of the Catholics to retain their own schools, another plan was tried. The Manitoba Act had provided for an appeal to the Dominion Government against any act of the provincial legislature " affecting any right or privilege of the Protestant or Roman Catholic minority of the Queen's subjects in relation to education." Such an appeal Gerald Brophy now made on behalf of the Catholic citizens. The Ottawa Government referred the matter to the Supreme Court, which decided against the right of appeal in this case. The case was then carried to the Privy Council where it was decided that the religious minority had a right of appeal and that the Dominion Government had power to pass remedial legislation.

The interest was now transferred to Ottawa where the Conservative party was in power. Since it was in close affiliation, in Ontario at least, with the Orange order, the Government was reluctant to take action. Yet it was held that there was a grievance and that some remedy must be found for it. An order was issued to Manitoba directing the Government of the province to restore to the Catholics the right to have their own schools supported by their share of the public tax. Six years had now passed since the Government of Manitoba under the same premier, Hon. Thomas Greenway, had forced the Federal Government to meet its wishes over the question of the disallowance of railway charters. It was, if anything, more determined now to have its own way. The order was disregarded. A memorandum was returned saying that the Federal Government should make a careful investigation of the facts. To which, after many discussions, the Dominion Cabinet replied that, if Manitoba did not make a reasonable settlement, Parliament would be called together by the beginning of the next year, 1896, and would pass a remedial law.

Thus the struggle was transferred to the Federal Parliament. It echoed throughout Canada in the months which followed, and forced men of both political parties into positions which were not in harmony with their usual associations. The Prime Minister, Sir Mackenzie Bowell, an ex-Grand Master of the Orange Order, brought into Parliament a bill designed to remedy the grievance of the Catholics of Manitoba. The bill was accepted by the official spokesmen of the Catholic Church in Canada. But Sir Wilfrid Laurier, though as Catholic in his associations as the Prime Minister was Protestant in his, refused to support it. With all his eloquence he argued that the

T. A. Burrows, Esq.

BUSINESS PREMISES OF THE FIRM THROUGH WHICH MANITOBA WHEAT WAS FIRST SHIPPED TO THE EAST.

T. A. Burrows, Esq.

A. W. BURROWS' LAND OFFICE.

The stone building at the right was put up to serve as a vault for the first Dominion Receiver—General Gilbert McMicken.

act was being passed in ignorance of actual facts and without any attempt to arrive at a peaceful settlement. Coercion of any province by the Dominion he steadfastly refused to support. Both in and out of Parliament there was the most intense controversy, and when, as the end of this Parliament drew near, the Government made an effort to force the bill through, Manitoba, which a quarter of a century before had been an almost unknown hinterland, became the focal point of one of the great political fights in Canadian history.

"There remained only a month before the House must dissolve in face of an election," writes O. D. Skelton in his life of Sir Wilfrid Laurier. "All other business was suspended. The House sat day and night. Relays of ministers and back benchers were organized to hold the fort. The effort was in vain. Tupper met his match. The North of Ireland insurgents in the Conservative ranks, aided by a few Ontario Liberals, blocked progress. It was in vain that Tupper read this man and that out of the party. . . . It was in vain that for a hundred hours the House was held in session. Dr. Sproule read the Nova Scotia school law, John Charlton read the Bible passages prescribed in the Ontario Schools, Colonel Tyrwhitt went through Mark Twain and Bihaud's *History of Canada*, always promising to come to the point, and barely a clause went through."

Finally the Prime Minister gave in. The bill was withdrawn and shortly the bitterly fought election of 1896 was in full swing. The Liberals came out of the fight with a decisive majority. Manitoba, it was made clear, was not to be coerced. But, by a curious turn of the political mind, Manitoba was no longer as excited by the attempted coercion as was the province of Ontario. She gave to the party which had been championing the bill of coercion, four out of her five seats thus creating a situation only less surprising than that which was revealed in Quebec. Though the authorities of the Catholic church had all been for the Remedial Bill, the French Canadian Catholic citizens of that province were more concerned that the Dominion Government should not have the right to coerce a province than they were over the matter of Catholic schools in Manitoba.   They gave a majority of thirty-three out of sixty-five seats to Sir Wilfrid Laurier, who had fought the election as the champion of the rights of the provinces of Canada.

With a Liberal Government at Ottawa and a Liberal Government in Manitoba, it was not difficult to arrive at a compromise.   Various amendments to the Public School Acts which sought to make it possible for the Catholics to accept the public schools, were arranged. Religious instruction might, under conditions, be permitted in the last half hour of the school day ; under certain circumstances Catholic teachers might be insisted upon.   In schools where there were ten French-speaking pupils or ten pupils speaking any language other than English, teaching on the bi-lingual system was to be permitted.

This settlement, known as the Laurier-Greenway Settlement, ended the open controversy and remained the basis of the school law for another twenty years. Laurier himself regarded it as a " happy solution of a very difficult question."   The minority were of another mind though there arose a measure of co-operation. With the exception of a number of parish schools in the cities of Winnipeg and Brandon, the Catholic schools accepted the public grant, were visited by Government inspectors and thus became public schools.   The question passed for twenty years out of the state of open controversy.   Once in the thirty-two years which lie between that fight of 1896 and the present, it came again into the state of open combat.   For the most part it lies under the surface—a live question in Manitoba politics for which a solution acceptable to all parties has not yet been found.

CHAPTER VIII

HOMES ON THE PRAIRIE

WHEN the rebellion of 1870 was over, and the arrival of the force of 200 men sent to repel the expected Fenian invasion had restored a feeling of security to Manitoba, the stream of immigration began to flow into this province, " penetrating everywhere in advance of surveys, as fancy dictated," to quote Major Boulton. That soldier-immigrant's fancy took him 250 miles north-west from Winnipeg to the Shell River, passing, as he journeyed thither, thousands of acres of the finest land in the world. There he had the satisfaction of seeing the town of Russell grow up.

For the most part, however, the newcomers were content to seek farms on the Portage Plains. It was now nearly twenty years since the courageous Archdeacon Cochrane had led his gallant little band out to begin the village of Portage la Prairie, and almost ten years since the first Canadian immigrant had found his way through this village to a home on the plains. This first settler, John McLean, who had brought with him his wife, his mother and seven children, had been followed a few weeks later by the second, Kenneth McBean, who had also a wife and seven children to help people the vacant spaces. Slowly they came—Kenneth Mackenzie, afterward one of the best known citizens of Manitoba, to Rat Creek, there to build up Burnside ; Dan Shea to the site of Totogan on Lake Manitoba, Tom Wallace to the Westbourne River—so that Hill, writing of the time just after the rebellion, is able to say :

" The fertile plains surrounding the Portage settlement, to the east as far as Poplar Point and west beyond Burnside, became the cynosure in those early days of travellers' eyes and after a time the home of a yeomen population of which any country might well be proud. Amongst those who at this early date sought what is now familiarly called the Portage Plains we find the names of Dilworth, Donnelly, McKay, Brydon, Green, Wilton, Marlatt, Smith, McKeown, Dr. Cowan and William Lyons."

By 1871, when the trickle of immigration began to take on the proportions of a stream, conditions in the Portage district were of that frontier simplicity when querns were still used to grind the grain. In this very year, however, W. M. Smith built the first steam grist mill. Now, too, began to come the men who established the early businesses of Portage la Prairie: Thomas Garland, T. B. Miller, W. P. Smith and Michael Blake. The stage, the steamboats on the river, the vision of the railway, the fertile plains immediately at hand, all combined to make this little town a mecca for Ontario men from the counties of Lanark, Huron and Bruce. By the time Manitoba was overtaken by her first boom, it had become a settlement of importance with a population of some 4,000 people.

While Portage la Prairie was growing into the largest place outside of Winnipeg, because it was the point of entry to lands unlimited in extent and productivity, transportation was creating the town of Selkirk to the north of Winnipeg, about twenty-five miles down the Red River. Because of the St. Andrew's Rapids this new town was the practical head of navigation. Two fine natural harbours, one on either side of the river, increased its advantages as the main port for the steam boats now traversing the lakes. It was hoped that it might soon be the head of a lucrative water traffic as far west as Edmonton. The report of the engineers on the Canadian Pacific route brought additional publicity to Selkirk by its recommendation that this was the most advantageous point for the crossing of the Red River, which barred the way to the west. When, in 1874, telegraph communication was established with the outside world, and the Canadian Pacific set up its offices at

Selkirk, its future as a great city seemed assured.   In the spring of the following year the grading of the railway to the east was begun, the contractor in charge being J. W. Sifton.   Shortly after came the first store, the first hotel, another store, a brickyard and a school, and " in 1876 Selkirk's future was brighter than that of any other place," says a historian of the period.   For three years the dream lasted, and then, the route of the railway having been changed, the glory passed to Winnipeg.   The rapidity with which the Canadian Pacific Railway was pushed to completion put an end to that other dream of water transport, with Selkirk as the seat of a great inland port.

But though the big offices and many of the buildings put up in anticipation of the coming of the railway were left to decay, Selkirk turned its attention to building up a town based on the natural resources of the area tributary to it.   First to be developed was the lumbering industry. Just as in the case of the village of Winnipeg, here again it was Henry McKenny who caught the first glimpse of what might be.   Coming as early as 1868 to Lake Winnipeg, in a small schooner which had been built for him out of oak trees found in the Pembina Hills, he began to cut timber on Big Island.   It does not seem that he remained interested long, but for a quarter of a century the lumbering business was the basis of much of the commercial activity of Selkirk.   One of the keen participants in it was T. A. Burrows, who bought from Lord Strathcona, into whose hands it had come, that first boat in the trade, the *Jessie McKenny*.

Lumbering was followed by fishing, which began when the firm of Reid and Clarke put a single sailing boat on the lake, and became flourishing when the big American firms, seeking new fishing grounds to replace those of the great lakes, found their way to Lake Winnipeg.   Reid and Clarke were, in a few years, able to sell out to a Chicago firm for $80,000 and by 1888 the output of fish coming down to Selkirk was 300 tons a year, valued at $150,000.   To-day the annual catch from Lake Winnipeg runs about seven million pounds and has a value of more than half a million dollars. As in the early days of the industry, it begins its land journey at Selkirk and practically all of it goes to the American market.

While Selkirk was enjoying its dream of future greatness, developments in transportation were creating another town which seemed to have an assured and rosy future. This was Emerson, also on the Red but about seventy miles up the river from Winnipeg, and just at the American boundary. A visitor to the site of Emerson in the early spring of 1874 would have found nothing there but vacant land. In all the district round about there were not more than 100 souls. But that spring four men, Thomas Carney, W. N. Fairbanks, F. T. Bradly and Captain Nash, laid out the town site and before the end of the summer 100 people were actually living there. Emerson became quickly not only the point of entry for all traffic from the United States and Eastern Canada, but also the gateway to the land lying along the rivers and lakes and the wooded areas around Pembina and Turtle Mountains in the southern part of the province, which was the second district into which the newcomers from Ontario went. To keep this territory tributary to it, the town in 1880 built a bridge across the river at a cost of $45,000. Its population was now 1,400 and its trade operations extended fully 200 miles to the west.

When, at the end of 1881, the people of Emerson took stock of their progress, it seemed certain that this town was to be a great metropolis in Western Canada. Like Selkirk, it had its dream of outgrowing Winnipeg. In that one year its population had increased to almost 3,000. It had built over $300,000 worth of new buildings. Its manufacturing output was well over half a million. It had fifty-eight places of business giving employment to 170 clerks and having an annual turnover of nearly a million and a half dollars. Across the river, where land was not so dear, the town of West Lynne was growing up. But already the cloud was on the horizon. In the spring of 1882 the Red River overflowed its banks and Emerson was a heavy sufferer. There the waters rose to such a height that the steamer *Cheyenne*, with a barge carrying lumber, sailed right up the main street and unloaded its cargo at the steps of the Presbyterian church. For weeks the citizens lived in the second storeys of their houses. The little town of West Lynne across the river practically disappeared. In the midst of this calamity the Pembina Mountain Railway was completed to Winnipeg and Emerson saw itself cut off from that traffic to the west which was its life-blood. It appealed to General Manager Van Horne of the Canadian Pacific for a branch line which would give the much-desired connexion to the west. On condition that the town would build an iron bridge three feet above high-water level, the wished-for branch was promised. The town let the contract for the bridge. The railway company graded the road and laid the rails for the branch line. But the boom, which affected outside towns as well as Winnipeg, had broken; the population, quick to perceive that the dream of a great Emerson was over, at least for generations, drifted away, and there were no funds to pay for the bridge. The town's bankers paid the contractors but ordered them to keep possession of the bridge. When finished, its swing section was turned up and down the river, and a party of workmen camped upon it.

" Seeing no other mode of taking possession but by taking the law into their own hands," says Hill, " the citizens procured a number of boats and ladders and rowed out into the middle of the stream, placed the ladders and, despite the opposition of the occupants of the bridge, took possession, pretty much the same as a man-of-war's men would an enemy's ship, threatening to throw the occupants into the river if they offered any opposition, swung the bridge across the river into position and having once gained possession, kept it."

But the end was not yet. Van Horne, never sympathetic to Emerson's claims, had grown weary of the strife and delay. One fine Sunday morning there appeared in Emerson a construction train, which, in spite of the protests of the citizens, removed the rails and destroyed the road-bed. Creditors dismantled the iron bridge and the following year the old wooden bridge, which in the flood had gone to the bottom of the river, was raised and restored to position at a further cost of $25,000. " With the decline of the boom," writes Hill, " Emerson went farther down than any other city in Manitoba."

In the summer of 1874 Manitoba received the first of the thousands of new Canadians who were to find their homes within her borders. In that year there came from Russia the first band of the 6,000 Mennonites who, within the next two years, were to establish themselves on land set apart for them by the Dominion Government— seventeen townships on the west side of the Red River, eight on the east side. Fifteen hundred strong they came that summer, more than 3,500 the next and still another 1,500 in 1876. The immigration officer in Quebec, when he looked at that first band of pilgrims, was moved to write in his annual report : " They were of a robust appearance, very mild, temperate and docile. . . . They brought a considerable amount of specie with them. . . . Their clothing was well adapted for the climate of Manitoba, consisting for the most part of heavy, home-made cloth, and they were nearly all supplied with fur coats, caps, and mitts." A comment on the suitability of their clothing for the climate of Manitoba is furnished by Mrs. E. H. Burnell, who still, in 1928, has a vivid memory of going down to the wharf to see these un-known people land on one of the hottest days of a hot summer. " We had thought they would be very strange," she said, " and they looked it—the women with hand-kerchiefs on their heads and wearing aprons and the men with their hot sheep-skin coats."

These German Quakers, who a century before had taken refuge in Russia from the military rule of Prussia, found themselves, because of the withdrawal of the regulation of the Empress Catharine exempting them from military service, compelled to seek a new home. Just as this order became known, William Hespeler, who years before had emigrated from his native Germany to Waterloo county in Ontario, was home on a visit. Hearing of the plight of the Mennonites, he hastened to suggest to the Dominion Government that they might prove desirable settlers, and to the Mennonites that in Canada they might find their land of promise. Not until their scouts had visited several countries, did the Mennonites decide to come to Manitoba. But once the decision was taken, arrangements were placed in the hands of Jacob Y. Shantz, one of their number, and William Hespeler, now Commissioner of Russian Immigration, and there was no halting either in their coming or in their determination to establish themselves at once in a settled mode of life.

When the distances and the difficulties of transportation are remembered, it seems almost incredible that J. C. McLagan should have found it possible to write, as he did two years later :

" Seldom have I beheld any spectacle more pregnant with prophecy, more fraught with promise of a successful future, than the Mennonite settlement. When I visited these interesting people, they had been only two years in the province, and yet, in a long ride I took across many miles of prairie, which but yesterday were absolutely bare, desolated and untenanted, the home of the wolf, the badger and the eagle, I passed village after village, homestead after homestead, furnished with all the conveniences and incidents of European comfort and a scientific agriculture, while on either side the road cornfields already ripe for harvest, and pastures populous with herds of cattle, stretched away to the horizon."

It is still possible to be enthusiastic over the service which the Mennonites rendered to Manitoba, and to all the North-west as well, for they were the first settlers to demonstrate that it was possible to live and farm well upon the open treeless prairie. Up to the time of their coming practically all settlement had been along the lines of the river courses, or close to the lakes, or in the wooded lands to the south-west. It is on record that when, in the early seventies, certain of the Red River people decided to leave the safe neighbourhood of the river and go back to Stonewall to take up land, they were thought to be mad and to be courting death from starvation and privation during the winter storms. " It is 1879 now," says one writer of the Mennonite settlement, " and farms on that plain are as hard to get and as valuable as our much wanted timber claims along the Mountain ; and west 100 miles to Turtle Mountain rolls the tide of immigration."

When the Mennonites settled upon their " reserve," the head of each family was given his homestead, but within their own organization all land was held in common and their districts soon were dotted with village communes of the Russian type, there being no fewer than sixty-two of those communal villages on the west side of the river. For about fifteen years this system persisted, but by the end of the century individual ownership was the usual order among these settlers, who, by their energy and thrift, their skill and resourcefulness in farming, added much to the wealth of the province. To give but one example, it was they who introduced the growing of flax which became a substantial crop in Manitoba.

Following rapidly upon the Mennonites came the second group of New Canadians—the Icelanders. Emigration from Iceland due to hard times in the island began in 1870, the first parties going to Wisconsin. Two years later the first Icelander to come to Canada, one Sygtryggur Jonasson, went to Ontario, and sent home such enthusiastic accounts that a party arrived in Canada a year later and took up land in Muskoka. The second party had a long pilgrimage, the course of which makes it easier to understand why they called its ultimate ending on the bleak shores of Lake Winnipeg Gimli, or Paradise. They went on their first arrival to Kinmount, in the back-woods of Ontario, where a railway was being constructed. Not long after their arrival work was suspended, and the Icelanders who, speaking generally, were able to bring very little with them in either goods or money, were in grave difficulties. Part of them went to Nova Scotia to the fisheries but most remained. They found a friend in John Taylor, a resident of the district, who devised the plan of moving them to Manitoba and, with the support of Lord Dufferin, persuaded the Dominion Government to adopt it. Delegates came out to view the land and with all the wheat-growing area to choose from, selected the inaccessible shores of Lake Winnipeg. One of their number has set out the reasons for their choice. The grasshoppers would not be so likely to do damage on the shores of the lake. There was abundant timber for building and for fuel. There was a waterway to Winnipeg and, likewise, an abundance of fine fish. Large tracts of land could be secured where the Icelanders might live by themselves. Lastly, the main line of the projected railway was going to cross the river at Selkirk, only forty miles away.

The whole party, impressed by the enthusiasm of their scouts, set out for Winnipeg. They were joined by those who had sought refuge in Nova Scotia, that province having been unwilling to give them any concessions. On October 11th, 1875, they arrived in Winnipeg—85 families, 285 souls. On the evening of the tenth day after they reached their Gimli, having been thirty-two days on the way. The winter that year was long and severe, but these new settlers built themselves shelters and carried on the work of making a home and winning a livelihood in the wilderness. Despite the hardships, the reports which went back to Iceland brought out another party the following year.

The difficulties which this settlement encountered would have defeated a less sturdy people. Especially sad is the story of the smallpox plague which visited it in the fall of 1877. The colony was cut off for weeks from communication with the world outside and more than fifty persons died. The growth of the fishing industry brought to them employment, but under conditions which called for courage and hardihood. Bad roads frustrated many of their efforts and thirty long years lay between their coming and that of the first railroad to Lake Winnipeg.

" The difficulties in a man's way often bring out the best that is in him. Whether or not this was the reason of the success of the Icelanders, it is certain that their progress has been phenomenal," wrote W. D. Scott, thirty years after their arrival. " In a power to acquire a knowledge of the English language, they are in a class by themselves. An Icelander who knows no word of English when the ground is being prepared for seed in the spring will speak that language with scarcely a trace of foreign accent by the time the harvest is being garnered in the fall. . . . No people show a stronger desire for the education of their children. As a result, they are, considering their numbers, prominent in mercantile, professional and political life."

In the course of years the Icelandic people have spread out into other parts of the province. Many went to Winnipeg; others to Selkirk. Material advancement has come to those who settled on wheat-bearing lands, as at Argyle and Posen. But wherever they may go, or in what work they may engage, it still remains true that they, of all the peoples who have come to Manitoba, have most quickly become identified with the British population, and have made most progress in the general life of the province. One of their number who came as a small boy, Hon. Thomas Johnson, became Attorney-General of Manitoba. Their most famous representative is the explorer Steffanson, who was born on the shores of Lake Winnipeg in 1879. At the time of the celebration of the fiftieth anniversary of their coming they claimed in the west 18 members of the legislatures, 2 Rhodes scholars, 19 professors, 40 lawyers and 40 doctors—a remarkable percentage out of the 16,000 who now live in Canada, of whom 12,000 are in Manitoba.

When the Mennonites had proved that the once feared treeless prairie was in reality the richest of rich farming

land, Canadian and British settlers were not slow to follow
in their footsteps.   Settlement then began to spread out
to the west, to the south-west and then to the north-west,
leaving the rivers and lakes.   Its direction was naturally
determined by the course of the railways, which, in the
period between 1880 and 1890, developed with almost
startling rapidity.   The first line was, of course, that
which connected St. Boniface with the American railroads.

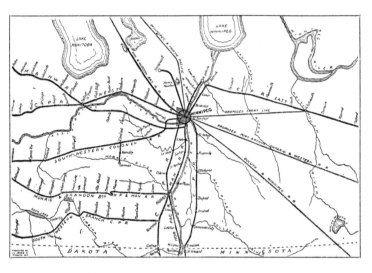

Fig. 13.—Map showing the railways of Manitoba as they were
in 1890.

———————— already built.   〰〰〰〰〰 proposed.

Then came the development of the main line of the
Canadian Pacific, the road between Port Arthur and
Winnipeg being completed in 1883, and the main line
reaching the Rockies in 1884.   While the main line
was being constructed, branch lines were being developed
in Manitoba by the railway company and other lines by
subsidiary companies.   Trains ran on these lines, especially
on the main line, as soon as steel was laid, and Portage la

Prairie and Brandon had train connection with Winnipeg in 1881. The Manitoba and South-western Railway was opened as far as Manitou in 1882 and four years later reached Deloraine. Another six years and it was beyond the boundary of Manitoba. The Manitoba and North-western Railway, running west from Portage la Prairie, completed in 1885 its line as far as Minnedosa and two years later was on its way past Birtle. The Souris branch of the Canadian Pacific reached Elm Creek in 1885, Cypress River in 1886, and by 1892 had gone through Souris to Reston. As has already been seen, the Northern Pacific in 1888 began to build its lines from the American border to Winnipeg, to Brandon and to Portage la Prairie. Altogether the railway mileage in Manitoba increased from 353 in 1880 to 1605 in 1890. This increase was at the cost of the alienation of much land. Sixty-four hundred acres per mile was the usual subsidy, and all the odd numbered sections of land were reserved that the railways might choose their portion from among them. In some cases it was twenty years before the selection was made, and much good land was thereby held out of settlement.

Naturally the new settlers were anxious to be as near the railway stations as possible, and new centres grew up about every fifteen or twenty miles along the lines, often in advance of the railway itself. The railway companies, themselves being great landowners, and especially the Canadian Pacific, the greatest landowner of them all, in order to induce settlement, carried on organized work in Eastern Canada, in Great Britain, and, at a comparatively early time, in Europe. The Canadian Pacific offered its lands at $2.50 per acre with the promise of a rebate of $1.25 for every acre cultivated. Homestead lands near the railways were taken up very rapidly and it soon became a choice between going far beyond the line or buying lands from the railways or the land companies which were early in the field. The energy of the Canadian Pacific in selling its lands had much to do with carrying settlement far beyond the boundaries of

Manitoba, while there were still thousands of fertile acres within the province awaiting cultivation.

To-day, with a network of railway lines, with motor and aeroplane transportation, and with quick communication by means of the telephone and the radio, it is not easy to realize the difficulties which these early settlers had to overcome. The abandonment of the Dawson route sent all traffic to the American railways until the Canadian Pacific Railway was built. There were only two ways of reaching Manitoba. In summer the route was by rail to Collingwood, steamer to Duluth, rail to Moorhead in Minnesota, and river boat to Winnipeg. The winter route was by rail, via Detroit and Chicago, to Moorhead and thence by stage, or in the later years by rail, to Winnipeg. " Either of these routes," says Begg, who travelled them often, " was inconvenient, expensive and attended with much hardship."

To begin with, the United States was eager for all possible immigration. Each trainload of would-be colonists had its American immigration agents aboard, praising the country through which they were passing, offering great inducements if only the newcomers would leave the trains and settle in the United States. Often too, when the immigrant reached Winnipeg, he found conditions so discouraging that he turned and went back to the Western States. Perhaps it was that he found all the land within a reasonable distance taken up, and dreaded the weary miles which must be travelled, often by ox-cart, before he found a home. Perhaps it was the isolation, or the mosquitoes making summer nights a long misery. Perhaps it was the mud—that all-pervasive mud about which everyone who ever wrote a word about Manitoba, tells. Not nearly everyone had the wisdom of Father Lacombe with regard to that mud. It is related that one day, returning to the station in Winnipeg, he found a party of immigrants whom he had just escorted from the New England states, so discouraged with the rain and the mud that they begged to be allowed to return. " Then go back, since you have not any more sense than to judge a country before you have looked into it," he said. " If there is deep mud here it is only because the soil is fat—the richest in America. But go back to your Massachusetts, if you want, where the soil is all pebbles, and work again in the factories."

They did not go, but joined with hundreds of other French Canadians brought through the efforts of Archbishop Taché and Father Lacombe from Quebec and from New England, whither they had gone from Canada, to people the villages of St. Agathe, St. Jean Baptiste, St. Joseph, St. Pierre and Letellier. Away to the north, on the Winnipeg River, Father Allard a little later settled the first families who came from Quebec to found the little community of St. George.

Indeed, for every intending settler who faltered and turned back, hundreds came on, drawn by the cheapness and fertility of the land, and by the spirit of youth and buoyancy and freedom which filled the western country. One difficulty, at least, these settlers did not have to meet. The North-west Mounted Police, organized by the Dominion Government in 1873 had, building in the foundations well laid by the Hudson's Bay Company, made the reign of law complete on the prairie. The newcomers built their homes and cultivated their lands with little of the lawlessness which has usually characterized frontier life in other new countries. Secure in this protection, the settlers pushed rapidly ahead of the railways and " at the close of 1879," says Begg, " farmhouses and cultivated fields were in sight all along the main road for 250 miles west of Winnipeg. Dr. Daniel M. Gordon, afterwards a much-respected pastor in Winnipeg, making a trip in 1879, records, " from Ellice to Winnipeg we saw every day the houses of new settlers, the country to this extent having already been surveyed into townships."

One by one the towns of to-day came into existence, each with its own story, each with its characteristics stamped upon it by the conditions of its origin. The oldest one in the north-western part of the province, or

THE LAST OX-CART TRAIN THROUGH PORTAGE LA PRAIRIE.

what was called the North-west in those early days, was
Rapid City, which was laid out in 1877 by an English
syndicate. This company got a large grant from the
Dominion Government on condition that it bring out
settlers. Under the guidance of J. C. Whellams, large
parties came out the following year from England, and in
1879, only two years after the site was laid out, Rapid
City was described as being " without a rival in the
province." A large English settlement came also to
Minnedosa, at first called Tanner's Crossing. By the
time the Manitoba and North-western Railway had reached
Neepawa the country round about was so settled and so
skilfully farmed that Neepawa was for a while the largest
wheat-shipping point in the province.

As early as 1875 James Oliver settled on his farm on the
plains around the present town of Carberry, and was the
first settler in all that district. Not for another three
years did Dougall and John McVicar push on farther west
near to the site of the city of Brandon, and build their sod
houses, calling the settlement Grand Valley. Though
they could easily have procured logs in the Brandon
Hills, they did not even know of their existence, but went
all the way to the Riding Mountains and floated logs
down the Little Saskatchewan. Their tools were limited
to an axe, a shovel, and a pickaxe, and the supplies of
seed grain and potatoes were seventy miles away. But by
the end of 1879 they had built themselves log houses and
secured a crop. By this time, too, they had easy access
to Winnipeg, in the summer at least, by steamer down the
Assiniboine River. Settlers came in quickly, and when
it became known that the Canadian Pacific would take
the southern route, Grand Valley grew like magic.
Tents dotted the ground. Every day saw new arrivals
coming by stage, in wagons, on foot, or by boat. Brandon
was not in existence, but such was the rush for land that
the new-comers pushed beyond where the new city was to
be, only two miles away. Had the McVicars been
willing to accept the offer for their land made to them by
General Rosser, when he was selecting town sites for the

12

new railway, the Brandon of to-day would have been Grand Valley. But they did not think $25,000 enough. Angered at their refusal, General Rosser went two miles to a farm of a settler named Adamson, and there bought the half-mile square which is the centre of Brandon. " Grand Valley," says Beecham Trotter, " became a living corpse."

Typical of many towns in Manitoba is the story of the founding of Crystal City in the summer of 1879. Thomas Greenway, afterwards Premier, was a member of the Dominion House, and, impressed by the opportunity offered, took a great interest in the settling of the new lands to the west, even to the extent of making a trip to Manitoba in the summer of 1878. He was filled with enthusiasm at what he saw and heard, and, returning to his home in Centralia, Ontario, he spent the winter urging his friends to go west and arranging for excursion trains to Manitoba in the spring. During that winter he organized the Rock Lake Colonization Company, composed of eight men who agreed to settle on adjacent land and to work their holdings in common for the first season. Spring found them at Emerson. There they were joined by James E. Parr, son of a member of the company, who had come out the fall before to learn the ways of the west, and who, after fifty years, is still in active business in Crystal City. Together they all journeyed across the unknown trails to the Crystal Creek, ninety miles to the west, floating their goods across the streams in the wagon boxes, and began to break their land. They were quickly followed by other settlers, so that before the end of the season all of the good land in that district was homesteaded. Thomas Greenway went on bringing more settlers and building the store and church and school and homes which the town, as a community, needed. Three years later Crystal City was a substantial town, with clothing, food, furniture, boot and shoe, and farm implement, stores and a good newspaper, from the columns of which it may be learned that the influence of American magazines was an early problem in Manitoba, for the

Canadian Illustrated News.

ICELANDERS EMBARKING AT POINT EDWARD ON THEIR WAY TO
LAKE WINNIPEG.

H. S. Seaman, Esq.

THE PAS IN 1877.

Philadelphia Saturday Post was carrying in it a good-sized advertisement. When, two years later, the railway decided to pass Crystal City at a distance of a mile, the town was able to pick itself up and transfer its buildings to the rail side.

The immigration to Crystal City and the towns along the southern border of the province went in from Emerson, but the territory between that and the main line of the Canadian Pacific Railway was mostly settled from Winnipeg. In 1878 Rodmond Roblin, afterwards Premier of the province, came from Picton, Ontario, and with his wife went out to Carman to engage in business. Two years later the first settler in the Souris district, Capt. Gilbert Wood, drove in a prairie schooner drawn by oxen 150 miles across the country to the beautiful valley of the Souris River. The surveyors followed hard after him, and then a colonization company of four men from Millbrook, Ontario, headed by the late Senator Kirchoffer, got large land grants and quickly settled this area with people from the township of Cavan in Ontario, from England, and even from the North of Ireland.

Of towns which were settled by people from Great Britain, Virden on the main line became the best known, though there was also a very distinctive group on the White Horse Plains, as the Headingly area was called in the early days. Including among their numbers graduates of British universities, and, as well, people of sufficient means to permit of their living the life of the English country gentlemen, so far as it might be lived on the prairies, these settlers, by their love of good books, art, music, flowers, and gentle ways of living, made a contribution to the life of Manitoba which no one has yet attempted to value. At the same time they did not seek to escape the hard work, which was necessarily the lot of all settlers. J. W. C. Haldane, who visited Western Canada in the nineties, gives in his book, *Thirty-eight Hundred Miles across Canada*, a quotation from an English settler in one of these towns.

" We had in our part of the country the sons of three earls. The nephews, nieces and cousins of earls were almost innumerable. I have heard the niece of a farmer, whose father was a general and whose brother is an admiral, declare with great pride that in summer and winter the week's washing was folded, ironed and mended all on a Monday, and also that she and her husband had together washed twenty-two blankets in one day."

The breaking of the land boom, the bad floods of 1882, poor crops, hard frosts, the fight with the C.P.R. over railway charters, and the rebellion of 1885, all combined, discouraged immigration, and for some time settlement fell off and there were hard times for those people already in the province, whether in Winnipeg or in the rural areas. Occasionally a brighter day seemed about to dawn. " I am glad to be able to report a decided improvement in mercantile affairs in Manitoba," the Commissioner of the Hudson's Bay Company wrote in the end of 1885. " The bank deposits are largely increasing, so much so that the rate of interest is being steadily reduced. The wholesale and retail business throughout the city has shown a marked improvement during the past six weeks." When wheat, which had reached an average production in 1876 of 32½ bushels to the acre, a record it has never equalled since, came back in 1887 to 25·7 bushels, it was thought that the end of hard times had come. But 1888 proved one of the worst years Manitoba has ever had. It was so disastrous that no records of what tiny crop may have been harvested, were kept. It was, however, the last of its kind and not again has Manitoba had anything which could be called a total crop failure. In the years which followed 1888, it won its title of " the Sure Crop Province."

But though settlers might be coming in slowly and though in Winnipeg business might seem to be very dull, in reality the province was developing at a creditable rate. By 1891 the population was two and a half times what it had been in 1881, and whereas in 1883 slightly over 200,000 acres were producing crops, by 1887 over 400,000 acres were under cultivation and over 750,000

TRAIN-LOAD OF SETTLERS AND THEIR EFFECTS.

Canadian Pacific Railway Company.

three years later. By this time also there were manufacturing enterprises in the province having an invested capital of $7,500,000 and employing 5,000 persons. The year 1888 seems to have been a turning point in more things than crops and the tide of immigration and business quickened perceptibly. Branch lines were being built rapidly, and into all parts of the province, except what is now known as Northern Manitoba, settlers were going. The latest district to attract was that around Dauphin, into which settlers began to go as early as 1885, though its real development had to await the coming of the railway, by which time Manitoba was beginning to write a new chapter in her romance.

Perhaps one of the earliest signs of the opening of that new chapter was the arrival in 1892 of the third group of new Canadians—the Ukrainians. In those days even the name of the country was unknown in Canada, and these people were called either Ruthenians or Galicians —sometimes, indeed, Galatians from the memory of the writings of St. Paul. Away off in the province of Galicia, which is now part of Poland, but in those days was in the Austro-Hungarian Empire, there was a small village called Nebilow, lying next to one of those German villages by means of which the Austrians had sought to make this territory German. Some of these Germans had made their way to Canada and the tales they sent home reached the people of Nebilow and filled them with a desire to go to the new world. They determined to send three of their number to spy out the land and, in August 1892, these three, Vasil Leynak, Ivan Pilipiwski and Jurko Panischak, set off in their peasant costumes to journey to Manitoba. Crossing the German border, they were arrested and made to tell whither they were bound and whether they had enough money to reach their destination. As it turned out Leynak had enough, Pilipiwski was five guelders short and Panischak lacked thirty guelders. Among themselves it was decided that Panischak should give some of his money to Pilipiwski and return then to Nebilow to await word from Canada.

The two adventurers reached Winnipeg just as there was demand for harvesters. No one could speak to them in their own language, but, falling in with a Mennonite, who remembered a little Russian, which they also understood, they were advised to go to Gretna, where they got work and earned, what was for them, a large sum of money.

Pilipiwski returned to his village just at Christmas-time with glad tidings from Canada and immediately preparations for the long journey were begun by the families of the three adventurers and by ten other families. Just as they were about to start, the leaders were arrested for sedition and kept three months in prison. But the ten families came bravely on. Six of them went to Alberta to be near their German friends, two went to Gretna, and two remained in Winnipeg, where Panischak and his family still live.

Two years later the Educational Society of Lemberg, disturbed by some of the stories which were coming from Brazil, to which country at that time there was a large immigration of their people, sent Professor Olesku to study Western Canada. His book, telling what he had seen, was published at the end of the year, and had the effect of making Canada, instead of Brazil, the land of heart's desire for those central Europeans. It is interesting to note the things which weighed with Professor Olesku. He was astonished to find that in three years one of the original two settlers owned a small house and had $80 in the bank.

Throughout the province in those days of slow development, life was lived in the simplest and most friendly fashion. " Those were the days when everybody helped the other fellow," said one who was through it all. Everybody knew everybody and whatever might have been their social position before coming west, a common friendliness drew them into one society here. In summer hard work was the order for all, for the land was plentiful and fertile, and labourers were few.

" So far as evening entertainments are concerned," wrote

Haldane, " winter is the time when they are in full swing just as they are in cities and as many who attend such gatherings have to traverse distances frequently of twenty miles, the phases of the moon are often carefully studied for very practical purposes. Although the thermometer may be down to 20 or 30 below zero, the usually dry atmosphere exhilarates those who are exposed to it, and renders them almost proof against pulmonary complaints, which, we may add, are hardly known. On this account, people when travelling, get along nicely over the dry snow on sleighs or on snow shoes, or by skating on lakes and rivers, or, if a large party, in a very comfortable vehicle drawn by horses or sometimes by a team of cattle."

As all shared in pleasures, so all shared in work, as Haldane was quick to notice.

" In some form or other this system of working for one's self is constantly being practised in the colonies of aristocracy and gentry, college professors, university, professional and commercial men of all ranks without the slightest fear of losing caste. But then it must be remembered that their manual arts . . . are ennobled on the prairie . . . by the fact that they are only used as means of eventually obtaining the prosperity which has, perhaps, been long denied them."

In Winnipeg, too, during the long period of recovery which lay between the breaking of the boom of 1882 and the years just at the turn of the century, life was lived upon the same simple friendly terms. There was no wealth to mark out a special social class. Twelve hundred dollars was still a good income even for those who were natural leaders in the community which found its diversions in amateur theatricals and concerts, in quiet card parties and occasional formal dances. The surprise party was one of the chief features of social life. Driving in summer, sleighing in winter, snow-shoeing, skating, cricket, horse-racing, curling and rowing were the chief sports. The comparative isolation of Winnipeg was no bar to the development of games and athletics. The first bonspiel was held in March 1889, and in the summer of the same year, the Rowing Club's Senior Four, composed of G. H. Garwood, J. H. Turnbull, A. C. L. Fox

and G. F. Galt, won the championship of America.
From this time, too, dates the first building of the
Y.M.C.A. and the founding of the Winnipeg Canoe Club.
The women of the city busied themselves, in what leisure
housekeeping, under conditions still difficult compared
with those of to-day, allowed them, in church and charity
work. The organization of several of the well-known
philanthropic institutions of Winnipeg date from this
time, among which are the Women's Hospital Aid, the
Children's Home, and the Home for Young Women
which has grown into the Canadian Women's Hostel.

With settlement advancing in the province and the
needs of the railroad builders continuing and even
increasing, business grew steadily, if slowly. Winnipeg,
lying in the " neck of the bottle " between the American
boundary and Lake Winnipeg, was regarded as the
necessary distributing point for the entire west. But the
weariness of waiting for the turn of the tide was discouraging to those who had come to the west twenty
years before, and who were still paying the price of the
folly of the boom. There was little in the outlook of
those who were either in Winnipeg or in the province in
1896—unless it might be the beginning of the Canadian
Northern Railway—to show that the turn had come ;
that the sun was rising on a new day in the story of
Manitoba.

CHAPTER IX

LOOKING back over the history of Manitoba, it is quite clear that by the time the year 1896 was drawing to a close, the province was passing another milestone and entering upon a day bright with the promise of future growth and prosperity. Two events seem to mark definitely the actual turn in the road.

The first cause of the change in her fortunes lay in the advent to power in the summer of this year of the Laurier Government. Like all new governments, it was full of zeal and energy. By common consent the Cabinet was able, quite beyond the ordinary run of cabinets, including, as it did, leaders from the political life of each province. Moreover it had the singularly good fortune to come to power at a time when world forces were favourable to the development of Canada. An increasing supply of gold was bringing better prices throughout the world and farming thus appeared a more attractive occupation. This change came just at the moment when the supply of fertile, free lands in the United States was exhausted. There was, therefore, at once a desire for the cheap lands of Canada and a good price awaiting the product of her prairies.

For the member of the Cabinet from Manitoba, Sir Wilfrid chose Clifford Sifton, Attorney-General in the Greenway Government. He had already served eight years in the Manitoba Legislature, where his father had been Speaker. For five of those years he had been a member of the Cabinet. In the Ottawa Government he was the sole representative of the West, and it was part of the West's good fortune that he was able to express

her needs with understanding and vigour. In the
Department of the Interior he found opportunity to display his great administrative capacity, and immediately
he turned all his energy towards supplying the West's
great need—settlers to cultivate her prairies.

In Winnipeg, men, wearied with long waiting for the
day of promise, laughed when they heard that Clifford
Sifton intended to seek the first settlers in the United
States. " We thought," said one who shared the burden
of that time, " that the Americans had a good country
of their own . . . a much better one than we had. Why
should they come to our west ? " So little up to this
time had American citizens thought of seeking cheap
land in Canada, that the census for the fiscal year 1896
records no immigration from the United States. Agents,
however, have left it on record that 49 American settlers
actually came. " The 49," said the *Free Press* at a later
date when the American immigration was in full tide,
" may be considered the pioneers of the present migration
to Manitoba and the Territories." Until this time there
had been no effort made by any Canadian agencies to set
before American farmers the advantages which the
Canadian west had to offer. Wholeheartedly, Clifford
Sifton plunged into the business not only of letting them
know, but of forcing them to learn. Advertisements
were placed in some 7,000 or 8,000 American papers,
daily and weekly. Every American fair of any size had
its Canadian exhibit. Agents were appointed in cities
at key points, and there was always available for the
interested farmer, or newspaper man, a free excursion
into the new country that he might be able to tell at first
hand of its wonders.

The response was almost immediate. The census,
which had shown no American immigration in 1896,
records nearly 2,500 entries in 1897. By 1900, 13,500
were reported. By the middle of the next decade the
number had risen to over 50,000 annually. This migration reached its peak in 1913 when 139,000 Americans
entered Canada seeking new homes. It is difficult to

visualize what a tremendous undertaking was the trans-
ference of so many people. As early as 1903 special
trains of immigrants and their effects were leaving points
in the Western States daily in the spring of the year.
Almost every state sent its quota. W. R. Callaway of
Minneapolis, who, as an officer of the " Soo Line,"
the Canadian Pacific Railway's American subsidiary,
was one of the most active organizers of the migration,
recalls that when, owing to bad spring floods he had to
turn over many of the immigrants to a rival road, he
transferred in one week alone five thousand passengers
and a thousand cars of effects. This particular immigration differed from all others which have come into Western
Canada, in that the settlers were for the most part familiar
with farming under western conditions and brought
with them not only household furniture and implements
of great value, but also large sums of money. A careful
estimate placed the average wealth of these new settlers
at $998.

The second event which marks the turning point of
1896 in the development of Manitoba, was the building
in the summer of that year of the 100 miles of railway
by which the settlements around Dauphin got railway
connection, and the whole of the fertile area in the north-
western part of the province became open for settlement. These 100 miles mark the commencement of the
enterprise later known as the Canadian Northern Railway,
which, from this small beginning, through the genius
and courage and persistence of William Mackenzie and
Donald Mann, became a transcontinental railway.

What happened in Dauphin while this railway, which
was to give quick connection with the world outside,
was being built reads like a fairy tale. It was but the
first of scores of such experiences which were to fill
the story of the next fifteen years. In September of
1896 the town site, then a wheat-field, was purchased.
Waiting only until the crop could be harvested, the surveyors laid out the town. Lots were offered for sale on
October 7th. By December 23rd the railway was opened

for business, and when at the end of the year the new-comers took stock of their progress, they found that the little new town had already seventy buildings. In March, 1898, the *Dauphin Press* issued a special publicity number wherein one may see that in much less than two years the town had become a substantial one of four hotels, a church, a school and all manner of businesses, including many which, in the earlier days of Manitoba, had come only after long waiting.

For ten years before this time the great fertility of this area, where crops of forty and forty-five bushels to the acre were not uncommon, had been attracting settlers, even though they had to live at a distance of from sixty to eighty miles from a railway. The first five settlers went in in 1885. By 1892 there were 2,500 people living in the district. By the end of 1897, just one year after the opening of the railway, the number had increased to 12,000, by far the greater proportion of whom had gone in that year. The expectations of Dauphin were further increased by the decision of the Manitoba Government to build a hundred-mile-long road into the Swan Lake country, where, sheltered by the Duck and Porcupine mountains, was some of the best land in the province. It is also a pleasant rolling land and better drained than even the Dauphin country. The mountains and river valley afford picturesque scenery, and offer a relief from the monotony of the level country, as it seems to those who have not yet caught the beauty of space and colour of the prairie.

The expansion of the Canadian Northern system was rapid. Charters of railways, built and unbuilt, in Manitoba and western Ontario were acquired. When in 1898 the Greenway Government thought it well for the province to have an outlet to Lake Superior independent of the Canadian Pacific, it assisted Mackenzie and Mann, by means of a guarantee of their bonds, to build a line to Port Arthur. Three years later, again with the help of the Manitoba Government, this new railway got a lease for 999 years at an annual rental of $300,000 of the lines of

BRANDON IN 1882.

Picturesque Canada.

AN EMIGRANT TRAIN.

the Northern Pacific within the province. This lease and the completing of the line to Port Arthur in 1902 gave to the Canadian Northern 1,240 miles of railway.

The expansion of this railway into a transcontinental does not belong to the story of Manitoba. The construction of the road did, however, especially in the first days, have an important bearing upon the settlement of the province. The Canadian Pacific Railway quite naturally wished to place the settlers it brought as far to the west as possible, since every extra mile meant more returns from freight. The Canadian Northern, on the other hand, had its land grants in Manitoba. It was vital to its progress to sell those lands and make them freight-producing. Under the direction of Theodore A. Burrows, now, in 1928, Lieutenant-Governor, who was Land Commissioner of the new railway as he was also the pioneer in the lumbering industry which flourished in this section, much was done to divert the tide of immigration, then sweeping past Manitoba to the North-west Territories, and to place settlers in this province, particularly those parts of it tributary to the Canadian Northern.

Once the tide of American immigration began to move into Western Canada, Clifford Sifton turned his attention to the United Kingdom and from that to the countries of Europe. To arouse interest there was much easier since the remarkable fact that Americans were actually preferring to find homes in Canada had attracted the attention of the entire European world, which up to that time had had its interest focussed upon the United States so far as emigration was concerned. The same methods of advertising and exhibits and lectures were employed. To these were added now in Great Britain a play upon the motive of patriotism. " Settlement should be kept within the Empire," " Keep Canada British," were the cries. British immigration to Canada, which in 1900 stood at 10,000, had seven years later risen to the astonishing yearly total of 132,000. Not all of this came to Western Canada, it is true, but the large proportion of it did, and went to swell the total of the population which fed the business houses of Winnipeg, even if it did not settle upon the lands of Manitoba.

Five or six years after the Laurier Government took office, the Department of the Interior, aided by the railways and the land companies, had made the prairies " the Mecca of the world's landless folk." From almost all quarters people were thronging to Western Canada. It has already been seen how from Iceland and Russia and the Austro-Hungarian Empire thousands of Europeans had come to Manitoba. Between the governmental machinery and the effect of Professor Olesku's book on opportunities in Western Canada for his Ruthenian people, it was not long before these people were coming in large numbers. A total of 5,000 in 1900 rose to 21,000 in 1907, at which figure it still stood in 1912. Many opinions have been expressed as to the value of immigration from this country—the largest which the province has yet received from any non-English-speaking country. The opinion of J. W. Dafoe, who has had ample opportunity for first-hand knowledge, may be quoted. " The Ruthenians in their own land are small farmers, and they proved themselves from the outset extremely valuable settlers. They were placed largely on second-class land, scrubby in character, which the homesteaders from the United States or Eastern Canada passed by, and they at once proceeded to make homes for themselves." These people, like the Icelanders and the Mennonites, preferred to settle largely in communities. Many of them, however, have found their way into Winnipeg, where they attend the public schools and mingle in industrial and commercial life with people of English-speaking origin. They have had one member of the Dominion Parliament and several members of the legislatures. Establishing their first newspaper in 1903 they now have nine or ten papers in Western Canada, and show every disposition to carry their share in the responsibilities of the life of the province.

But this immigration, which swept down upon Mani-

The T. Eaton Company, Winnipeg.

Portage Avenue when the T. Eaton store was being built. The green-
houses were on the present site of the Enderton Building.

T. A. Burrows, Esq.

Driving the last spike in the Canadian Northern Railway. The party
included several men who contributed largely to the making of Mani-
toba :—Lt.-Gov. Burrows, Sir William Mackenzie, Sir Donald Mann,
Sir Edmund Walker, Sir John Aird, F. H. Brydges, Hugh Sutherland,
D. B. Hanna, Z. A. Lash, Andrew Strang, George Marks, Archie
McKeller, G. H. Shaw, and R. J. Mackenzie.

toba and the Territories, or the provinces of Saskatchewan and Alberta as they became in the middle of the period, was not limited to people from two or three countries. Russians, including those strange and fanatical people the Doukhobours, Italians, French, Germans, Finns, Swedes and Norwegians—they came seeking land in order to make homes for themselves in this new country. Through this immigration Manitoba found settlers, but she found also opportunities of development quite beyond settlement. In supplying goods and services for the thousands thronging to the prairies, great businesses were built up and men rose to fortune rapidly. In 1901 Manitoba got in all a little more than 11,000 immigrants. Two years later she was called upon to welcome and find homes for almost 40,000 who came in that one year. Just what this meant within the province is indicated by the names of towns which appeared in the Manitoba list of that year which were not in existence at the beginning of the period—Teulon, Steinbach, Swan River, Dauphin, Gilbert Plains, Makinak, Plumas, Edrans, Lyleton, Beaver, Winnipegosis, Wellwood, Brookdale, Bradwardine, Lenore, Grandview and Mineola. Somewhat under the 1903 rate immigration into Manitoba continued until in the year just before the Great War it had attained the mark of 43,000. During this same time the total immigration into Canada rose from 49,000 in 1901 to 400,000 in 1913.

In the middle of this period the building of the Grand Trunk Pacific Railway from Winnipeg to the Pacific coast and of the National Transcontinental from Winnipeg to Moncton was begun. This construction furnished a never-failing source of work for the new settlers, who, coming for the most part with little money, would, without this aid, undoubtedly have found the first years of developing their farms very difficult. As each section of the railway was completed, traffic was opened and thus good land hitherto inaccessible was made available. The Canadian Pacific, slow to hear the calls of the settlers for railways when there was no competition, entered now into a feverish activity in the construction of branch lines. The Canadian Northern was likewise busy constructing " feeders." There followed a period of unprecedented activity and rapidity in the opening of branch lines. By the time this period of expansion reached its end in 1914, there were in Western Canada more than 12,000 miles of railway where thirty-five years earlier not a mile of track had existed. In order to get these railways built with this unparalleled speed, much of the land of Western Canada had been alienated. But by the time the two later transcontinental lines were undertaken, the Federal policy had changed and lands were no longer granted. Such governmental aid as was extended was now in the form of subsidies, or of the guaranteeing of the railway bonds.

Towards the end of the period the Federal Government entered upon the building of the railway to Hudson Bay which had been the dream of the western people for thirty years. By the time war broke out, the entire road from The Pas to Nelson was under contract, and ninety-five miles of steel had been laid. Much had also been done in the improvement of the harbour at Nelson and it was confidently expected that this railway, which would bring the wheat-fields of the prairies fifteen hundred miles nearer Liverpool, would be completed in 1916. In 1912 an extension of the boundaries gave Manitoba the two best harbours on Hudson Bay, Nelson and Churchill, and 500 miles of coast-line. By this change the tiny " postage stamp " province of 13,000 square miles, already once extended to 73,000, reached its present size of 251,000 square miles (page xiv), just double that of the British Isles.

The economic gain to Manitoba of this great influx of new settlers and the accompanying extension of railway facilities, may be measured in a comparison of the figures found in the census returns. In 1901, thirty-four years after Confederation, the land under crop in Manitoba was 2,756,106 acres, just a million more than it had been five years earlier. By the end of the period this figure had increased to more than 5,000,000. The value of field crops had increased from $16,680,000 to $76,500,000 in 1911. The wheat crop, which in the previous ten years had averaged twenty million bushels, rose to an average of forty-seven million in the decade following 1901.

It was not, however, out in the province that the change took on such tremendous proportions. It is in what happened in Winnipeg in those years which lie between the opening of the century and the coming of the Great War, that the true mirror of the effect of the movement of peoples from all over the world to the western plains is to be found. In those years Winnipeg was the business centre for all the prairies. Through her poured the stream of immigrants ; through her, too, poured the streams of manufactured articles which went to supply their wants ; and through her, on its journey to the markets of the world, went the ever-increasing stream of wheat to the production of which the great majority of the new settlers devoted themselves. In the minds of the people of Winnipeg, it was as a distribution centre that the city would have a great future. It was still the neck of the bottle through which all must come and go, leaving on the journey some payment for services rendered. To perform these services thousands of people flocked to Winnipeg. In the five years between 1901 and 1906 it grew from a city of just over 40,000 to one of a little more than 100,000. Before the coming of the war that 100,000 had been more than doubled.

William E. Curtis, special correspondent of the *Chicago Record Herald*, who visited Winnipeg in September of 1911, sent back to his paper his impressions on this point.

" All roads lead to Winnipeg. It is the focal point of the three transcontinental lines of Canada, and nobody, neither manufacturer, capitalist, farmer, mechanic, lawyer, doctor, merchant, priest nor labourer, can pass from one part of Canada to another without going through Winnipeg. It is a gateway through which all the commerce of the east and the west, and the north and the south must flow. No city, in America at least, has such absolute and complete command over the wholesale trade of so vast an

13

area. It is destined to become one of the greatest distributing commercial centres of the continent as well as a manufacturing community of great importance."

The old spirit of far-sighted courage, combined with shrewd enterprise, somewhat dulled in the long years of what had seemed stagnation, though in fact it was only relatively so, returned to the people of Winnipeg. In the light of the somewhat dazzling vision induced by the crowding in of population, they began to lay the foundations of the great Winnipeg of the future. The provincial Government, now a Conservative one under the premiership of Rodmond Roblin, joined with the civic authorities in constructive programmes not alone of actual buildings but of plans and legislation for the benefit of the people of Winnipeg and Manitoba.

The university which had been founded in the 'seventies was in the beginning an examining body only. Increasingly as time went on, the colleges found it difficult to continue the teaching of the sciences and began to look for aid from the university. Upon the urging of interested citizens it was decided to build the university a home, and in 1900 the corner-stone of the original building was laid by the Duke of York, now King George. In 1904 six professors were appointed, and teaching under university authority, as distinct from that of the four colleges which composed it, for to the original three—St. John's, St. Boniface and Manitoba—had recently been added Wesley College, was commenced. Little by little the university extended until it was teaching practically every subject and in 1913 its work was given executive direction by the appointment of a president. Brandon College, founded by the Baptist connection, and serving the cause of higher education in the western part of the province, dates from this time, having received its charter in 1901. Two years later the Agricultural College was founded, and buildings erected for it on the present site of the Tuxedo Barracks.

Increasing population brought many problems in the provision of adequate schools throughout the province

George W. Batho, Esq.

IN THE VALLEY OF THE ASSINIBOINE.

Hill's " History of Manitoba."

HOMESTEAD NEAR RAPID CITY.

where a school population of 63,000 in 1901 grew into one of 107,000 in 1914. In 1908 the Department of Education became the charge of one minister, with Hon. G. R. Coldwell as the first Minister of Education and Robert Fletcher, who had already been for five years the administrative head, the first deputy minister. In that position he still is the director of education in Manitoba, the friend and counsellor of thousands of teachers and school trustees. It was in Winnipeg, however, that the most serious problems for school children arose. To those problems successive school boards gave their best endeavour under the wise guidance of Daniel McIntyre, who, becoming superintendent of schools in 1885 when the teaching staff numbered 42 and the schools 11, is still superintendent when that staff has grown to 980 and the schools to 67. Each year it was necessary to build new schools to take care of the school children who grew in number from 6,000 in 1896 to 13,000 in 1906, and 25,000 in the year before the war. In 1910 the increasing number of children in the high schools caused the adoption of plans for two new technical high schools to be built at the cost of three quarters of a million dollars. Steadily the citizens voted the necessary funds for all expansions. Schools and their administration became a centre of civic pride and satisfaction in a community where almost any view included a school or a church.

Naturally as more and more land came under cultivation, the question of the methods of marketing wheat became of ever increasing importance. As early in the history of the province as 1883 an effort had been made to organize a grain exchange but there was not enough business to keep it going. In 1887 another attempt was made and the Grain Exchange of Winnipeg was organized with C. N. Bell, who continued in that office for twenty-nine years, as secretary. It was not until the influx of population began to make itself felt that there was sufficient business to warrant a futures market. This was first opened in 1903 and from that time membership in the Exchange grew rapidly.

Grain companies dealing through the Exchange put up elevators along the lines of railway, to which the farmers had, perforce, to sell their grain. The railroads co-operated with these companies by making the rule that they would only handle such grain as was shipped through elevators. Very early in the history of the grain trade, the farmers felt they were not getting the full price for their wheat. Even a small charge made for handling grain swells into a great total when thousands of bushels are handled, and it appeared that the men of the elevator companies, and the members of the Grain Exchange who furnished the handling services, were growing rich much faster than were the farmers. In an effort to protect their interests, the farmers put up their own elevators, and there were about sixty of these throughout the west as early as 1900. But the farmers operating these elevators found competition very difficult. Their resources were restricted and over and above every other cause stood the fact that the " line companies," as the regular elevator companies were called, could and would pay a little more for the wheat for just long enough to put the farmer elevator out of business.

As early as 1899 this dissatisfaction felt by the farmers resulted in the appointment of a Royal Commission. Out of the inquiry came the Canada Grain Act, passed first in 1900 and to-day, with many changes, still the act governing the grain trade. By it control was placed in the hands of the Dominion Government, the grain business thus having a form of supervision not applied to any other business in Canada. Some of the grievances were now removed and the farmers got two highly prized rights, that of having cars into which they might ship their grain directly, and that of requiring the railways to build loading platforms for the convenience of shippers.

Again in 1906 a Royal Commission of investigation was appointed, and again it was found that the farmers had cause of complaint. Rightly or wrongly the farmers believed that the trade was controlled by a few large concerns represented in the Grain Exchange and at other points. These firms, they believed, restricted competition and controlled prices. While some of the farmers were clamouring for commissions or for legislation others turned their minds towards the formation of a company to handle their own grain co-operatively. Though the main body did not endorse the scheme, thirty members of the Territorial Grain Growers Association at their meeting in February 1906 organized a joint stock company and called it the Grain Growers Grain Company, Limited. By the autumn a thousand shares of the value of $25 had been subscribed, and on September 1st, with $5,000 paid-up capital and a seat on the Grain Exchange, it began business. A few months later T. A. Crerar came in from Russell to become manager and later president, his experience in the grain trade up to that moment being such as might be gained from the occupations of farming and of managing a small country elevator. Under his organizing genius the company developed rapidly and very quickly became the largest grain handling company on a commission basis in Western Canada.

Before long the new company came into sharp conflict with the Grain Exchange over its plan to pro-rate profits with its members. This, the Exchange decided, came within the rules against rebating, and so the new company was expelled. Finding that the plan was a violation of its own charter, the Grain Growers Grain Company modified its position and applied to be reinstated. The application was refused. It then abandoned its plan and again applied for membership, only to be once more refused. While this was going on the Royal Commission was investigating the Grain Exchange and the grain trade generally. Without waiting for its findings angry members of the new company had brought suit against members of the Grain Exchange. Both in the courts and by the commission the Grain Exchange was exonerated from any wrong-doing, but the state of the public mind, and especially the state of mind of the farmers, may easily be imagined. The Manitoba Government met the popular clamour by demanding certain revisions in the charter of the Exchange. The Exchange refused to comply and, in protest, dissolved its organization in February 1908. In September of that year, it reorganized as a voluntary association, in which form it has continued until the present day. Shortly after the reorganization the Grain Growers Grain Company was again admitted to membership.

The way of the grain trade continued to be a stormy one. As a later commission of inquiry has said: " Between the year 1897 and the outbreak of the Great War in 1914, thirteen investigations into various departments of the grain trade were held by Royal Commissioners in some cases appointed by Federal and in other cases by provincial authority. All of these investigations were prompted by complaints emanating from the producers of grain, and they all resulted in bringing about at least some beneficial changes in the conditions complained of."

At each crisis the Grain Growers Grain Company was successful in its appeals to the farmers for support. Dissatisfaction with the elevator business continued, and in 1910 the Manitoba Government, with the support of the farmers, took the courageous step, not before tried by any Government, of going into the elevator business itself. It acquired 174 elevators and operated them for two years, thus giving the " line companies " effective competition. But the operation involved a heavy loss and at the end of this time these elevators were leased to the Grain Growers Grain Company. A recent *Washington Bulletin* commenting on this phase of the struggle within the grain trade says: " It is doubtful if these facilities could have been acquired by the farmers themselves at that time. The Manitoba Government's venture may, therefore, have had more significance and a greater bearing on later developments than has at any time been credited to it." With the financial failure of the Government elevators in Manitoba, the Grain Growers Grain Company saw that the campaign which it had been carrying on for Government ownership and operation of all terminal elevators was not likely to meet with success. It, therefore, secured a lease of two of the Canadian Pacific Railway elevators at Fort William which it has been operating ever since.

In Winnipeg commercial growth was keeping pace with the development of field crops which underlay all the life of the city. The total area under crop, which was 3,000,000 acres throughout the prairie in 1900, was by 1910 13,000,000. In that time building permits in the city had risen from $1,750,000 to $15,000,000. They went on increasing until in 1912 they were $20,000,000. Whereas at the beginning of this time of expansion $550,000 was a sufficient revenue to run the city and school business of Winnipeg, in 1913 the sum necessary was $3,500,000. Bank clearings rose in the same time from $106,900,000 to $1,600,000,000.

From Great Britain, from Eastern Canada and from the United States came the agents of banks, trust companies, insurance companies, and wholesale concerns to open branches, their business increasing with a rapidity which made it difficult to find experienced men to man their offices. Each new business coming from the outside confirmed the men already here in their confidence in the great destiny of Winnipeg. Perhaps the most emphatic assurance that in the world outside the faith of Winnipeg in its own future was shared by men of great vision and experience came when Timothy Eaton, the merchant prince of Canada, decided to build a store in Winnipeg. When, in 1906, this store, much larger than any store yet built, was opened, it represented to all the city a new stage in its development.

But however stimulating and comforting signs of confidence in the future of Winnipeg which came from the outside may have been, it was the men who were in charge of affairs in both the city and province who set themselves to lay the foundations for the future with faith and courage. In 1905 the City Council, being convinced that a supply of cheap hydro-electric energy would be of great value in building up the city, decided to undertake the enterprise as a civic business if they could win the consent of the rate payers. There was a great contest over the by-law which was finally submitted in June 1906. At that time the cost of current for domestic purposes was twenty cents a kilowatt hour. The proposal advocated by the Mayor, Thomas Sharpe, and Alderman Cockburn, to whom more than to anyone else is due the credit of initiating the enterprise, involved the development of a plant on the Winnipeg River at a cost which would put current for lighting into the homes in Winnipeg at a price of three cents a kilowatt hour. There were many citizens who scoffed openly at the plan, feeling that the proposed reduction in rates was an impossible one. However, those who favoured public ownership persisted and were, in the end, able to win the citizens to their view. The by-law for the expenditure of $3,500,000 on the plant at Point du Bois on the Winnipeg River carried, and on October 16th, 1911, the first power was delivered in Winnipeg. At once the price of current for domestic lighting which had already been cut to ten cents fell to three cents a kilowatt hour. The expectations with which the City Council entered upon this project have been justified by the fact that with this price both the Winnipeg Hydro and the Winnipeg Electric, its private competitor, have been able to develop and to keep themselves in good financial condition. The use of electric power has been continually on the increase. Three years after its power was first delivered the Winnipeg Hydro had almost 30,000 customers and was engaged in doubling the capacity of its plant. Evidence of the care with which the seventy-seven miles of transmission line necessary to bring the power from the river to the city was constructed lies in the fact that in the first five years of operation the most serious interruption lasted less than two minutes. The foresight of the men who urged the project upon the city has been much more than justified in the fact that never since the first has there been a year in which the number of its customers has not increased (Fig. 23).

Scarcely were the ballots of the citizens on the hydro-electric enterprise counted when the City Council turned its attention to the matter of an adequate water-supply and appointed a commission to investigate the question. At that time the city was drawing its water from artesian wells and there was a fear that with the rapidly increasing population the supply might be exhausted. A year later the commission reported in favour of the Winnipeg River as the best source of supply. But by that time the city was spending huge sums on the hydro-electric proposition, and, under the financial guidance of J. H. Ashdown, who was by this time Mayor of the city as well as chairman of the commission, it was decided to keep the city's financial condition sound and not to undertake both projects at one time. Five years later the water question became active, and a second commission of enquiry recommended Shoal Lake, almost a hundred miles from Winnipeg in the Lake of the Woods area, as the best available source of supply. From this lake, which could be kept uncontaminated, might be drawn a supply of pure soft water sufficient for the needs of Winnipeg and the surrounding suburbs until they should have a population of 850,000. Under the leadership of T. R. Deacon, now Mayor, the City Council decided on this plan, and, in the spring of May 1913, the citizens of the Greater Winnipeg Water District voted about seven to one in favour of the scheme. By a much greater proportion they voted the expenditure of $13,000,000 required for the construction of the aqueduct by which the water was to be brought to the city. Though the work was commenced just before the Great War, it was not until shortly after the Armistice that this water was actually flowing into the homes of the citizens who in happier days had had the courage to embark on this enterprise. Only four communities in all the world have gone to a greater distance to seek their water-supply. Flowing through 96·5 miles of concrete conduit and iron pipes, the water of Shoal Lake comes all the way under its own pressure.

At the Parliament Buildings there was the same faith in the future of Winnipeg as at the City Hall and the

same courage to prepare for that future. The telephone
system was purchased from the Bell Telephone Company
at the end of 1907 at a cost of $3,300,000. To ensure
that the other utilities of the province should be operated
with a just regard for the interest of the citizens, a Public
Utilities Commission was established in 1911. The growing industrial life caused the establishment of a system of
factory inspection. But the faith of the Government
in the future of the city and province was perhaps best
seen in the huge building programme which it undertook
towards the end of this period, when the flood of new
settlers was at its high point, and when the growth of the
city had reached its most rapid pace. A new Court House
was erected at a cost of $1,250,000. The Agricultural
College was moved to a site in St. Vital where a
$4,000,000 plant was erected. These two large under-
takings were not completed before the great project of
a new Parliament Buildings planned to cost about
$3,000,000 was launched. It was well under way when
the current of development was changed by the outbreak
of the war.

The same characteristics were being shown through the
period by men in industrial and commercial life. New
enterprises were constantly being launched and achieving
success even beyond the hopes of their originators. In all
those businesses which are included in census returns
under the heading of manufactures there was great
development. Some small beginnings had been made
before this time of expansion, and by 1901 the value of
the manufacturing output was placed at $8,000,000.
Five years later this had increased to $18,000,000.
Another five years and it mounted to $32,000,000,
putting Winnipeg in the fourth place in Canada. In 1914,
just before the outbreak of the war, it was confidently
expected that this output would reach $40,000,000.

All this activity had its effect upon the individual
citizen. Such strenuous expansion in building and in
mercantile and industrial realms forced up the price of
land. Then entered the speculator, and the price of land

mounted higher and higher and higher. The entire area of the city, sufficient for a population of more than 500,000 was divided up into lots and eagerly bought. For miles in every direction around the city sub-divisions were laid out and suburban municipalities with great expectations were organized. Beautiful new residence areas sprang up. Churches sold their valuable down-town properties and moved up town. Wealthy banks and corporations built themselves handsome homes. Lastly, came the small speculator drawn into the game by tales of easily made fortunes. Then the tide began to ebb. The vast capital expenditure on railway building which had so largely contributed to the abnormal prosperity was nearing its end, and the inflation of land values could not continue. By 1913 the boom was over, though the development on which the permanent future of the country rested was still in full stride.

Then came the war.

CHAPTER X

THE TEST OF WAR

On the outbreak of the War Canadian opinion was at once clear. To the measure of her strength Canada was ready, in an hour of deadly peril, to fight side by side with Britain in a great cause. It should be said that Canadian national opinion demurred to the widely received view that Canada went into the war blindly ' to help England,' as the phrase ran. The desire to stand by England was, indeed, dominant in the public mind, but conviction went deeper than this. Canada was looking, for herself, at the issues of the war, and, like England, was convinced of the German menace to freedom.''

These words, written by Professor George M. Wrong of Toronto University from the point of vantage of ten years after war was declared on that fateful August 4th, 1914, were as true of the province of Manitoba as they were of the whole Dominion. Though in early years the people of Manitoba had been quite isolated from world currents, though even at the beginning of the war period there was still in this province a sense of isolation amid the sparsely settled spaces of the North-west, there was no section of Canada in which her citizens responded with greater speed and thoroughness. This is, perhaps, the more surprising when it is recalled that by the census of 1916 only 57 per cent. of her population was British. It may be that the years during which Manitoba had stood holding the north-western part of the continent for Britain had put into her tradition a force which, un-realized, compelled her now to action. Whatever may be the explanation, there is no doubt of the fact. With a single-minded enthusiasm this province entered into the war. In a spirit of determination she continued to the end. "We are war weary but not disheartened," said Premier Norris in the spring of 1918, when the long struggle was at one of its most intense moments. "We have helped to bear the brunt of the struggle for the past three and a half years, and with a stout heart and a firm conviction of our ability to work out our own salvation we can face the future without flinching."

Within three weeks of the day war was declared men were enlisted, marshalled into regiments, and on their way to Valcartier, there to become part of the force of 33,000 Canadian soldiers who reached England in October. Steadily the march of men from Manitoba to the battle-fields of the world continued until war ceased. From the beginning to the end there were enrolled for active service from this province 66,234 men and 171 women. Of the 52,000 Canadians who made the supreme sacrifice, 7,813 went to war from Manitoba, this number including three women. The mere tabulation of the names of the regiments with which the men of Manitoba enlisted revives memories poignant and stirring of a time when almost every day brought its thrill of pride mingled so deeply with heartfelt sorrow (Chap. XII).

At home the work of providing for the soldiers and their dependents, everything which could render the burden of war service more tolerable, was taken up with enthusiasm. The difficulty was not to find workers but to give employment to all the hands which were offered. Within a few days of the outbreak, women were at work throughout the province making hospital supplies and soldiers' comforts—work which they did not lay down until the day of the Armistice. The Soldiers' Comforts Commission, which provided for men on service was the first in the field in Manitoba. It was followed very shortly by the Manitoba Red Cross, which steadily extended its efforts, both in the making of all kinds of supplies for the wounded and in collecting money, as the war went on, and, all told, contributed from this province almost $2,000,000 in money and supplies.

The Legislature met early in September. It voted at

once a gift of 50,000 bags of flour and $5,000 to the
Belgian Relief Fund ; it suspended mortgage payments
by means of a Moratorium Act, and it organized the
Manitoba Patriotic Fund. From the day of its inception
this fund received generous contributions. Hundreds of
citizens pledged the gift of a day's pay each month. In
a little more than a year it had received $500,000.
But, as the months passed on, there arose a certain
dissatisfaction over the fact that there were some
well-to-do people who steadily evaded contributing,
and, after a time, this fund was raised by a tax collected
through the municipalities, which rose to the rate of
two mills. From first to last there passed through this
fund, administered solely for the benefit of the families
of the men who went on service, $5,450,000.

In these years no appeal for aid went unanswered.
In addition to the principal national and provincial funds
there were many smaller ones. The Red Cross organizations of the poorer countries had their workers here.
The relief funds of Belgium, Poland, Serbia, and Armenia
all had their regular contributors. Within six weeks
from the time war was declared, the women of the city,
under the leadership of the I.O.D.E. and the Local
Council of Women, had contributed several thousand
dollars for a hospital ship which the women of Canada
were providing. Every unit had its own auxiliary
working at top speed that their own men might not lack
supplies, nor their families at home want for friendship
and necessary aid. The work of the Y.M.C.A., in supplying food close to the firing line and comforts and amusements for the men when in reserve, was supported to the
amount of $250,000. Altogether it is estimated that
nearly $9,000,000 was contributed through various
funds and agencies. This, of course, takes no account
of the continuous and rapid stream of private parcels
which went forward to men upon the firing line, known
and unknown, from the women of the city who, through
this work, found some relief from the strain of waiting
for news from the front.

J. C. Davies, Esq.

THE RELATIVES' MEMORIAL IN

Hilliard Tayler, Esq.

FIGURE OF THE RELATIVES' MEMORIAL,

For the men, who not many months after the outbreak of the war began to come home, there was another set of activities, as, indeed, there was for the men in camp preparing to go overseas. For the aid of the returned men there was organized in 1915 a Provincial Returned Soldiers' Committee. For the men who had not yet gone, no effort was too great for any group to undertake for their entertainment or to keep up the morale through the tedious months of necessary preparation. No account of the services so freely given would approach completeness without mention of the devoted men and women who, through the four years of war, let no train of soldiers leave or approach Winnipeg without their word of farewell or welcome. No outline which could be presented would adequately present the sum of war activities or make mention of the men and women whose names deserve to be honoured.

When in 1917 the Government of Canada decided to raise money from the people of the country for the prosecution of the war, Manitoba's efforts compared well with those of other provinces. Committees, which included the leading business men of the city and province, directed this work. To the first loan there were no less than 78,856 subscribers, and the amount raised was $32,326,000, which meant a *per capita* subscription of $85.23—the highest rate of any of the provinces. In the following year the province was asked for $33,000,000. It did actually subscribe $44,000,000, the subscribers this time numbering over 86,000. All told, Manitoba contributed to war loans a total of $76,000,000.

It is not, however, the services rendered at home, nor the material givings of this province which, ten years later, are remembered and talked about. That which makes hearts beat faster with a thrill of pride and thankfulness is the heroic record of the men who went overseas. No record of decorations can give the measure of this heroism—nor has it any relation to the achievements of the men. Yet it is impossible not to feel pride in the honours which came to men from Manitoba.

Last to be mentioned but standing first in affection and esteem are those men who won the greatest honour of all—the Victoria Cross. Of these the official Ottawa list names fifteen men who were attached to Manitoba battalions or to the Royal Flying Corps. They are :

> Lieutenant-Colonel W. G. Barker.
> Sergeant Alexander Brereton.
> Lieutenant R. G. Combe.
> Sergeant F. G. Coppins.
> Lieutenant G. M. Flowerdew.
> Company Sergeant-Major F. W. Hall.
> Lieutenant F. M. W. Harvey.
> Lieutenant S. L. Honey.
> Lieutenant A. A. McLeod.
> Captain C. N. Mitchell.
> Captain C. P. J. O'Kelly.
> Private J. P. Robertson.
> Captain Robert Shankland.
> Major Harens Strachan.
> Lieutenant J. E. Tait.

To this list must be added the names of three other Manitoba men who also won the coveted honour :

> Sergeant Leo Clark.
> Sergeant Ralph Small.
> Sergeant Raphael Zengal.

By a curious coincidence three of these men went to war, all unknown to each other, from a single street in the western end of Winnipeg. To their perpetual memory the City Council changed the name of their street to Valour Road, and the Women's Canadian Club erected at the point where it intersects Portage Avenue special lights and a tablet in their honour.

The tale of the valour and heroism of the men of Manitoba, who helped to change the course of history upon the plains of Flanders, lies outside the scope of this story, which concerns itself with what the war brought within the confines of the province. Yet it is not possible to recall those days of stirring deeds without an added

PROVINCIAL PARLIAMENT BUILDINGS.

TABLET ERECTED
AT THE CORNER OF
VALOUR ROAD AND
PORTAGE AVENUE
TO THREE WINNERS
OF THE VICTORIA
CROSS.

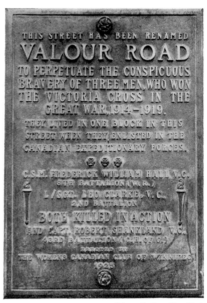

THIS STREET HAS BEEN RENAMED
VALOUR ROAD
TO PERPETUATE THE CONSPICUOUS
BRAVERY OF THREE MEN, WHO WON
THE VICTORIA CROSS IN THE
GREAT WAR, 1914-1919.
THEY LIVED IN ONE BLOCK IN THIS
STREET WHEN THEY ENLISTED IN THE
CANADIAN EXPEDITIONARY FORCES.

C.S.M. FREDERICK WILLIAM HALL, V.C.
8TH BATTALION (W.R.)
L/SGT. LEO CLARKE, V.C.
2ND BATTALION
BOTH KILLED IN ACTION
AND CAPT. ROBERT SHANKLAND, V.C.
43RD BATTALION (CEF OF C.)
ERECTED BY
THE WOMEN'S CANADIAN CLUB OF WINNIPEG
1925

Women's Canadian Club.

prayer of gratitude for those sons of the province who wrote her name in the history of the world at St. Julien, with its deadly surprise of poison gas, at Courcelette, at Vimy Ridge, and at Passchendaele. The story of the achievements on the battlefields is the story of the whole Canadian Army, but the people of Manitoba will ever walk with surer tread because their sons upheld the best traditions and shared in the greatest achievements of those heroic battalions.

Two incidents brought the past history of the province into living connection with the war. In the spring of 1916 many visitors to London saw in the window of British Columbia House a rifle with a silver plate bearing the following inscription:

" This rifle was used by Sniper N 1295 Pte. P. Riel, nephew of Louis Riel of the Riel Rebellion, 8th Battalion, 90th Rifles. With it he accounted for thirty Germans between March 1915, and January 15th, 1916, when he was killed by a shell at Anton's Farm, near Messines."

The second incident concerned the Hudson's Bay Company, which, though now its business of gathering furs had to be carried on more in the unsettled districts far to the north and west, had, nevertheless, remained a great force in the city of Winnipeg. Early in the war it offered its services to the French Government. For that Government it arranged credits and later acted as its purchasing and transport agent. It served the Russian Government also, the experience of its captains in bringing ships into Hudson Bay proving of the greatest value in transporting goods to Archangel. It is interesting to note that during the years 1918 and 1919 the company was unloading from its ships every seven minutes supplies equivalent to the entire cargo which its first ship, the *Nonsuch*, brought home from North America almost two hundred and fifty years before.

It was not, however, in the realm of war work alone that life in Manitoba became an absorbing interest in those years of the conflict. For most of the period

14

political life was a turmoil when one excitement followed hard upon another. The Roblin Government, which had been in office since 1900, went to the country in the summer of 1914. It was a bitterly fought election in which many charges of corruption in connection with the extensive building programme were urged against the party in power. The result of the election was to return the Roblin Government to power with 27 seats to 22 for the Liberals, now under the leadership of T. C. Norris. It was a matter of general agreement that an effective force in lowering the Government majority were the speeches of Mrs. Nellie McClung, who made vigorous attacks upon the Government, not so much for corruption as for their course in regard to the administration of the liquor laws, and their refusal of the franchise to women. This appearance of Mrs. McClung marks the entry of women into active political work in Canada.

At the special session of the Legislature, called because of the war, the Government was obliged to ask for an increased grant of $1,000,000 for the completion of the Parliament Buildings, the cost of which it was now said would be $4,500,000 instead of the $3,000,000 at first expected. From this point on the struggle between the two parties was constant and bitter. It centred upon two points—the money spent in building the Court House, the Agricultural College, and the Parliament Buildings, and the refusal of the Government to pass any of the social legislation now being demanded throughout the province. Of the social questions temperance was the foremost. Writing of the Conservative party in Manitoba at this time, the *Canadian Annual Review* says :

" The temperance element were against the Government, so were the women's organizations, many church bodies and leaders, and the chief men in the farmers' organizations. Sir Rodmond Roblin was not popular in a personal sense, though a vigorous, hard-hitting, and capable politician. As Prime Minister he had done many good things ; it remained for this year (1915) to bring out the dark shadings."

The Liberals continued their campaign against the Government, charging " gross and culpable negligence " and the payment to the contractors of undue profit to the amount of $850,000, the further charge being that these undue profits had, in some degree, found their way back into the campaign funds of the Government party. When the Cabinet refused to appoint a Royal Commission to investigate the charges, the Liberal members of the Legislature presented to the Lieutenant-Governor, Sir Douglas Cameron, a Memorial praying him not to permit the house to prorogue until such a commission had been appointed. Within a few hours the situation was completely changed. The Lieutenant-Governor, accepting the recommendations of the Memorial, insisted upon the commission, and Chief Justice Mathers, Justice D. A. Macdonald, and the Police Magistrate, Hugh John Macdonald, one time Premier of the province, were appointed to conduct the investigation.

Six weeks later the Roblin Government resigned and the Liberals, with T. C. Norris as Premier, took office. Thomas Johnson became Minister of Public Works, A. B. Hudson, Attorney-General, Edward Brown, Provincial Treasurer, and Dr. R. S. Thornton, Minister of Education. A week later work was stopped on the Parliament Buildings and the business of auditing the books of the province began. During the summer the Royal Commission gave its finding that the charges made by the Liberal members had been " fully proven."

A stormy time followed in which charge and counter charge brought commission after commission. Thomas Kelly, the contractor for the Parliament Buildings, was arrested in Chicago, brought back to Winnipeg, tried, convicted, and sentenced to two and one-half years in the penitentiary and to make repayment to the province to the amount of $1,250,000. The late ministers Sir Rodmond Roblin, Hon. G. R. Coldwell, and Hon. J. H. Howden were arrested and put on trial for conspiracy to defraud the province. The jury disagreed, and

subsequently they were discharged, on the ground of
" a serious condition of health."

The new Government went to the country in August
1915 and won a sweeping victory, only six seats going to
the opposition. " The general result," says the *Canadian
Annual* of that year, " was a great victory for new men,
new methods and a new policy." Although much of its
attention, and in particular much of the attention of
the new Attorney-General, Hon. A. B. Hudson, was for
the next two years absorbed in questions arising out of
the trials of Kelly and the late ministers, as well as out
of the several commissions, the Government proceeded
at once to fulfil the pledges of a new policy made freely
during the election. Nothing, perhaps, in the whole
history of Manitoba is more interesting or stimulating
than the speed with which, from being generally counted
as one of the backward provinces, this province came to
stand in the forefront of the whole Dominion in laws
concerning social matters.

On January 27th, 1916, two years to the day after Sir
Rodmond had bluntly refused their request, women filled
the galleries of the legislative chamber to hear the bill
giving them the franchise receive its third reading. They
had already presented a petition with 40,000 signatures
asking for this measure which gave to the women of
Manitoba the distinction of being the first women in
Canada to be enfranchised. When, in 1920, Mrs. Edith
Rogers, great grand-daughter of Sir George Simpson,
was elected for one of the Winnipeg seats, Manitoba
became the second province to count a woman among
its law-makers.

After women's suffrage came the liquor legislation.
Around this problem had centred some interesting events
in the political history of Manitoba. The first plebiscite
ever to be held in Canada on the question of prohibition
took place in Manitoba in 1892, and resulted in a vote in
favour of the measure of 19,000 to 7,000. When, in 1898,
the Dominion Government took a vote, this province
registered 12,000 to 3,000 in favour of prohibition. Going

Rust Research Laboratory, Winnipeg.

SPRAYING SULPHUR FROM AN AEROPLANE TO PREVENT RUST. TAKEN FROM THE AIR IN 1927.

Manitoba Department of Agriculture.

A. P. STEVENSON OF MORDEN UNDER ONE OF HIS OWN APPLE TREES—THIRTY-THREE YEARS OLD, AND STILL BEARING FRUIT.

to the country in the following year Hugh John Macdonald and his party were elected on a platform of temperance. In the first session of the Legislature after the election, under the direction of Premier Macdonald, the Manitoba Temperance Act drafted by J. A. M. Aikins, K.C., was introduced and carried. There were, however, many doubts as to its constitutionality and the question was, therefore, referred to the courts. When, a few months later, the Privy Council decided that the act was within the power of the province, the provincial Government, led by Sir Rodmond Roblin, who had succeeded Macdonald on the latter's entry into Dominion politics, announced that it would hold another plebiscite before putting the act into effect. The temperance forces charged bad faith and counselled their people not to go to the polls, with the result that the referendum was defeated and the Government felt justified in not putting the act into force.

All through the time of the Roblin ministry a bitter fight was carried on between the Government and the temperance forces, and, towards the end of its tenure of office, charges were freely made against the Government over the administration of the liquor laws, the private clubs, of which there were a large number, being a special point of attack. The phrase used in connection with a famous murder trial, " clubs of that class," became a slogan in the fight, and the Norris party had, in their election pledges, definitely promised legislation which, if supported by a referendum vote, would " banish the bar." This legislation, a revised Manitoba Temperance Act, was passed through the Legislature early in 1916 and on March 13th was submitted to a referendum. The Government would not allow the new enfranchised women to vote, declaring that such a law could not be enforced if carried by their votes. Without their aid the referendum resulted in a two to one vote in favour of the legislation and Manitoba became the first province to have prohibition. The act came into force on June 1st, and three months later the Mayor of Winnipeg went on record as saying that drunkenness had decreased 80 per cent. in Winnipeg and crime throughout the province 58 per cent. over the same period in 1915. When, towards the end of the war, the Dominion Government gave to the province the right to forbid importation of liquor, Manitoba took still another vote and endorsed this further restriction of the liquor traffic.

With the knowledge that there had been a great increase in the number of non-English-speaking people in Manitoba during the years of rapid expansion, the question of the education of the children of the province in the English language had come to occupy a large place in public attention. It will be remembered that the Laurier-Greenway settlement, made in 1897, had provided that wherever in any school there were ten children speaking a language other than English, they should be entitled to instruction upon the bi-lingual system. In the years that had passed, the conditions in Manitoba had changed radically. Now, in addition to 30,000 French-speaking citizens, there were out of a population of 500,000 no fewer than 100,000 whose language was neither French nor English. It was known that there were districts in Manitoba where the children could not speak a word of English and the Norris Government, in appealing to the country, had promised that they would introduce the compulsory and effective teaching of English into all the schools of the province.

To this task they set themselves in the fruitful session of 1916. A survey disclosed that conditions were even worse than had been alleged. One-sixth of the school population of the province were in the French, German, Ruthenian or Polish bi-lingual schools. At least one quarter of these children were being taught in a language which was neither English nor their own tongue. This situation arose owing to the mixing of several nationalities in the one school, the nationality with the largest number of pupils determining the language to be used. Bi-lingualism was thus reduced to an absurdity. But, further than this, the survey disclosed that of the 16,000 children registered in these schools only 9,000 were in attendance. The Government thereupon decided to go further than its platform demanded. It would amend the Laurier-Greenway settlement, and it would pass a compulsory attendance act which would ensure that children should go to school until they were fourteen years old.

Bitter resentment was felt among the non-English people at this drastic change. The Minister of Education, Dr. R. S. Thornton, sought to allay the feeling by promising a sympathetic administration of the new act. " The immediate effect of the repeal," he said, speaking in the Legislature, " will be to stop the process of converting our regular schools into bi-lingual schools. No more bi-lingual schools will be created, but the changing of conditions is a matter which will require much time, patience and consideration."

But the French, for whom the compromise of the Laurier-Greenway settlement had been primarily arranged, were at once aroused against the Government. Indignation meetings were held. Members in the house— all but one of the opposition were French-speaking— declaimed against what they called " the criminal treatment of a minority." The Archbishop of St. Boniface proclaimed in a pastoral letter that he would never cease standing for the rights of the French minority. The Government was charged with treating the famous settlement as " a scrap of paper." With that charge the Attorney-General dealt. " As to the Laurier-Greenway settlement," he said, " it is said to be a sacred compact. But you never accepted it as a final statement. This means it is sacred so far as we are concerned, but not so with you."

Within the Liberal party were many who felt that, while all children should be taught English, the French language was deserving of special consideration. Certain compromises, none of them acceptable to the French, were offered and in the end the Government decided to proceed according to their announced policy. The act amending the Laurier-Greenway settlement was passed on March 10th, and a week later the Compulsory Education Act had its third reading. Both acts came into force the following August. Every effort was made to enforce the act in a spirit of conciliation. The device of putting schools under an official trustee instead of under a board of locally elected trustees, was adopted to meet difficult situations and successfully applied. When, after some years of experimenting, the Minister of Education decided to use somewhat sterner methods to bring the only thoroughly irreconcilable group, the Mennonites, to a compliance with the law, the Government was met first with passive resistance, and then with the departure of large groups of these settlers for Mexico. Their places were in some measure taken by a somewhat similar group, the Hutterites, who, however, came into the province promising to respect the school laws. The school population, which was 100,000 in 1915, had by the end of the war, with no immigration to speak of, risen to 138,000. It now stands at 170,000, with an average attendance of 148,000.

Unwearied with his efforts in relation to the public school, the Minister of Education in the following session turned his attention to the request of the university council. The constitution of the university was re-modelled to make it more of a provincial institution, since the province was now responsible for its finances, its needs having quite outgrown the original endowments. The system of a board of governors, supreme in all matters of policy and finance, with a council directing the educational side, was adopted. The first board was appointed soon after the passing of the act with Isaac Pitblado, K.C., who years before had acted as registrar, and whose services to the institution had been many, as the first chairman. His Grace the Archbishop of Rupert's Land, Dr. Samuel Pritchard Matheson, the primate of all Canada, and the most distinguished of the descendants of the original Selkirk settlers, continued to be chancellor. Monseigneur Cherrier, who from the beginning of the university had been closely connected with its administration, was continued in the office of vice-chancellor, which he still holds.

But not yet was the tale of the social legislation complete. The first session of the Norris Government saw, in addition to those measures already enumerated, the passage, in response to the urging of a large group of women, of the Mothers' Pensions Act. The board to administer this act, which had E. D. Martin as its first chairman, would, it was expected, have to spend about $15,000 a year. Its work has developed until now more than $400,000 a year is spent and nearly 900 mothers are cared for. Following close upon this came another response to the demands of the newly enfranchised women when a board to censor motion pictures was established. The next year saw the passage of two acts designed to aid the farmers. The Rural Credits Act provided for the creation of local groups of farmers, who by means of their own credit and Government backing, were to be in a position to make short term loans to the farmers of their district. The Farm Loans Act provided for the making of long term loans upon the amortization plan for more permanent purposes. Within two years this board had loaned more than $2,000,000 to some 800 farmers, of whom only nine were in arrears. Labour had some of its wishes gratified in the establishment of a labour bureau, and in a revision which greatly widened the scope of the Workmen's Compensation Act. The bill providing for direct legislation passed through the Legislature. A Public Welfare commission of citizens specially interested in social matters was created with instructions to study the institutions of the province and make recommendations to the Government.

In the same year, 1917, came the Minimum Wage Board, urged by groups of women who had made careful study of the wage conditions among young women, particularly in Winnipeg. This, the first commission of its kind to be established in Canada, was given control not only of wages but of conditions and hours of labour, and has wider powers than have yet been given to any other

minimum wage board in the Dominion.   The Dower Act,
also the result of agitation on the part of the women of
the province, was passed this year.   Under it a wife gets
a life interest in the homestead or the city home, and is
also assured of a share of her husband's estate.   The
provincial system of public health, inaugurated the
year before, was extended this year by the opening at
Brandon by Hon. T. H. Johnson, Minister of Public Works,
of the first child welfare station in Canada, and by an
increase in the number of nurses employed.   This department was steadily developed until, in 1921, there were
fifty nurses on duty throughout the province.   The new
Civil Service Act and the new Winnipeg City Charter
also belong to the work of this year.

In the following year, 1918, the Government's interest
in social matters was further shown by the appointment
of a psychiatrist to begin work in the interest of the
feeble-minded, 5,000 of whom, it was estimated, were to
be found in Manitoba.   In the interests of the rural
population, the provincial hydro system was inaugurated.
Still later a new election act established proportional
representation for provincial elections in the city of
Winnipeg.   In an endeavour to prevent labour disputes,
the Industrial Conditions Board, with Dr. C. W. Gordon
as chairman, was organized.   The Direct Legislation
Act, to which the party was pledged and which it had
passed in its early days, was now adjudged by the Privy
Council to be ultra vires, but the Government stood by
the principle of the measure and applied it when modifica-
tion of its temperance legislation was proposed.   Through
the application of its provisions, the Moderation League,
in 1924, got its bill providing for Government control
and sale of liquor upon the statute books.

Early in the summer of 1919 Winnipeg was called upon
to meet what was, perhaps, the most severe test of any
which the war period brought.   Here, as in practically
all parts of the western world, there was to be observed a
growing unrest on the part of labour.   It had first shown
itself at Winnipeg in the brief strike of the telephone

operators in 1917 and again in the strike of civic employees in 1918. The cost of living was rising rapidly. There was a feeling that there had been, during the war, profiteering in the necessities of life, and that this profiteering still continued. The unrest was further quickened by the revolutions taking place in many countries towards the end of the war, and, in particular, by the Russian revolution to which the extremists among the socialist and labour groups looked for leadership. Gradually these extremists won control of the Trades and Labour councils in Winnipeg, and the other cities of Western Canada. The One Big Union, a new idea of labour organization, and opposed to the usual craft union, was organized in British Columbia and spread rapidly. The cry was that, if all the workers would strike at one time, the capitalist world would be on its knees. Quite openly, plans were laid for a general strike throughout Western Canada in the summer of 1919, when the forces of labour would make a sudden effort to overthrow the existing system. Events precipitated action in Winnipeg, and the city found itself engaged in a struggle more severe, more prolonged, than any which has occurred upon this continent. In this city was tested out the efficacy of the plan by which the sympathisers of the soviet system in Russia hoped to introduce the same system in Canada.

On May 1st two large groups—the metal workers and the building trades—went on strike. They did so because of the refusal of the employers to treat with the group as a whole, instead of with the individual unions, as had hitherto been done. Each side stood firm in its determination not to yield the point, and the extremists preached that now was the time to try a sympathetic strike. Over and over again the workers were told that if they would all join in a sympathetic strike, in two days the affair would be over with victory on the side of labour. Strike votes were taken, and, while there is reason to doubt the validity of some of the votes, it seems, on the whole, clear that labour was ready to make its great experiment. How general that readiness was is shown by

the fact that the number of strikers was officially estimated at 22,000, of whom about half were organized in
unions. With their families, therefore, the strikers made
up about 40 per cent. of the population of Winnipeg, then
reckoned to be about 200,000.

On May 15th the sympathetic strike took place. All
services ceased. There was no delivery of bread or milk
or ice or of parcels from stores. Telephones ceased to
ring, street cars and elevators to run. Telegrams remained undelivered. Postmen and firemen no longer
went on duty. For days there was no newspaper save
the *Western Labour News*. In all the factories work
ceased. Many clerks left the stores. Even the washer-
women failed to come to work. For a few hours there
was fear that even the water-supply would be cut off.
From this extreme, however, the workers recoiled.
The police, though known to be in sympathy with the
strikers, were not called out, the strike committee recog-
nizing the danger from rioting and looting. Otherwise,
the paralysis was complete. There was great jubilation
among the workers at its very completeness. Within
forty-eight hours, or very little more, it was declared, the
strike committee would occupy the seats of Government
at the Parliament Buildings and the City Hall.

In much less than forty-eight hours the strikers had
learned, to their sorrow, that their children no more than
the children of the rich could do without bread and milk.
Indeed, they could not do so well, since the better-off
people in the city had motors and could go for necessities
for their families. They had also learned that there was
to be no easy victory over other sections of the city.
The Citizens' Committee, already organized in case the
strike should occur, took up the services the workers had
left. Hundreds of volunteers, both men and women,
came forward. Delivery depots for milk and bread and
ice were organized at the schools. Business men became
for the time being firemen, and delivery men, and jitney
drivers. They enlisted as a militia and lived in constant
readiness at Minto Barracks. Women became telephone

Roses blooming in a Manitoba garden on a bush which lived through
the winter without protection.

Display of fruit gathered on one Manitoba farm in the month of
September. It includes eight varieties of apples, seven of plums,
two of cherries, everbearing strawberries and raspberries.

operators. They also organized a widespread system of meals for the men engaged in the voluntary services. The response of the community was complete. To the threat of violence from one class other classes would not yield.

Less than forty-eight hours after the strike had begun the strike committee ordered the men engaged in the preparation and delivery of bread and milk to return to work. Looking back, it is clear that at that moment the strike was broken. The rest was endurance—an endurance test which ran for six long weeks in the beautiful warm days of early summer. On both sides there was manifest a grim determination to see the fight through to a finish. The enthusiasm with which citizens left their homes and their businesses to perform unaccustomed and arduous duties was no less remarkable than the solidarity of the workers and their friends.

Throughout the entire period pressure was being brought upon the provincial Government to break the strike by the application of military force. This pressure the Government steadily resisted. Moderate-minded men and women sought to find a way out which might permit both sides to withdraw from the struggle. Appeal for military intervention was, towards the end of the strike, made to the Dominion Government. The ministers at Ottawa, not sharing the view of the local Government that the strike was being slowly, but surely and safely, won by the Citizens' Committee, and that the appearance of soldiers might endanger the victory, sent a detachment of mounted police to Winnipeg and ordered the arrest of the leaders. These arrests were easily accomplished for no resistance was offered. The workers, now at the point where they were glad of an excuse to end the strike, threw up their hands. Where employers would take them back, they returned at once to their old jobs, but as some would not do this—the Dominion Government leading the way in the case of the post office—the resultant disorganization and bitterness were very great. Even now, after nine years, much of the bitterness remains. It shows itself most clearly in the City Council, to which members are still elected upon labour and citizen tickets and in which votes are constantly recorded showing the two sides aligned one against the other.

Charges of sedition were laid against the strike leaders. One of them was sentenced to the penitentiary. Six others went to jail. Their supporters retaliated by electing three of them to the Legislature in the election of 1920. Not the least extraordinary in the whole strange occurrence is that, in spite of the constant tension and the high feeling which ran through the city on certain of the more difficult days, there was not, except once, any open encounter. Even this conflict would not have taken place had the prohibition of parades and processions been observed. Towards the end of the strike the strikers and their sympathizers among the returned soldiers undertook to hold a silent massed parade. Mounted police, who were in the city to maintain order, endeavoured to prevent the demonstration, and a riot followed, in which one life was lost and several persons injured. The *Free Press*, commenting on the struggle, said : " In its essence this was a victory for the plain people, who rose in wrath against the pretensions of the strike committee ; and in this demonstration that the people as a whole are greater and more powerful than even the most thoroughly organized minority, we have our most hopeful guarantee that we shall not again see in this town revolution in the garb of a general strike."

Economically, Manitoba met the test of war with gallant spirit. The call for more food for the forces, and for the people of the fighting countries in Europe, was met by greatly increased production, though that production was carried on with difficulty owing to the increasing scarcity of workers. The rise in the price of wheat, which reached $2 for Number One Hard in 1916 and continued to rise until on September 11th, 1920, it was quoted on the Winnipeg Exchange at 285½, was in itself a great incentive to production. High prices for other food products helped the movement towards diversified farming and further increased the prosperity of the farm. Prices of farm products rose at first more rapidly than prices of other commodities, and in the war years the farmers were among the most prosperous people in the country. After the war, to their surprise, they found themselves more prosperous than ever. The Minister of Agriculture, reporting early in 1919 to the Legislature, had much exhilarating news. The acreage under crop had risen to 6,000,000. The dairy returns for the year were $65,000,000, to be compared with a return of $11,000,000 in 1915, only three years before. The stockyards at Winnipeg had handled livestock to the value of $38,000,000. There was a new egg crop worth $2,000,000. Even the potato crop rose in value to $21,000,000.

In Winnipeg the experience was the same. Rents rose rapidly, and houses, which had been a drug in the market, began to sell well. Prices continued high, production of manufactured goods continued at the old rate. A feeling of security prevailed, and especially among the farmers. There was an eager reaching out for every opportunity which came in sight. In large numbers the farmers bought more and more, mortgaging their earlier holdings to do so.

Then all over the world prices fell suddenly—and, first, the prices of agricultural products. The same wheat which had sold in September 1920 for $2.85 by the end of November was being quoted at $1.78. By November of the next year, it had touched $1.02. Conditions were made worse for the farmer since the crop of 1921 had been put in at the old high costs, for wages and manufactured articles were still high. It was a hopeless situation for the farmers who had bought more land and who had to go on paying for that land, though it was no longer of the same value now that the price of its product was much lower. Their dollar, which had been worth one hundred cents in 1913 and one hundred and forty cents in 1917 was, in 1922, worth only ninety-two cents and was still declining. Many farmers saw their savings of years disappear. Others found their once free farms heavily encumbered. In despair many farms were abandoned. Loan companies and banks suffered heavily. The Rural Credits scheme, which had expanded rapidly, almost foundered. Bitterness of feeling among the farmers was increased by the fact that some classes in the country seemed still to be prosperous, and that in some employments wages were still high. They believed themselves to be exploited. In Winnipeg, so dependent upon the prosperity of the farmers, this condition was reflected. The land boom which had seemed to have so hopeful a beginning collapsed completely. All over the province men wondered in their despair whether Manitoba had, indeed, a future. Out of the depths of that bitterness and despair was born a new movement. Its rise marks the passing of another milestone in Manitoba's history.

Department of Natural Resources, Canada.

THE PAS IN 1927, TAKEN FROM THE AIR.

CHAPTER XI

NEW TIMES, NEW FORCES

THE years which lie between 1914, when the Great War broke out, and 1922, when the reaction from the war began to spend itself, constitute a period apart from the general course of the life of Manitoba. All those forces which make for the development of a new country—the inflow of capital, the coming of new settlers, the grasping of every new opportunity—diminished almost to the vanishing point. The energy of the people of the province was completely absorbed in war and in the application of those many social measures which made such progress during the war. True, under the impetus of war demands, more land had been put under crop, but the bad fortune which befell most of those who so increased their holdings, made this expansion of little value. In almost all things the Manitoba of four years after the war stood in the same position as it had in those months of 1914, preceding the war, when the impetus of the great expansion had noticeably begun to spend itself. There was, however, one difference. In 1914 men were still under the encouragement of the days when Manitoba grew with startling rapidity. In 1922 they were, as in the days before that expansion, worn down by a long period of discouragement —discouragement all the more intense because of the exhaustion of body, mind and spirit felt all over the western world when the demands of war no longer had to be faced. The recovery from that condition makes the last, and in some ways the most exhilarating, of all the tales which Manitoba has yet written upon the pages of British history. It is a new time and in this new time Manitoba is seen to go about her business in a new way.

New forces play upon her people and her future seems to be a different one from that which would have been foretold for her in the days before the war.

As the farmers were the first to feel the war deflation, as they were the class upon whom it bore most heavily, so they were the first to seek and to find a way out. In those years of 1920, 1921 and 1922 when it was difficult for the farmer to make money, there was much suspicion and fault-finding. The methods of marketing, the railways, the banks—all were blamed. Even the farmers' organizations themselves were harshly criticized. Looking back over the years, the farmer could not escape the fact that, under the Government control and the Wheat Board of the war period, prices had been high. It is not surprising that he came to the conclusion that there must again be a Wheat Board to control the marketing of the greatest resource of Western Canada.

In their somewhat grim determination to remedy conditions, the farmers turned first to political action. The Progressive party went from triumph to triumph until it held the balance of power at Ottawa, and had captured the Governments of three of the provinces, Ontario, Alberta and Manitoba. But their efforts to obtain the re-establishment of the Wheat Board met with defeat. The Manitoba Legislature, even under the farmers' Government, which had succeeded the Norris Government in 1922, refused to endorse the proposal, and without the co-operation of the three prairie provinces there could be no national board.

The hope of Government control died. The farmers were thrown back upon themselves. Their response in that moment was magnificent. It carries the mind back to those old settlers who simply would not be beaten by famine, flood or war. If there could not be a Government pool, to which all farmers would send their wheat to be sold, there should be a voluntary pool. In the early summer of 1923, within two weeks after it was clear there would be no Wheat Board, the United Farmers of all three western provinces had met and declared for the

Winnipeg from the Air in May 1928, looking down Portage Avenue.

voluntary pool idea. The farmers returned home from these meetings to take up the work of organization. Aaron Sapiro, a leader in the egg and butter and fruit pools of the United States, was brought to the west to preach the gospel of co-operation. Almost like a prairie fire, the movement spread. With a fervour which can only be described as religious, men and women joined in the work of organizing. The original farmers' groups gave place to large organization committees on which were representatives of the grain trade, the boards of trade, the press, the retail merchants, the banks and the provincial governments. Professional and business men left their offices to share in the campaign for members. The United Grain Growers and other co-operative companies advanced money to meet the cost of organization.

The Alberta pool was ready in time to handle part of the crop of 1923, but the Saskatchewan and Manitoba pools did not get under way until 1924. Since that time the march of the pools has been remarkable. They have established a central selling agency which handles approximately half of the entire wheat crop. They have added pools for the sale of oats, barley and rye. They have acquired elevators and are building terminal elevators at Fort William, Vancouver, with a combined capacity of 9,500,000 bushels. In many ways they have sought to extend their services to the farmers, and they carry on a constant campaign of education in co-operative methods. Like all other wheat-handling agencies, they have come on good days, since Europe has begun to feel that it can once more afford wheat bread, and Russia still remains out of the market. Whether they have, or have not, actually affected world prices, and whether they have secured for their members a higher price per bushel than has been received by those who sold through the commission houses are questions to which there is, as yet, no generally satisfactory answer. The fact which cannot be denied, and which has been and still is a most important factor in securing members and renewals of first contracts, is that in times of government boards and the voluntary pools, the price of wheat has been higher than it was when the marketing was left to the decision of the individual farmers selling through the commission houses. But, beyond any material gain, has been the new hope, and courage, and enterprise which the great success of their pools has brought to thousands of men and women engaged in farming. A new life flows through the rural areas of the west.

Meantime, the other wheat-handling agencies go serenely on their way, sharing in the better times which higher prices have brought. The Grain Exchange, from its small beginnings forty years ago, has now a membership of 300 and its seats have reached a value of $12,000. Through it passes much of the share of the crop handled by the pools, to which the Exchange adopts, as it were, a waiting attitude. " We still tend to the belief," said a recent president, " that the free play of opinion of farmers, merchants and millers, and exporters and importers the world over, year in and year out, will record in the future, as it has in the past, a wheat price that has an uncanny way of reflecting true conditions, and reflecting them better than any body of men can possibly forecast them."

It is interesting to speculate how far the United Grain Growers Company paved the way for the success of the newer form of co-operative organization seen in the pools. An outcome of an earlier time of desperate struggle for the farmers of Manitoba, this Company has had an astonishing progress. In 1927 it came to the celebration of its twenty-first birthday with a membership of 34,000 and with its tiny original paid-up capital of $5,000 swollen to $3,000,000 and a reserve fund of $1,500,000. Midway in that journey the first Grain Growers Grain Company and the Alberta Farmers Co-operative Elevator Company were amalgamated, taking the present name of the United Grain Growers Company. Though grown to such dimensions, the Company still retains the rigid democracy of its early years. No one not financially interested in farming may hold so much as a single share, and no one, no matter how great his stake in farming may be, can hold more than 100 of the $25 shares.

While improvement has thus been sought in the marketing of wheat, the development of the wheat itself has not been neglected. Off in a corner of the grounds at the Agricultural College is a small building owned by the Federal Government. It is the only building in the world devoted exclusively to research into the ways of that dreaded parasite of the wheat plant—rust. Much has already been discovered of vital interest. It is now known that rust spores are blown along by the winds all the way from Texas, ravaging the wheat crops on the way if climatic conditions are favourable to their development. By use of aeroplanes the approach of rust is detected, and the farmers are warned of its coming. In the summer of 1927 hundreds of acres of wheat were sprayed from an aeroplane with the fine sulphur dust which the laboratory workers discovered would prevent rust developing. And there, in the unromantic-looking building, half a dozen workers, under the leadership of skilled scientists, seek to create a kind of wheat which will resist all the twenty-five forms of wheat rust which have been distinguished, and equal the Marquis wheat in milling and baking qualities.

On the production side of agriculture the most notable change has been the spread of diversified farming. The pressure of deflation in wheat prices forced a development which had been slowly coming. Herds of cattle and creameries have multiplied astonishingly since that time in the 'eighties when the Shoal Lake creamery initiated the butter industry. Up to the period of the war, Manitoba was importing a large portion of her supplies of butter, eggs and poultry, and even vegetables. Now she exports all of them. In 1922 a co-operative poultry marketing association was organized. In five years the shipments of poultry grew from 117,000 pounds to 1,062,000 pounds. In 1924 the same association organized an egg pool, and in three years the exports of eggs increased from eleven to 100 cars.

So fast the changes come: the perfecting of the vegetable crop and its increase, so that now cabbages and cauliflower find their way out to the choicest markets of the continent ; the first carload of honey in 1925 winning instant approval and sale because of its peculiarly fine flavour ; the flowering of the effort of A. P. Stevenson, of Morden, to bring apples to perfection in Manitoba, in the production of many varieties of apples in different sections of the province ; the appearance in Winnipeg markets of locally grown strawberries, and raspberries, and currants ; rumours that out of university experiments will come presently new varieties of grapes and blueberries ; more sheep and a yearly auction of their wool ; more hogs and a packing industry running the milling industry a close second in the value of its products. Year by year the Manitoba farmer widens his interests. Year by year he makes other resources than wheat yield him a return.

Even the fur-bearing animals must now pay toll to the farmer. Once Indians and hunters and trappers left civilization for long weary months to bring back the pelts of the fur-bearing animals. But now 5,000 farmers find diversion and profit as they share in this traffic. New methods are employed. No longer are the furs coming only from the free, roaming animals, increasing as climatic and food conditions would let them. Furs are now " farmed." Within easy distance of Winnipeg may be found several farms producing different varieties of fox skins. Further away in the swamps and muskegs the musk-rat is also being farmed—one day to be, it is said, a source of large revenue to Manitoba. Still others of this new variety of farmers experiment with mink. Chinchilla rabbits engross the attention of others. The story of the new fur trade of Manitoba becomes a fascinating tale of modern resourcefulness.

Somewhat slower than the farmers were the people of the cities in lifting themselves out of the depression. But even while the wheat pools were bringing fresh hope and courage in the country, it began to be clear that big

PORTAGE AVENUE, WINNIPEG, 1896.

The high building on the right is the old Clarendon Hotel. The
two vacant lots opposite are the sites of the Somerset Block and the
T. Eaton store.

PORTAGE AVENUE, WINNIPEG, IN 1928.

The two-storey building in the centre on the right is on the site of
the old Clarendon Hotel. Opposite are the Somerset Block and the
T. Eaton Store.

business men here and outside the province—even outside of Canada—had great confidence in the future of Manitoba. The earliest evidence of this—at first not given its true value—came when, in 1921, the Winnipeg Electric Company induced a group of New York capitalists to undertake the investment of $9,000,000 in a new power development at Great Falls on the Winnipeg River. Where, the doubters asked, would a market be found for 168,000 horse-power? The confidence of those big business men found its complete justification in the fact that only five years later the last unit was being installed and the investment had reached $14,000,000. So great had been the development in the use of electric power, that by 1928 the Winnipeg Hydro had started the development of Slave Falls and the Winnipeg Electric was looking for new power at Seven Sisters Falls. On cheap power as well as on cheap farm lands, Manitoba begins to build.

But in addition to the capitalists interested in power development, there were other far-seeing men who had confidence in the future of Manitoba. It was in these years that the eagerly-awaited new store of the Hudson's Bay Company was erected. For so long had this building been expected that it stood almost in the public mind as a symbol of better days. This store, generally acknowledged to be one of the finest on the continent, brought the Hudson's Bay Company again to a leading position in the commercial life of Winnipeg. Less spectacularly, the T. Eaton Company, which twenty years before had marked a new era, began to build ware-houses, and a printing plant, and to develop that research department which makes it a leader among all the great merchandising firms of North America. In another direction outside capital showed its confidence in Manitoba. In 1926 the Manitoba Pulp and Paper Company erected a mill of 300 tons capacity on the Winnipeg River and began the construction at Pine Falls of the first model town the Canadian west has yet seen. On February 8th, 1927, the *Manitoba Free Press* was printed on the first shipment of paper produced from the forests of Manitoba.

In the old days the prosperity of Winnipeg was identified with its future as a distributing centre of the entire west. But the growth of smaller cities and the changes resulting from the opening of the Panama Canal seriously altered the situation for Winnipeg. Business men began to realize that the future of the city must have a broader basis. With abundant cheap power close at hand, with 4,000,000 additional horse-power available in the Nelson River, with the history of the middle western states before their eyes, men's minds turned naturally to manufacturing, which already had made a healthy beginning. The capital involved had reached $100,000,000 and the gross annual output almost the same figure. In the spring of 1925, the Bracken Government, with the co-operation of the Winnipeg City Council and the Greater Winnipeg Board of Trade, appointed an industrial development board, " to make a survey of the resources, the markets, existing industries, transportation and power, raw material and labour, and to compile related data on all phases of information which might be sought by intending investors and promoters." Three years later the board was able to report that seventy-six new industries had come to Winnipeg, and that sixty-four already here had enlarged their plants. The number of manufacturing plants in Manitoba, according to the latest figures available, had grown to over 800, the wage bill to over $30,000,000, and the value of the product had increased by more than fifty per cent. In this expansion of manufacturing is seen, in part at least, the answer to the query as to where a market would be found for the power when it was produced.

In the words of John Bracken, head of a farmers' Government but always alert to the value of industrial development, " since 1924 we have discovered four-fifths of Manitoba." Commenting on this the *Winnipeg Tribune* expresses the general opinion when it says :

" That is not altogether creditable to the people of Manitoba.

J. H. Stovel, Esq.

CENTRAL MANITOBA MINE IN 1928.

Department of Natural Resources, Canada.

FLIN FLON FROM THE AIR LATE IN 1927.

but it is very largely true. Manitoba is a vast and wealthy province, but until the last two or three years there has been little effort to develop its wealth anywhere save in the comparatively small triangle of purely agricultural land in the south-west of the province. Now other resources are being investigated. Manitoba has caught the vision of what it will mean when our manufacturing possibilities are fully explored ; when our mineral fields are opened up ; our forest resources developed, the fisheries of our sea-coast exploited, and our agriculture made supplementary to the economic life of the province rather than an export industry."

It was, however, when the mines of Manitoba began to attract the attention of the outside world that the people of the province became sure that a new era of prosperity had begun. The earliest days of the mining industry go back a long time to the period when the Hudson's Bay Company found its salt supply in the brine springs on the west side of Lake Manitoba. A later stage was reached when the non-metallic minerals began to be developed. Since attention was called to the beauty and fine working qualities of Tyndall stone through its use in the Parliament Buildings at Winnipeg, the demand for it has much increased. Both for interior decoration and as building stone it is being largely used in Eastern Canada. It is seen in the fine interior of the new Houses of Parliament at Ottawa and in the new Eaton store in Montreal. Further development of the non-metallic materials is seen in the cement and gypsum industries in Winnipeg, which draw their supplies from Steep Rock Lake and from Lake St. Martin, and in the marble quarries being opened on the east side of Lake Winnipeg.

But it is in the gold and copper mines that the interest has centred. For ten years stories of gold discoveries had been coming into Winnipeg and there had been some small production of gold at Herb Lake and Rice Lake. Scores of prospects were, in the summer of 1928, being explored. But the only gold-bearing property which reached a production stage was that of the Central Manitoba Mines, Limited, at Long Lake, about 100 miles north-east of Winnipeg. As soon as that company had

16

secured a transmission line to bring it power, once it had put its mill into operation, and had actually begun shipping gold, many other prospects secured the necessary backing. For the past ten years, also, much was heard of the marvellous values of the Flin Flon copper deposit eighty miles north-west of The Pas. War delayed its development, but, in December 1927, American capitalists took up their option to purchase the property, and began at once to plan extensive operations. The construction of the necessary railway was at once undertaken by the Canadian National Railway with the assistance of the Manitoba Government. Of the stupendous values of this deposit there is no longer any doubt. With the completion of the smelter, probably in 1931, daily shipments from the Flin Flon will include approximately 60 tons of copper, 120 tons of zinc, $6,000 gold and $3,000 silver bullion. Where in 1928 nothing existed but muskeg and rock, a town of 5,000 will serve the needs of this country. The development of the mining industry is greatly aided by the re-opening of work on the Hudson Bay railway, the construction of which was suspended during the war. After much pressure from the west, the Federal Government decided to finish the road and once more the dream of Manitoba of fifty years ago seems likely to reach fulfilment. In the meantime, the port on Hudson Bay has been shifted from Nelson to Churchill, but Manitobans care little to which port the railway goes, as long as this new outlet to the sea is provided for her products.

Not the least of the romance connected with the new mining fields lies in the use of the aeroplane in their development. In June 1927 the first commercial aeroplane made its appearance in the Central Manitoba mining field. Less than a year later, on May 15th, 1928, the first bullion ever to be shipped by air was brought from that mine to Winnipeg. Into The Pas and the Flin Flon area, the flying machines carry men and materials. The summer of 1928 brought a daily air passenger service from Winnipeg into the mining

From a portrait by J. W. L. Forster, photographed by Mr. and Mrs. C. Jessup.

HIS GRACE THE ARCHBISHOP OF RUPERT'S LAND, PRIMATE
OF ALL CANADA.

fields most easily reached from this point. A company was organized to survey the whole Pre-Cambrian area of Manitoba with the aid of a fleet of aeroplanes, carrying prospectors into hitherto inaccessible districts.

Into this province, quickened to a new life, the tide of immigration flows once more. From the British Isles, from the United States, from every country in Europe people again come seeking homes in the Canadian West, and Manitoba shares in this new settlement. The new-comers find conditions very different from those which met the newcomers of an earlier day. New opportunities await them, and also railways, near at hand wherever they may go, and churches, and schools for their children, and social and marketing agencies beyond the dreams of the earlier settlers. Industry and mining offer more varied fields. There is no longer the drastic change from the conditions of long-settled communities to the hardships of pioneer settlement. Manitoba's problem now is to build a united and progressive people out of elements as varied as those of all Europe.

But the progress of the new times has not been confined to material things. From the earliest days churches and schools have been the first care of the people and the most conspicuous buildings in every community. From the first school at St. John's in Winnipeg, the educational system has grown until it is now one of the first objects of public interest. In 1927 the curriculum of the elementary schools was re-made, in the following year that of the high schools. The number of girls and boys who receive a high school education is perhaps twenty times as great in proportion to the population as it was in the days of the expansion. The university has become the second in point of attendance in Canada. Study clubs multiply on every hand. The love of books and music and pictures, and the desire for travel, have developed with a greater ease of life. Perhaps better than anything else, the flower gardens both of the cities and the country reflect that growth of mind and spirit which has kept pace with material prosperity.

Thus, in a pleasant land shining once more under the sun of a promise of better days, the people of Manitoba are engaged in the work of manufacturing and distribution, and of the development of natural resources. Agriculture in all its phases, the water powers, the forests, the fisheries, the mines—all these are resources of untold fertility and strength and wealth. But the greatest heritage lies not in the material resources, vast though they may be, but in those qualities of energy, of courage, of hardihood and of steadfastness in adversity no less than in prosperity, which are the greatest gifts of the first settlers to all who, following in their footsteps, seek homes in Manitoba, " the meeting place of the Great Spirit."

CHAPTER XII

HE WHO RUNS MAY READ

Evolution of the name Winnipeg as outlined by Dr. C. N. Bell in the proceedings of the Historical and Scientific Society of Manitoba

Ouinipigon	.	.	.	.	La Vérendrye, 1734
Ouinipique	.	.	.	.	Dobbs, 1742
Vnipignon	.	.	.	.	Galissoniere, 1750
Ouinipeg	.	.	.	.	Bougainville, 1757
Ouinipigon	.	.	.	.	Jefferys, 1760
Ouinipique	.	.	.	.	French Map, 1766
Winnepeck	.	.	.	.	Carver, 1768
Winipegon	.	.	.	.	Henry, 1775
Winipic	.	.	.	.	Mackenzie, 1789
Winipick	.	.	.	.	Harmon, 1800
Winipic	.	.	.	.	Pike, 1805
Winipic	.	.	.	.	Lord Selkirk, 1816
Winepic	.	.	.	.	Ross Cox, 1817
Winnipic	.	.	.	.	Schoolcraft, 1820
Winnepeek	.	.	.	.	Keating, 1823
Winipeg	.	.	.	.	Beltrami, 1823
Winnipeg	.	.	.	.	Capt. Black, 1833

The name is derived from the Cree words—" Win," dirty ; and " Nepe," water.

The Premiers of Manitoba

Boyd, Alfred .	.	Sept. 16, 1870 to Dec. 14, 1871
Girard, Marc Amable	.	Dec. 14, 1871 ,, Mar. 14, 1872
Clarke, Henry James	.	Mar. 14, 1872 ,, July 8, 1874
Girard, Marc Amable	.	July 8, 1874 ,, Dec. 2, 1874
Davis, Robert Atkinson .	.	Dec. 3, 1874 ,, Oct. 16, 1878
Norquay, John	.	Oct. 16, 1878 ,, Dec. 23, 1887
Harrison, David Howard .	.	Dec. 26, 1887 ,, Jan. 19, 1888
Greenway, Thomas .	.	Jan. 19, 1888 ,, Jan. 6, 1900
Macdonald, Hugh John .	.	Jan. 8, 1900 ,, Oct. 29, 1900
Roblin, Rodmond Palen .	.	Oct. 29, 1900 ,, May 12, 1915
Norris, Tobias Crawford .	.	May 12, 1915 ,, Aug. 8, 1922
Bracken, John	.	Aug. 8, 1922

The Lieutenant-Governors of Manitoba

Archibald, Adams G.	May 20, 1870
Morris, Alexander	Dec. 2, 1872
Cauchon, Edouard	Dec. 2, 1877
Aikins, James Cox	Dec. 2, 1882
Schultz, Sir John Christian	July 2, 1888
Patterson, James Colebrook	Sept. 2, 1895
McMillan, Sir Daniel Hunter	Oct. 15, 1900
Cameron, Sir Douglas Colin	Aug. 1, 1911
Aikins, Sir James A. M.	Aug. 3, 1916
Burrows, Theodore Arthur	Oct. 26, 1926

Developed Water Power in Manitoba

River	Company or owner	Location of plant	Head in feet	1926 installation, h.p.	Ultimate installation, h.p.
Winnipeg	City of Winnipeg	Point du Bois	46	102,900	102,000
Winnipeg	Winnipeg Electric Co.	Pinewa channel	40	37,800	37,800
Winnipeg	Manitoba Power Co.	Great Falls	56	84,000	168,000
		Total		224,700	307,800

Undeveloped Water Power in Manitoba

River	Estimated horse-power at 80 per cent. efficiency	
	At ordinary minimum flow	At ordinary six-month flow
Berens	11,450	18,570
Burntwood	9,060	27,185
Churchill	325,500	467,600
Dauphin	16,960	19,540
Grass	5,131	15,380
Hayes	7,611	22,800
Nelson	2,443,320	3,948,200
Pigeon	24,880	40,420
Saskatchewan	58,600	197,445
Winnipeg	171,290	305,300
Total	3,073,802	5,062,440

MGR. ALEXANDRE-ANTONIN TACHÉ.
First Archbishop of St. Boniface.

REV. JOHN WEST.
The first Protestant clergyman
in Manitoba.

FATHER LACOMBE.
First Rector of St. Mary's, the
first Roman Catholic church in
Winnipeg.

Manitoba Units on service in the Great War, with the names of their commanding officers furnished through the courtesy of Major-General Ketchen, C.B., C.M.G.

5TH BATTALION C.E.F. (WESTERN CAVALRY).
Lt.-Col. H. M. Dyer, D.S.O.

8TH BATTALION (WINNIPEG RIFLES).
Lt.-Col. A. L. Saunders, D.S.O., M.C.

10TH BATTALION.
Lt.-Col. J. G. Rattray, D.S.O.
Lt.-Col. D. M. Ormonde, D.S.O.

11TH BATTALION.
Lt.-Col. R. Burritt, D.S.O.

16TH BATTALION (part).
Capt. John Geddes.

27TH (CITY OF WINNIPEG) BATTALION.
Lt.-Col. I. R. Snider, O.B.E.
Lt.-Col. P. J. Daly, C.M.G., D.S.O.
Lt.-Col. H. J. Riley, D.S.O.

32ND BATTALION C.E.F. (absorbed by 15th Reserve Battn.).
Lt -Col. H. J. Cowan.
Lt.-Col. C. D. McPherson.
Lt.-Col. F. J. Clarke.

43RD BATTALION CAMERON HIGHLANDERS OF CANADA.
Lt.-Col. R. McD. Thomson.
Lt.-Col. W. Grassie, D.S.O.
Lt.-Col. W. K. Chandler, D.S.O.
Lt.-Col. H. M. Urquhuart, D.S.O., M.C.

44TH BATTALION C.E.F. (transferred to New Brunswick Area).
Lt.-Col. E. R. Wayland, C.M.G.

45TH BATTALION C.E.F. (absorbed by 11th Reserve Battn.).
Lt.-Col. F. J. Clarke.

61ST BATTALION C.E.F.
Lt.-Col. D. McLean.
Lt.-Col. F. J. Murray.

78TH BATTALION (WINNIPEG GRENADIERS).
Lt.-Col. J. B. Mitchell.
Lt.-Col. J. Kirkaldy, D.S.O.
Lt.-Col. J. Semmens, D.S.O.

79TH BATTALION C.E.F. (absorbed by 17th Reserve Battn.).
Lt.-Col. G. Clingan.

90TH BATTALION C.E.F. (absorbed by 11th Reserve Battn.).
Lt.-Col. W. A. Munro.

100TH BATTALION C.E.F. (absorbed by 11th Reserve Battn.).
Lt.-Col. J. B. Mitchell.

101ST BATTALION C.E.F. (absorbed by 17th Reserve Battn.).
Lt.-Col. D. McLean.

107TH (Pioneer Battalion of C.E.F).
Lt.-Col. G. Campbell, D.S.O.

108TH BATTALION C.E.F. (absorbed 14th Reserve Battn.).
Lt.-Col. G. H. Bradbury.

144TH BATTALION C.E.F. (absorbed 18th Reserve Battn.).
    Lt.-Col. A. W. Morley, M.C.
174TH BATTALION C.E.F. (absorbed 11th Reserve Battn.).
    Lt.-Col. H. F. Osler.
179TH BATTALION C.E.F. (absorbed 14th Reserve Battn.).
    Lt.-Col. J. Y. Reid.
181ST BATTALION C.E.F. (absorbed 18th Reserve Battn.).
    Lt.-Col. D. W. Beaubier.
184TH BATTALION C.E.F. (absorbed 11th Reserve Battn.).
    Lt.-Col. W. H. Sharpe.
190TH BATTALION C.E.F. (absorbed 11th Reserve Battn.).
    Lt.-Col. G. K. W. Watson.
196TH BATTALION C.E.F. (Western Universities) (absorbed 19th Re-
    serve Battn.).
    Lt.-Col. D. S. Mackay, O.B.E.
200TH BATTALION C.E.F. (absorbed 11th Reserve Battn.).
    Lt.-Col. A. L. Bonnycastle.
203RD BATTALION C.E.F. (absorbed 18th Reserve Battn.).
    Lt.-Col. J. E. Hansford.
221ST BATTALION C.E.F. (absorbed 11th Reserve Battn.).
    Lt.-Col. V. A. N. McMeans.
222ND BATTALION C.E.F. (absorbed 19th Reserve Battn.).
    Lt.-Col. J. Lightfoot.
223RD BATTALION C.E.F. (absorbed 11th Reserve Battn.).
    Lt.-Col. H. M. Hanneson.
226TH BATTALION C.E.F. (absorbed 14th Reserve Battn.).
    Lt.-Col. R. A. Gillespie.
1ST CANADIAN MOUNTED RIFLES, C.E.F. (raised as Cavalry Regt.
    Turned into Infantry Battn.).
    Lt. Col. H. I. Stevenson, D.S.O.
    Lt.-Col. A. E. Shaw.
    Lt.-Col. R. C. Andros, D.S.O.
    Lt.-Col. B. Laws.

CANADIAN CAVALRY BRIGADE.
LORD STRATHCONA'S HORSE R.C.
    Lt.-Col. A. C. Macdonell, D.S.O.
    Lt.-Col. J. A. Hesketh, D.S.O.
    Lt.-Col. M Doherty, D.S.O.
    Lt.-Col. D. G. Macdonald, D.S.O., M.C.
    Lt.-Col. C. Gooday.
FORT GARRY HORSE.
    Lt.-Col. R. W. Patterson, D.S.O.
    Lt.-Col. H. I. Stevenson, D.S.O.

CANADIAN ARMY MEDICAL CORPS.
D.D.M.S. CANADIAN CORPS.
    Col. R. M. Simpson, D.S.O.
A.D.M.S. 3RD CANADIAN DIVISION.
    Col. C. P. Templeton, C.B., D.S.O.
A.D.M.S. 4TH CANADIAN DIVISION.
    Col. P. G. Bell, C.B., D.S.O.
No. 3 CANADIAN FIELD AMBULANCE.
    Lt.-Col. W. L. Watt, C.B.

REV. GEORGE YOUNG, D.D.
(Methodist).

REV. ALEXANDER McDONALD.
(Baptist).

REV. JOHN BLACK, D.D.
The Apostle of the Red River.

(Presbyterian).

First ministers of the Methodist, Presbyterian, and Baptist churches
in Manitoba.

Lt.-Col. J. A. Gunn, C.B.
Lt.-Col. C. P. Templeton, C.B., D.S.O.
Lt.-Col. A. S. Donaldson.
No. 4 CANADIAN FIELD AMBULANCE.
Lt.-Col. W. Webster, D.S.O.
Lt.-Col. C. F. McGuffin, D.S.O.
Lt.-Col. R. H. Macdonald, M.C.
Lt.-Col. G. W. Treleaven, D.S.O., M.C.
Maj. T. H. Bell, M.C.
No. 11 CANADIAN FIELD AMBULANCE.
Lt.-Col. J. D. McQueen.
No. 12 CANADIAN FIELD AMBULANCE.
Lt.-Col. H. F. Gordon.
Lt.-Col. P. G. Bell, D.S.O.
No. 3 CANADIAN CASUALTY CLEARING STATION.
Lt.-Col. R. J. Blanchard.
Lt.-Col. F. A. Young.
No. 4 CANADIAN CASUALTY CLEARING STATION.
Lt.-Col. G. W. Prowse.
Lt.-Col. S. Campbell.
No. 2 CANADIAN STATIONARY HOSPITAL.
Lt.-Col. G. Clingan.

The province of Manitoba also furnished many detachments and drafts for the various Units of :

Canadian Artillery (Batteries and Ammunition Columns).
Canadian Engineers—Companies and Battalions.
Cyclists Units.
Machine Gun Units and Battalions.
Signal Companies.
Tunnelling Companies.
Entrenching Battalions.
Infantry Works Battalions.
Labour Battalions.
Divisional Trains.
Supply Columns.
Mechanical Transport.
Ammunition Parts.
Railway Troops Battalions.
Canadian Forestry Corps.
General Hospitals.
Royal Naval Air Service.
Royal Air Force.

Divisions and Brigades Commanded by Manitoba men, with the names of their commanders furnished through the courtesy of Major-General Ketchen, C.B., C.M.G.

2ND CANADIAN DIVISION.
Maj.-Gen. Sir S. B. Steele, K.C.M.G., C.B., M.V.O.
1ST CANADIAN DIVISION.
Maj.-Gen. Sir A. C. Macdonnell, K.C.B., C.M.G., D.S.O.
2ND CANADIAN DIVISION.
Brig.-Gen. (later Maj.-Gen.) H. D. B. Ketchen, C.B., C.M.G.

17

6TH CANADIAN INFANTRY BRIGADE.
Brig.-Gen. (later Maj.-Gen.) H. D. B. Ketchen, C.B., C.M.G.
Brig.-Gen. A. H. Bell, C.M.G., D.S.O.
Brig.-Gen. A. Ross, C.M.G., D.S.O.
7TH CANADIAN INFANTRY BRIGADE.
Brig.-Gen. (later Maj.-Gen.) A. C. Macdonell, C.M.G., D.S.O.
Brig.-Gen. H. M. Dyer, C.M.G., D.S.O.
9TH CANADIAN INFANTRY BRIGADE.
Brig.-Gen. D. M. Ormonde, C.M.G., D.S.O.
12TH CANADIAN INFANTRY BRIGADE.
Brig.-Gen. J. H. Kirkcaldy, C.M.G., D.S.O.
CANADIAN CAVALRY BRIGADE.
Brig.-Gen. R. W. Patterson, C.M.G., D.S.O.

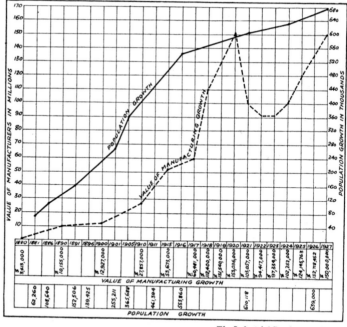

The Industrial Development Board.

Fig. 14.—The growth of the population of Manitoba compared
with the growth of manufacturing output,

Hon. John Bracken.

Hon. John Norquay.

Premiers of Manitoba.

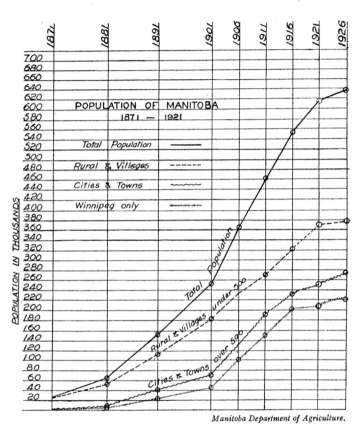

Fig. 15.—Growth of the population of Manitoba from 1871 to 1926.

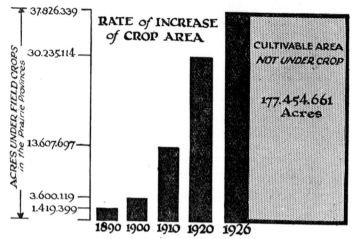

W. Sanford Evans Statistical Service.

Fig. 16.—The rate of increase in the crop area of the three prairie provinces.

W. Sanford Evans Statistical Service.

Fig. 17.—The growth of mixed farms in the prairie provinces in 25 years.

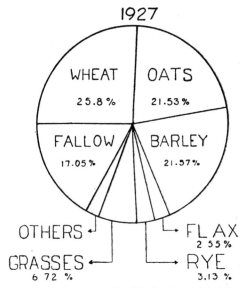

Manitoba Department of Agriculture.

Fig. 18.—The extent of mixed-grain farming in Manitoba.

MINERALIZED AREAS IN THE PRAIRIE PROVINCES

Principal Minerals

Gold	Oil
Silver	Gas
Copper	Gypsum
Zinc	Cement
Lead	Salt
Iron	Tar
Nickel	Soapstone
Lithium	Mineral Pigment
Coal	Bldg. Stone

W. Sanford Evans Statistical Service.

Fig. 19.

CHART SHOWING ANNUAL PRODUCTION OF CREAMERY BUTTER IN MANITOBA.

Manitoba Department of Agriculture.

Fig. 20.

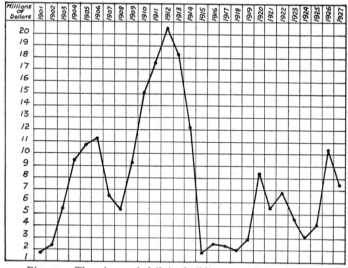

Fig. 21.—The rise and fall in building permits in Winnipeg from 1901–1927.

SIR RODMOND P. ROBLIN.   HON. T. CRAWFORD NORRIS.

HON. THOMAS GREENWAY.   SIR HUGH JOHN MACDONALD.

Premiers of Manitoba.

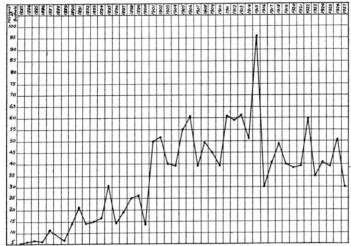

Fig. 22.—Fluctuations in the wheat crop—the basic crop of Manitoba—from 1883–1927.

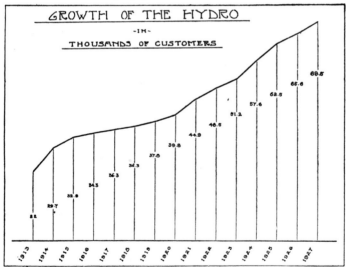

Winnipeg Hydro-Electric.

Fig. 23.—The steady growth in numbers of customers of the Winnipeg Hydro-Electric enterprises.

A SELECT BIBLIOGRAPHY

The following books will be of interest to the reader who may wish, without undertaking a serious course of study, to know more of the events described in this book.

The Search for the Western Sea, Lawrence J. Burpee.

Pathfinders of the West, Agnes Laut.

Lord Selkirk's Work in Canada, Chester Martin.

Red River Settlement, Alexander Ross.

Red River, J. J. Hargrave.

History of Manitoba, Hon. Donald Gunn.

History of Manitoba, Robert B. Hill.

History of the Great North-west, Alexander Begg.

Manitoba Memories, Rev. Dr. George Young.

Remarkable History of the Hudson's Bay Company, Rev. Dr. George Bryce.

Reminiscences of the North-west Rebellions, Major Boulton.

Women of Red River, W. J. Healey.

Canada and its Provinces—Articles in several volumes, but particularly in the two on the Prairie Provinces.

Makers of Canada, particularly lives of Mackenzie, Selkirk, and Simpson.

SUMMARY OF EVENTS

1610.	1 Nov.	Hudson aground in James Bay.
1612.	15 Aug.	Button at Nelson River.
1619.	5 Sept.	Munck sailed into Churchill Harbour.
1620.	20 Sept.	Munck reached Copenhagen.
1652.	Spring.	Radisson taken prisoner by Indians.
1658–9.	Winter.	Radisson and Groseilliers reached Lake Michigan.
1662.	Fall.	Radisson and Groseilliers built the first fort in the North-west.
1667.		Radisson and Groseilliers reached England and visited Charles II at Oxford.
1668.	3 June.	Radisson and Groseilliers sailed for Hudson Bay.
1670.	2 May.	Charter granted to Hudson's Bay Company.
1683.		Henry Kelsey sailed for Hudson Bay.
1683.	Oct.	Radisson up the Hayes in the service of France.
1684.	10 May.	Radisson became a British subject.
1685.	17 Nov.	La Vérendrye born at Three Rivers.
1686.	8 Aug.	Fort Nelson the only post in possession of H.B.C.
1688.		The first Fort Prince of Wales built at Churchill.
1690.	12 June.	Kelsey set out from York on his inland explorations.
1690.		H.B.C. trebled its stock and paid a dividend of 25 per cent.
1691.	23 Aug.	Kelsey saw the first buffalo hunt ever witnessed by a white man.
1693.		H.B.C., aided by the British Navy, recovered its posts from the French.
1697.		H.B.C. had lost to the French all their posts except Fort Albany.
1700.		Radisson, aged 65, refused the post of Warehouse Keeper by H.B.C.
1710.	12 June.	Radisson's widow given £6 by H.B.C. " as a charity."

18   235

1713.		Posts restored to H.B.C. by Treaty of Utrecht.
1720.		H.B.C. trebled its stock.
1722.		Kelsey recalled to London and pensioned.
1729.		Radisson's widow given £10 by H.B.C. " as a charity."
1731.	9 June.	La Vérendrye set out on his first journey West.
1731.	26 Aug.	La Vérendrye reached the Grande Portage.
1735–6.	Winter.	Jean La Vérendrye and party at Lake Winnipeg.
1736.	6 June.	Vérendrye party killed at Massacre Island.
1738.	24 Sept.	La Vérendrye reached the Forks.
1738.	18 Oct.	La Vérendrye set out to visit the Mandans.
1739.	10 Feb.	La Vérendrye returned to Fort de la Reine.
1743.	12 Jan.	The La Vérendryes reached the Bighorn Mountains.
1749.		Effort in British Parliament to upset H.B.C. Charter.
1749.	6 Dec.	La Vérendrye died at Three Rivers.
1754.	26 June.	Hendry left York to explore the interior.
1763.		French traders disappeared from the West.
1774.		Samuel Hearne built Cumberland House.
1782.	8 Aug.	Fort Prince of Wales surrendered to the French.
1782.	21 Aug.	York Factory surrendered to the French.
1784.		The North-West Company was organized at Montreal.
1784.	20 June.	Treaty of Paris restored all posts to H.B.C.
1787.	12 Feb.	Bishop Provencher born at Nicolet, Quebec.
1797.	7 Dec.	David Thompson reached the Souris River.
1800.	18 Aug.	Alexander Henry Jr. reached the Forks.
1801.	Spring.	Alexander Henry Jr. built Fort Pembina.
1801.		The first Red River cart built at Fort Pembina.
1803.		Alexander Henry Jr. built the first Fort Gibraltar.
1804.	4 Nov.	North-West and X.Y. Companies became one.
1811.	21 June.	H.B.C. ceded to Selkirk the District of Assiniboia.
1811.	24 Sept.	First party for Red River arrived at York.
1812.	6 July.	The first party arrived at Red River.
1812.	27 Oct.	The second party reached Red River.
1814.	21 June.	The third party reached Red River.
1815.	15 June.	140 Colonists left Red River for Upper Canada.
1815.	June.	Red River Settlement burnt to the ground.
1815.	19 Aug.	Settlers began to return to Red River.
1815.	3 Nov.	Fourth Selkirk party reached Red River.

1816.	19 June.	The Battle of Seven Oaks.
1816.	13 Aug.	Fort William captured by Lord Selkirk.
1817.	10 Jan.	Lord Selkirk's forces retook Fort Douglas.
1817.	June.	Lord Selkirk was at Red River Settlement.
1817.	18 July.	Lord Selkirk made a treaty with the Indians.
1818.	16 July.	Fathers Provencher and Dumoulin reached Red River.
1818.	Summer.	The first plague of grasshoppers at Red River.
1820.	8 April.	Lord Selkirk died at Pau, France, aged 49.
1820.	June.	Seed wheat brought from U.S. to Red River.
1820.	9 Sept.	First baptism at Red River by Rev. John West.
1820.	Oct.	First school opened at Red River.
1821.	1 June.	H.B.C. and N.W.C. became one.
1822.	12 May.	Father Provencher was consecrated Bishop.
1823.	10 June.	Rev. John West consecrated first Protestant Church.
1823.	23 July.	Archbishop Taché born at Rivière du Loup.
1825.	Spring.	Ploughs were first used at Red River.
1825.	9 July.	Old Fort Douglas sold to Robert Logan for £400.
1826.	Spring.	A great flood almost destroyed the Settlement.
1826.	24 June.	The De Meurons and the Swiss settlers left for U.S.
1829.	Summer.	Sixty families came to Red River from James Bay.
1830.		The first stone building was erected in Red River.
1831.	17 May.	Archbishop Machray born at Aberdeen.
1832.	13 April.	Rev. Mr. Cochrane chose a site for his Indian village.
1835.	12 Feb.	First meeting reorganized Council of Assiniboia.
1835.	23 Aug.	Selkirk grant bought back by H.B.C. for £84,000.
1838.	30 May.	H.B.C. rights extended to 1859.
1839.	13 June.	George Simpson appointed Governor of Rupert's Land.
1840.	Spring.	First Wesleyan Mission established by Rev. Mr. Rundel.
1844.	23 Oct.	Louis David Riel born at St. Boniface.
1845.	25 Aug.	Brother (Archbishop) Taché arrived at St. Boniface.
1846.	Sept.	Four hundred British soldiers arrived at Red River.
1849.	17 May.	The trial of William Sayer.
1849.	Oct.	Bishop David Anderson arrived at Red River.

1851. 18 Sept.	Rev. John Black arrived at Kildonan.
1852. Spring.	Severe floods injured Red River Settlement.
1852. 20 Sept.	Archbishop Matheson born at Kildonan.
1853. Summer.	A monthly mail service to Fort Ripley instituted.
1854. 5 Jan.	Kildonan church dedicated, free of debt.
1857. 5 Feb.	British Parliament ordered enquiry into H.B.C. affairs.
1859. Summer.	H.B.C. began to import goods via St. Paul.
1859. 19 May.	The first steamboat on the Red arrived at Fort Garry.
1859. 20 Dec.	Dr. Bird took up permanent residence at Red River.
1859. 22 Dec.	The first newspaper in the North-west was published.
1860. 7 Sept.	Sir George Simpson died at Lachine.
1862. Spring.	Henry McKenny built the first house in Winnipeg.
1862. August.	Milton and Cheadle began their explorations.
1864. 8 Nov.	The first Masonic Lodge in Fort Garry met.
1864. 4 Oct.	Bishop Anderson resigned : Bishop Machray succeeded.
1867. 1 July.	First Dominion Day.
1868. 4 July.	The Rev. George Young arrived in Winnipeg.
1868.	Henry McKenny began the lumber business in Manitoba.
1868. 31 July.	Act providing for surrender of H.B.C. rights.
1868. Fall.	Famine threatened Red River.
1868. 4 Dec.	The first Holy Trinity Church consecrated.
1869. Oct.	The survey party under Colonel Dennis began work.
1869. 11 Oct.	French Métis under Riel stopped the survey.
1869. 3 Nov.	Riel seized Fort Garry.
1870. 19 Jan.	Donald A. Smith made public statement.
1870. 25 Jan.	The first convention called by Riel met.
1870. 4 Mar.	Scott executed at Fort Garry.
1870. 9 March.	Archbishop Taché returned to St. Boniface.
1870. 12 May.	The Act creating the Province of Manitoba passed.
1870. 21 May.	Colonel Wolseley set out from Collingwood.
1870. 15 July.	Manitoba incorporated in the Dominion of Canada.
1870. 24 Aug.	Colonel Wolseley landed at Point Douglas.

1870. 2 Sept.	Lt.-Gov. Adams G. Archibald arrived at Fort Garry.
1870. 30 Dec.	Election for the first Legislature of Manitoba.
1870. 26. Nov.	United States Consul Taylor opened his office.
1871. 15 Mar.	The first session of the first Legislature opened.
1871. 26 April.	The first immigrants to the new province arrived.
1871. 8 July.	The first election of School Trustees in Winnipeg.
1871. 1 Aug.	Meeting to organize the first Congregational church.
1871. 3 Aug.	Lt.-Gov. Archibald signed a treaty with the Indians.
1871. Summer.	First steam grist mill in Manitoba.
1871. 5 Oct.	The attempted Fenian raid at Fort Daer.
1871. 31 Oct.	First public school in Winnipeg opened.
1871. 10 Nov.	Manitoba College opened at Kildonan.
1871. 20 Nov.	The first telegram sent from Manitoba.
1872. 4 Jan.	First bank opened and first cheques issued.
1872. 24 Mar.	Knox church organized as a mission.
1872. Summer.	The steamer " Selkirk " began to make regular trips.
1872. 9 Nov.	The first number of the *Manitoba Free Press* appeared.
1873. 11 Feb.	Meeting to organize Board of Trade called.
1873. 6 March.	First street light in Winnipeg.
1873. 23 May.	Act establishing R.N.W. Mounted Police passed.
1873. June.	The first Baptist Minister arrived in Winnipeg.
1873. 8 Nov.	The City of Winnipeg incorporated.
1874. 19 Jan.	First meeting of Winnipeg City Council.
1874. January.	The first Californian fruit arrived in Winnipeg.
1874. Spring.	The townsite of Emerson was surveyed.
1874. 5 July.	First iron casting in Manitoba by Mulvey and McKechine.
1874. 16 July.	The Manitoba Club organized.
1874. 18 July.	The first ticket to the old country was bought.
1874. 31 July.	The first party of Mennonites arrived from Russia.
1874. Summer.	Reid and Clarke began the fishing industry.
1874. 14 Oct.	The Rev. James Robertson came to Knox church.
1874. 9 Nov.	First regular meeting of the Y.M.C.A.
1875. Spring.	The first settler went to the Carberry district.
1875. 11 Oct.	The first Icelandic party of settlers arrived.

1875.	4 Nov.	Dr. John Maconn returned from Peace River.
1876.	4 Feb.	The Legislative Council of Manitoba abolished.
1876.	21 Oct.	First wheat shipped out of Manitoba.
1877.	6 Jan.	McLean's Flour Mill—the first—began operations.
1877.	28 Feb.	The Law Society of Manitoba incorporated.
1877.	28 Feb.	The University of Manitoba received its charter.
1877.	Summer.	The " Prince Rupert " went up the Assiniboine.
1877.	21 Sept.	First meeting of University Council.
1877.	8 Oct.	The first railway locomotive arrived in St. Boniface.
1877.	17 Oct.	First shipment of wheat direct to Europe.
1877.	3 Nov.	The first telephone in Winnipeg installed.
1878.	27 May.	The first University of Manitoba Examinations.
1878.	Summer.	The first settlement near Brandon.
1878.	16 Oct.	Hon. John Norquay formed his first government.
1878–9.	Dec.	First train to St. Paul.
1879.	9 Jan.	The first mail to travel by train left Winnipeg.
1879.	Summer.	Rock Lake Colonization Co. founded Crystal City.
1881.	21 Mar.	Boundaries of Manitoba extended.
1881.	17 Feb.	Contract for building C.P.R. signed.
1881.	26 July.	The first train crossed the Louise bridge.
1882.	1 Feb.	The first delivery of letters in Winnipeg.
1882.	11 Feb.	Rev. Dr. John Black died at Kildonan.
1882.	14 April.	The sale of Edmonton lots which marks the break of " the boom."
1882.	15 Oct.	The first electric light appeared on Main Street.
1882.	21 Nov.	The first steam plough came to the west.
1883.	23 April.	The Board of Trade of Brandon incorporated.
1884.	7 Sept.	The Red River Expedition left for service in Egypt.
1884.	7 Oct.	First block of first pavement in Winnipeg laid.
1885.	March.	Riel set up his government in N.W.T.
1885.	Spring.	The first settlers went to the Dauphin district.
1885.	24 April.	The engagement at Fish Creek.
1885.	2 May.	The engagement at Cut Knife Creek.
1885.	9–12 May.	Battle of Batoche.
1885.	15 May.	Daily railway service—Winnipeg–Port Arthur.
1885.	2 July.	The capture of Big Bear.
1885.	4 Aug.	First Torrens Title issued in Manitoba.
1885.	16 Nov.	Riel executed at Regina.

1887.	3 July.	Land for St. Boniface Hospital purchased.
1887.	23 Nov.	The Winnipeg Grain Exchange organized.
1888.	13 Jan.	Hon. Thomas Greenway became Premier.
1888.	Fall.	Struggle over Nor. Pac. & Man. Railway.
1888.		The last year of a complete crop failure.
1889.	March.	The first bonspiel held in Winnipeg.
1890.	3 March.	Dual system of schools abolished.
1892.	Fall.	The first two Ukrainians reached Winnipeg.
1892.	26 July.	The first electric street cars in Winnipeg.
1894.	1 Jan.	J. B. Tyrell returned from exploring the Barren Lands.
1894.	21 June.	Archbishop Taché died.
1895.	8 Jan.	Archbishop Langevin consecrated.
1896.	January.	The federal elections.
1896.	3 June.	Wesley College, Winnipeg, formally opened.
1896.	Sept.	The town site of Dauphin surveyed.
1896.		The first 100 miles of C.N.R. were built.
1897.		The Laurier-Greenway Settlement.
1897.	22 Aug.	Wheat touched $100 a bushel in Winnipeg.
1897.		Immigration on a large scale began.
1899.		First Royal Commission on the grain trade.
1901.		Brandon College received its charter.
1901.	14 June.	The first motor appeared, owned by Prof. Kenrick.
1903.		A future market in wheat opened in Winnipeg.
1904.		Six professors were called to the University.
1904.	9 March.	Archbishop Machray died.
1905.	2 March.	Bishop Matheson became Archbishop.
1905.		The third transcontinental railway begun.
1906.	February.	The Grain Growers' Grain Company organized.
1906.	8 July.	Street cars began to run on Sunday.
1906.	17 July.	The T. Eaton stores opened.
1907.		The telephone system purchased by the Man. Govt.
1907.		British immigration to Canada reached 132,000.
1908.	February.	The Grain Exchange gave up its charter.
1909.	August.	The B.A.A.S. met in Winnipeg.
1910.	10 May.	The first boat passed through St. Andrew's Lock.
1910.	2 July.	The first O.E.L. party of teachers left Winnipeg.
1910.		Erection of two Technical High Schools begun.
1911.	28 June.	First municipal hospital opened at Winnipeg.

1911.		The Public Utilities Commission established.
1911. 16 Oct.		Power developed by civic enterprise delivered.
1911.		Winnipeg Bank Clearings passed $1,000,000.
1912. 26 Feb.		The new boundaries of Manitoba announced.
1912. 5 May.		Opening of Vaughan Street Y.M.C.A.
1912. 6 May.		First public baths in Pritchard Avenue opened.
1913. 1 Oct.		Work began in Shoal Lakes project.
1913.		American immigration to Canada reached 139,000.
1914.		Entire H.B.C. Railway under contract.
1914. 4 Aug.		The Great War began.
1914. 3 Oct.		The first Canadian contingent sailed.
1915. 12 May.		Hon. T. C. Norris succeeded Sir R. P. Roblin.
1915. 22 May.		The first three men returned from the war.
1915. 15 June.		Archbishop Langevin died : Archbishop Bellivean succeeded.
1916. 27 Jan.		Women's Suffrage Bill given third reading.
1916. 13 March.		Bill to banish the Bar carried.
1916.		The Mothers' Pensions Act passed.
1916. August.		Compulsory Education Act came into force.
1917. 9 March.		The Rural Credits and Farm Loans Acts came into force.
1917.		The Minimum Wage Board established.
1918. 11 Oct.		Ban on public meetings owing to " Flu " epidemic.
1918. 11 Nov.		Armistice Day.
1919. 31 March.		Shoal Lake water turned on in Winnipeg.
1919. 13 May.		Opening of first Manitoba Musical Festival.
1919. 15 May.		The Winnipeg Strike began.
1920. 11 Sept.		Hard wheat quoted in Winnipeg at $2.85½.
1920. 1 June.		First deposit in Provincial Savings Bank.
1920. 29 June.		Mrs. Edith Rogers became first woman M.P.P.
1920. 15 July.		Manitoba's new Parliament Buildings opened.
1921. Nov.		Price of 1 Hard Wheat fell in Winnipeg to $1.02.
1922.		Co-operative Poultry Marketing Ass'n organized.
1922. August.		Hon. John Bracken became Premier.
1922. 28 Dec.		Work on Great Falls, development project begun.
1923. 10 June.		Bill to permit Sunday trains to the beaches passed.
1923. Fall.		Alberta Wheat Pool began operations.
1925. Spring.		The Industrial Development Board established.

1926. 18 Nov.   The new store of the Hudson's Bay Company opened.

1927.   8 Feb.   The *Free Press* printed on paper made in Manitoba.

1927. Summer.   Wheat sprayed with sulphur from aeroplane.

1927. Summer.   Commercial airplanes began their services to the mining camps.

1927. December. Option on Flin Flon mine taken up.

1928. 15 May.   Central Manitoba Mine shipped bullion by air.

INDEX